BECKETT A
POSTSTRUCTURALISM

ANTHONY UHLMANN

CAMBRIDGE
UNIVERSITY PRESS

CAMBRIDGE UNIVERSITY PRESS
Cambridge, New York, Melbourne, Madrid, Cape Town, Singapore, São Paulo

Cambridge University Press
The Edinburgh Building, Cambridge CB2 8RU, UK

Published in the United States of America by Cambridge University Press, New York

www.cambridge.org
Information on this title: www.cambridge.org/9780521640763

First published 1999
This digitally printed version 2008

A catalogue record for this publication is available from the British Library

Library of Congress Cataloguing in Publication data

Uhlmann, Anthony.
Beckett and poststructuralism / Anthony Uhlmann.
p.   cm.
Includes bibliographical references and index.
ISBN 0 521 64076 8 hardback
1. Beckett, Samuel, 1906–89 – Philosophy. 2. Philosophy, Modern – 20th century.
3. Beckett, Samuel, 1906–89 – Ethics. 4. Ethics, Modern – 20th century.
5. Poststructuralism – Ireland. 6. Poststructuralism – France. 7. Philosophy in literature.
8. Ethics in literature. 9. Philosophy, French. 10. Ethics, French. I. Title.
PR6003, E282Z86 1999
848' .91409 – dc21 98-43276–CIP

ISBN 978-0-521-64076-3 hardback
ISBN 978-0-521-05243-6 paperback

To Andrea Curr

Contents

Acknowledgements

I would like to thank a number of people who have made contributions to the way in which I have come to think about the questions addressed here. Firstly, Don Anderson, who has been involved with this project from the beginning, for his unfailing support and encouragement. Brian Massumi, Steven Connor, Leslie Hill and David Kelly, whose insightful and thorough criticisms contributed enormously to the final form of the book. Paul Patton, Moira Gatens, Genevieve Lloyd, Tom Gibson, Carl Power and Robert Sinnerbrink, who read chapters in draft form and whose enthusiasm and advice gave me the confidence to continue. I owe a debt to the careful and intelligent editors at Cambridge University Press, Ray Ryan (who saw the book through to press from its earliest draft to its final form) and Hilary Hammond for her excellent copy-editing. I would also like to thank James Knowlson, Mary Bryden, John Pilling and the staff at the Beckett Archives of the Beckett International Foundation at the University of Reading, and the staff at Dartmouth Library, Trinity College, Dublin and Boston College for their assistance during my research; my family and friends for their moral support; the Molony family for their hospitality when I stayed with them in Dublin; and especially Andrea Curr, who kept me sane and with whom I kept company travelling through recent French history.

Parts of this book have appeared in different version in *Law, Text, Culture, Southern Review* and *Substance*. Extracts from Beckett's published works are reproduced by kind permission of Grove Press, Calder Publications Limited, the Beckett International Foundation, University of Reading and the Samuel Beckett Estate. Extracts from Beckett's unpublished letter to Georges Duthuit, held at the Reading Archives, are reproduced by kind permission of Beckett's literary executor Jérôme Lindon on behalf of the Samuel Beckett Estate. The jacket photograph of Samuel Beckett was taken by Jerry Bauer in 1965 and I also thank him here for his good humour and for his kind permission to use this photograph. Finally I would like to acknowledge the three institutions that allowed me to complete this study: the Department of English at Queen's University in Canada, where I first began to think about Beckett; the Department of English at the University of Sydney, where I completed my Ph.D thesis on Beckett; and the School of Humanities at the University of Western Sydney, Hawkesbury, where I transformed that thesis into this book.

Introduction

THE FRIENDS OF BECKETT

In setting out on any theoretical or critical undertaking, it is helpful to have some general notion of the nature of the object of study. Deleuze and Guattari begin *What is Philosophy?* with a meditation on the nature of the 'friend'. The philosopher is the lover or the friend of wisdom and so in considering the nature of philosophy it is necessary to think the nature of the friend who is presupposed within it. A similar approach might be worthwhile in considering the tasks required of literary criticism in general, and of those critics concerned with the work of Beckett in particular.

There is clearly a field of study which calls itself 'Beckett studies', and in attempting to understand the works of Beckett one will inevitably add to, or be implicated within, this field of study. Implicated in this field are any number of thinkers who share aspects of the set of the works of Beckett in common. It might be claimed that just as philosophers are linked as friends of wisdom these thinkers might usefully be grouped together as 'friends of Beckett'. Indeed, given that Samuel Beckett died only a few years ago the field includes many critics who literally counted themselves as friends of the man, and these critics, in part because of their real friendships with Beckett, might still be said to be the most prominent in the field. I would also claim that, even amongst those who did not know Beckett personally, even those who claim only to be interested in the works, there is a sense of obligation. This might be considered to involve fidelity: a friend must, or should, be faithful. With the critics reading one another's works, it would be easy enough to offer examples as to how this notion of fidelity has real effects within the field. The friends of Beckett are not only faithful to Beckett but see it as part of their duty to check that this faithfulness (be it to the work or the man) is maintained by all the other suitors. Following the line of thought developed by Deleuze and Guattari a little further, the friends become rivals, and the struggles of the rivals turn about notions of fidelity (1994: 107). The question becomes: who is the true friend?

In *Nietzsche and Philosophy* Deleuze praises Nietzsche for indicating that the form of the question one asks is of the utmost importance. Philosophers often fall into the trap of asking 'what is? . . .' at times when they really should be asking 'who is? . . .' or 'which one is? . . .' (1983: 77). Rather than attempting to explicate this distinction, it might be worth attempting to test it.

When I ask 'what is literary criticism?', or even, 'what is Beckett studies?', I find myself developing a series of apparently heterogeneous generalizations; whereas in this particular case it seems much more useful to ask 'which one? . . .', which aspect of Beckett? Which aspect of Beckett's works? Which, or what kind of literary criticism? Which Beckett critic?

According to Nietzsche the question 'which one?' (qui) means this: what are the forces which take hold of a given thing, what is the will that possesses it? (Deleuze, 1983: 77)

Put in this way the question sounds very much like a personal accusation. Put in this way many a Beckett critic might struggle to affirm disinterestedness, to defeat his or her own jealousy and deflect the jealousy of the rivals by appealing to the notion of fidelity ('I might wish to possess this thing, "Samuel Beckett", but only because I am a true friend').

Further, however, when we force ourselves to ask 'which one?' we already presuppose that there are multiple aspects to the field. Following Proust as he is interpreted by Beckett, the lover wants to possess the whole of the loved one, but this proves impossible; absolute love itself proves impossible because the loved one is so dispersed in time and space that there is no way one could ever touch all of its points. To quote Beckett quoting Proust:

'We imagine that the object of our desire is a being that can be laid down before us, enclosed within a body. Alas! it is the extension of that being to all the points of space and time that it has occupied and will occupy. If we do not possess contact with such a place and with such an hour we do not possess that being. But we cannot touch all these points.' (Beckett, 1987: 58)

In asking 'which one?', then, as a friend you are forced to recognize the impossibility of absolute possession. If this is not recognized, the only option is to find sanctuary in an immobilized totalizing ideal of the loved one which, in the end, can only do injustice to the real loved one who, sooner or later, will break free of these imposed limits and betray you (behind your back, if you are lucky). It is clear, then, that the field of Beckett studies must divide; it also becomes apparent how the field must also always be constantly expanding as the works continue to touch more points in time and space and that this expansion will inevitably cause it to cross, as it has crossed already, numerous disciplinary boundaries.

ANSWERING THE QUESTION 'WHICH ONE?'

In general terms this book will seek to situate *Molloy*, *Malone Dies*, and *The Unnamable* within a French intellectual and historical milieu: specifically by relating these works to concepts and ways of seeing developed by French poststructuralists (focusing on the works of Deleuze and Guattari, Derrida and Foucault in particular) so as to shed light on Beckett's novels. This approach requires both that some explanations be given, as a number of problems become immediately apparent, and that some qualifications be made.

The qualifications concern what I will not be attempting and could not hope to do, and so I will treat them first. There is an enormous amount which might be written about Beckett's relationship to French thought and the French milieu in which he lived most of his life, and I can only hope to treat a fraction of this question. For example, I will not attempt a biographical survey, nor will I attempt to compare Beckett's works with those of contemporary French writers of fiction.[1] I will also in no way attempt to exhaustively survey the range of philosophical and aesthetic thought with which Beckett might have come into contact.[2]

With regard to the explanations, then, I will focus on key concepts and ways of thinking developed by one or two thinkers. My reasons for doing this largely relate to my answer to the question 'which one?' I am interested in that Beckett who is loosely described as a 'philosophical' writer. A number of critics have suggested that the question which most

---

[1] A comparative study of Beckett and his French literary contemporaries is no doubt overdue: one of the few English-language critics to write about Beckett with, to an extent, reference to post-war French literature, is Scott, whose book last appeared in 1969.

[2] This book adds to a body of works within Beckett studies which consider different aspects of Beckett's relationship with philosophy: see, for example, Adorno, 1988; Blanchot, 1986; Bryden, 1993; Butler, 1984; Connor, 1988,1992; Dearlove, 1982; Deleuze, 1995; Dobrez, 1986; Hill, 1990; Locatelli, 1990; Murphy, 1994; Rosen, 1976; Trezise, 1990; Watson, 1991; Wood, 1993.

concerned Beckett in his writings was the question of Being. This is a very large question, but it was one which Beckett approached in particular and fairly consistent ways. Further, his particular approach creates a striking resonance with certain recent trends in French poststructuralism, particularly as they are developed in the works of Deleuze and Guattari, Foucault, and Derrida. While I in no way claim that these resonances are the only ones, they are important nevertheless and will, in being followed through and in some fashion explicated, add to that body of work which seeks to better understand the achievement of Beckett's works.

In brief, I will be attempting to show two things. Firstly, that such resonance exists and that it thereby produces certain effects. Secondly, I will bring to light the question of whether this resonance, this proximity or neighbourhood (through which the writer and the philosophers seem to encounter similar questions and develop responses that are also in proximity), might be considered necessary rather than contingent. I will hope to show, in effect, that a certain climate or milieu (determined by historical necessity and certain convergences of traditions of thought) might be implicated in the production of this proximity, as certain urgent questions appear and require confrontation.

Two important problems emerge, which I will in part attempt to outline in this introduction: the first concerns the problem of how one might relate the separate disciplines (in Foucault's sense) of philosophy and literature. The second concerns the problem of how one might relate both of these disciplines to history.

LITERATURE AND PHILOSOPHY: ANTI-PLATONISM

It is likely that a reader, questioning my critical fidelity to Beckett's works, will question how it is possible to relate to Beckett's works notions developed by thinkers with whom Beckett was unlikely to have been familiar; thinkers who, while more or less contemporary, came after (at least in relation to the novels under consideration) Beckett, and to Beckett's own methods and works. The answer to this, which I will hope to develop throughout this introduction, will have two parts. Firstly, I will hope to indicate that these thinkers might be shown to draw upon similar intellectual traditions to those developed by Beckett. Secondly, I will hope to show throughout the book as a whole that the new situations confronted by Beckett on an aesthetic plane constituted urgent questions which confronted a whole generation of thinkers across different disciplines; further, that they thereby required a new philosophical approach (one which, and I will define this term more precisely below, might be termed 'anti-Platonic') in order to be understood conceptually, and that this approach emerges clearly in the works of Foucault, Deleuze and Guattari and Derrida. That is, I am suggesting that in a real sense Beckett 'thought differently', to use Foucault's term, and that his manner of thinking differently might best be described through recourse to those thinkers whose manner of thinking differently was analogous to his own.

THINKING DIFFERENTLY: 'ANTI-PLATONISM'

Literature and philosophy have long been considered to comprise separate and distinct spheres within the dominant tradition of Western thought. Plato's Socrates opposed the dialectic method of thought (which seeks to systematically trace the causes of things through logic, thereby appealing to reason alone and so 'teaching' rather than merely 'convincing' those to whom it is addressed) to the rhetorical method (which seeks to convince through describing the appearance of things and appealing to the emotions). The first method, the dialectic, was that adopted by the true philosopher (the lover of wisdom), while the second method, rhetoric, was that adopted by the sophist (the *soi-disant* 'wise-one').[3] Further, the methods of the sophist have often been equated with literary technique: through, for example, the use of devices which allow one to imitate something without understanding it (in a rational sense) and to convince others through an appeal to the emotions rather than to reason. Plato, then, found it necessary to cast the poet (once considered the seer, the prophet) from his Republic,[4] which was to be founded upon reason alone. From then on, to speak no doubt far too generally, literature and philosophy became fairly clearly separated domains. A central concern of philosophers labelled 'poststructuralist', however, has been the on-going effort to breach or pass beyond many of these well-policed borders.

To outline what is involved in 'anti-Platonism' is extremely difficult and therefore I will only attempt to provide a general idea of Deleuze's anti-Platonism here (which differs somewhat from that of Derrida, which is given its most explicit form in his reading of Plato found in *Dissemination*).

---

[3] Cf. Plato, 'Protagoras'.   [4] Cf. Plato, *The Republic*, Book 2.

In 'Theatrum Philosophicum', an article discussing Deleuze's ontology in *Difference and Repetition* and his aesthetics in *The Logic of Sense*, Foucault begins by asking what it means to 'reverse' or 'overturn' Plato in philosophy and suggests that in fact all philosophy might be called anti-Platonism. Indeed this seems to be how philosophy is defined: Plato provides a kind of model for philosophers so that 'the philosophical nature of a discourse is its Platonic differential' (Foucault, 1977: 166). All philosophical works, then, are both related to those of Plato and necessarily diverge from them. We should be aware that 'Platonism' is a philosophical term which refers specifically to the notion of Forms or Ideas developed by Plato.

So, Foucault suggests that all philosophy, including that of Plato, is anti-Platonic. Plato is anti-Platonic when we are unable to tell Socrates from the Sophists in the dialogues: philosophy is anti-Platonic when it attempts to derive any 'truth' from something other than an ideal Form; whenever it suggests that the truth might be variable rather than fixed; whenever it suggests that the truth might be paradoxical or ambiguous. Plato, says Foucault, was searching for the authentic, the pure gold; a savage purity, more pure than anything we might actually experience (Foucault, 1977: 167).

So how do you overturn Plato? Not, Foucault states, by just reversing the equation and putting appearance above essence, for all we do then is give a paltry kind of ideal Form to appearance. Rather than opposing the single model with a single appearance, he suggests, we should oppose the single model with the multitude of supposed appearances, a multitude so great and so divergent from the model as to render the model meaningless (Foucault, 1977: 168).

It would be far too large a task to attempt to completely define 'anti-Platonism' here: this would lead us into mazes of thought which would carry us too far from the questions at hand. For those that are interested, good summaries of 'anti-Platonism' can be found in Foucault's article, and, with relation to the differences between Deleuze's and Derrida's methods of 'reversing' Plato, in Paul Patton's 'Anti-Platonism and Art' (1994). What is of most importance to my argument here is simply the recognition of the importance of 'literary' kinds of thinking to both Deleuze's ontology of pure difference or chaos and Derrida's deconstruction.

In his essay on reversing Plato in *The Logic of Sense*, for example, Deleuze looks to Aesthetics to show how there is a disparity between our general view of experience (a view based on the invariable Forms, the

Ideas of Plato) and the conditions of our real experience (which involves constant change, constant flux, chaos). He suggests that what we need is a general view of experience which conforms to our actual experience. This he suggests, exists in modern literature, where divergent series, unrelated stories, are not unified but nevertheless resonate with one another. The structure of this kind of art, then, is reunited with our real experience, which does not proceed through well-ordered single story-lines but through the simultaneous sounding of various different and perhaps otherwise unrelated series of events (Deleuze, 1990: 260–2). Clearly, then, for Deleuze, philosophy must learn from literature of this type, the type created by Beckett, amongst others.

Derrida's deconstruction, on the other hand, affirms the importance of ambivalence, of the relation *between* terms rather than the choice of one term over another. Following Patton, Derrida 'seek[s] to undermine the Platonic order of representation from within, by arguing that the very concept of imitation/representation is infected with the same kind of ambivalence or indeterminacy found in other terms such as *pharmakon*' (Patton, 1994: 148), a term which, as Derrida shows in 'Plato's Pharmakon' means both 'poison' and 'remedy' at once (Derrida, 1981). Ambivalence, indeterminacy, one might contend, are the tools poets have been working with ever since when, and it is because of his insistence on the importance of such indeterminacy that Habermas accuses Derrida of 'leveling the genre distinctions' between literature and philosophy. Philosophy is that discipline which is supposed to be serious and to search for truth, the single meaning, through logic alone while literature requires ambiguity (an ambiguity which might allow the coexistence of logic and rhetoric, for example), uncertainty, several meanings at once.[5]

Deleuze and Guattari suggest that a work of art reaches the infinite through the finite (1994: 197), whereas Philosophy is commonly thought to approach the particular through the general. Beckett says much the same in 'Dante . . . Bruno . Vico . . Joyce': 'Poetry is essentially the antithesis of Metaphysics: Metaphysics purge the mind of the senses and

---

[5] Habermas's essay attempts to demolish Derrida's entire project by insisting that the border between Literature and Philosophy must be forcefully patrolled. Habermas suggests that while it is impossible for any discipline to be completely pure, nevertheless one should respect the dominant mode of any form of writing. Tellingly, however, he himself is forced to turn to rhetorical techniques in order to maintain his logical position by having us believe he, who clearly has a subtle mind, is ill-equipped to understand Derrida. This move is made so that he might turn to critiquing the more clearly inconsistent positions of Derrida's 'disciples' which are then quite unfairly taken as perfectly representing Derrida's own positions. This is a means of argument through sleight of hand which at best might be called disingenuous. See Habermas 1992: 185–210.

cultivate the disembodiment of the spiritual; Poetry is all passion and feeling and animates the inanimate; Metaphysics are most perfect when most concerned with universals; Poetry, when most concerned with particulars. Poets are the sense, philosophers the intelligence of humanity' (Beckett, 1983: 24). With Platonism, the infinite, the essence, the general or universal, is conflated with the 'Form' or 'Idea' which alone is considered eternal. So-called 'anti-Platonism', on the other hand, is a philosophy of existence rather than of Forms. It does not do away with essence; rather, it contends that essences cannot be disconnected from particulars as existence involves the play of differences (that which we understand as particular). This play of the general and the particular within an essence is sometimes called the 'indefinite' in Deleuze (Deleuze, 1995; Foucault, 1977: 167–70).[6]

So, if one wishes to speak of existence in this way, the rigid disciplinary boundaries between literature and philosophy (the one concerned with the particular the other with the general) must be breached, otherwise it is not possible to encounter existence or difference which requires the particular and the general at once. One might rightly contend that literature, at its best, has long been testing or ignoring this boundary. Indeed, this is precisely my point: that literature can be 'philosophical'. This, of course, does not mean reducing one to the other. Clearly, while they are concerned with the same questions they move in different directions and approach from opposite sides; literature moving from the particular towards the general, philosophy from the general towards the particular.

GILLES DELEUZE, 'POSTSTRUCTURALISM' AND SAMUEL BECKETT

While the reader might now be ready to concede the validity of comparing works of literature with works of philosophy in general the question still remains as to why one should specifically compare Samuel Beckett's works to the philosophy of Gilles Deleuze, Michel Foucault or Jacques Derrida. Firstly, this point might be in part defended anecdotally: in fact all of these philosophers indicate Beckett as a thinker whose project was in accord with their own. Foucault has stated, 'I belong to that generation of people, who, when they were students, were

---

[6] Where we stop talking, for example, of a particular woman or woman in general and begin to speak of 'a woman' as an indefinite term which is at once general and particular; any woman whatever, a being who is both determined and indeterminate.

enclosed within an horizon marked by Marxism, Phenomenology, Existentialism, etc. . . . I was like all the other students of philosophy at that time, and for me, the rupture came with Beckett: *Waiting for Godot*, a breath-taking spectacle' (Foucault, 1985: 105). Deleuze and Guattari frequently refer to Beckett's work to illustrate and even isolate concepts with which they work,[7] and, asked why he has never written on Beckett, Derrida replied: 'This is an author to whom I feel very close, or to whom I would like to feel myself very close' (Derrida, 1992: 60).

However, a more detailed response to the above question can also be given. My answer in the following discussion will primarily concern the relation between Beckett and Deleuze as the greater part of this book draws upon this relation. Although I will also briefly discuss Derrida in this introduction I will endeavour to sketch the relations to Foucault, Levinas and Derrida more fully later in the specific chapters which deal with those thinkers.

The proximity between the thinking which occurs in the work of Gilles Deleuze and Samuel Beckett is at once striking and paradoxical. Clearly Deleuze feels an affinity of some sort with Beckett: in *A Thousand Plateaus* he and Guattari include Beckett, along with Kafka and Godard, among writers of whom they are fond (97–8); and, as I have stated above, there are numerous examples of their use of Beckett's works to illustrate concepts that are being developed. On the other hand, as far as we know Beckett read little of Deleuze, although his young friend André Bernold discussed the work of both Deleuze and Derrida at length with him in the early to mid 1980s (Bernold, 1992a: 85–6).

Yet, if we are to believe the publicity which follows Beckett and Deleuze, then, strictly speaking, their projects should be considered irreconcilable. After all, Beckett is, in caricature, associated with negation, the expression of nothing, failure, the misery of being; all of these are (no doubt justifiably) critical commonplaces in the field of Beckett studies. On the other hand Deleuze is, like Spinoza, seen as a philosopher of affirmation, of joy, of positive Being which requires no negation.

To get us started, to bring together these irreconcilables, it might be worth considering Beckett's aesthetic writings beginning with the con-

---

[7] Concerning, for example, the problem of whether the body belongs to me and what belongs to it in *The Fold*, 109; the stroll of the schizo (2, 84), the inclusive disjunction (12, 76), the decentred subject (20) and the absence of links between disparate elements (324, 338) in *The Anti-Oedipus*; style as continuous variation (97–8), the rupture as opposed the voyage (199) and territorial assemblages (503) in *A Thousand Plateaus*; the perception-image; the action-image and the affection-image in *Cinema 1*. In addition Deleuze has dedicated two essays to Beckett: 'The Greatest Irish Film'(Deleuze, 1993a: 36–9) and 'The Exhausted'.

cept of 'identified contraries' in 'Dante . . . Bruno . Vico . . Joyce' which
Beckett borrowed from Giordano Bruno:

The maxima and minima of particular contraries are one and indifferent.
Minimal heat equals minimal cold. Consequently transmutations are circular.
The principle (minimum) of one contrary takes its movement from the principle (maximum) of another. Therefore not only do the minima coincide with
the minima, the maxima with the maxima, but the minima with the maxima in
the succession of transmutations. Maximal speed is a state of rest. The maximum of corruption and the minimum of generation are identical: in principle,
corruption is generation. And all things are ultimately identified with God, the
universal monad, Monad of monads. (Beckett, 1983: 21)

While clearly Beckett is paraphrasing Bruno in relation to Joyce there
are, already in this passage, one or two things which indicate how we
might begin to think the proximity between Beckett and Deleuze: in
particular, there is an emphasis on movement, and a reference, via
Bruno's pantheism and with a nod to Leibniz, to the plane of immanence, the one substance. Indeed, the notion of the monad develops this
further, indicating an identification of the microcosm with the macrocosm (cf. Leibniz, 1973: 179–94).

In the same essay Beckett affirms that while Joyce makes use of the
concepts of philosophers, his position is that of the artist, not the
philosopher. In consequence, rather than having to develop a conceptual consistency in the earnest manner demanded of philosophers he is
able to play with these concepts in a detached and disinterested way;
developing variations on the themes these concepts expound without
necessarily taking the process seriously (at least not with the seriousness
of a philosopher: 'Dante . . . Bruno . Vico . . Joyce': 22). The same can be
said of Beckett, with the qualification (good for Joyce as for Beckett) that
that which results from this disinterested play is not necessarily without
interest for the philosopher, especially one like Deleuze, who, like
Derrida, and following Nietzsche, at times sets about laughing down the
seriousness of philosophers.

Having said this, then, it is worth briefly recounting how Beckett
read, admired and played disinterestedly with the concepts of many of
the philosophers whom Deleuze counts as his antecedents, working in
what Michael Hardt has called a counter-tradition of philosophy; one
primarily defined, for Hardt, by the affirmation of the univocity of
Being (the plane of immanence). Among others Beckett read ('studied'
has overtones which are too serious), and clearly read closely, many of
the Pre-Socratics, Bruno, Vico, Descartes, Spinoza, Leibniz, Maleb-

ranche, Geulincx, Kant, Schopenhauer and Bergson (cf. Knowlson, 1996; on Bergson cf. Pilling, 1976: 7; Cronin, 1996: 127). He also knew something of Nietzsche. While Deleuze might not share Beckett's enthusiasm for all of these (particularly for Schopenhauer, demolished by Nietzsche's later critique although very influential for the early Nietzsche), and while Beckett may have read them with an eye more attuned to his own literary interests, it is worth noting how crucial many of these thinkers are to the development of Deleuze's own thought. Hardt particularly draws attention to the line of correspondence which passes through Spinoza, Nietzsche and Bergson, although Kant, Leibniz and the Pre-Socratics are also clearly important to Deleuze.

If I were to make a similar point from the opposite angle it is clear that like Beckett Deleuze was well versed in the traditions of Western literature (although it might be to push the point too far to say that Beckett's cardinal points – Dante and Joyce being among the most prominent – are shared with Deleuze). So too, it is clear that, like Beckett, Deleuze has often read philosophy for what might be called its literary style, as much as for its philosophical consistency (for example, Deleuze's essays 'on literature' collected in *Critique et Clinique* include essays on Spinoza, Nietzsche and Plato). So too, if Beckett's non-serious philosophizing has perfectly serious results, Deleuze, while not seriously considered a writer of literature, offers us play with literary materials which have startling effects. What might be further asserted here is that not only do Beckett and Deleuze share some of the same antecedents, they also share a method (a manner of creation) which for Deleuze involves the borrowing and transformation of concepts taken from his antecedents, and, for Beckett involves a similar 'perversion' or transformation of ideas and images taken from his antecedents (either literary or philosophical).

In some sense, then, each encounters the other. This encounter might be considered through the identified contrary; where Beckett, working towards the maximum of negation through aesthetic processes which have often been termed minimalist, in a 'circular transmutation' encounters the philosopher Deleuze whose philosophical project leads towards a maximum of affirmation, a pure affirmation, like that of Spinoza, which seems to admit no negation. The identity here is like that of a negative for a photograph. It is interesting that in developing the concepts of the perception-image, the affection-image and the action-image in *Cinema 1*, Deleuze turns to Beckett, but he does so to offer what he calls a reverse proof, which Beckett brings to light in *extinguishing* these three forms (1986: 66–70).

Yet understanding the proximity of Beckett and Deleuze through the identified contrary does not really seem to go far enough. Part of the problem is that while this concept might serve when attempting to consider opposites such as negation and affirmation, it is of little help when one wishes to consider other aspects of the proximity: particularly the nature of the relation between literature and philosophy, terms which, while somehow linked and somehow distinct, could not be usefully understood to be opposites. The problem here, rather than being one of opposition, is a problem of impurity, of interference, of mixing or overlapping.

Some of the key ideas which Beckett uses in working towards negation seem closely aligned with key ideas Deleuze uses in moving towards affirmation. In short, these ideas, which are all interrelated, are: immanence (the univocity of Being, with Being identified with Chaos); a kind of 'anti-Platonism'; and an emphasis on movement (as change, becoming). While the identification of these terms is never complete, the proximity is sufficient to allow, at times, striking resonances between their works. These, perhaps, are not the only points of contact, but they seem to me to be the most important. I will now attempt to briefly outline the nature of these terms.

UNIVOCITY OF BEING

It is clear, through *What is Philosophy?* and other works, how Deleuze underlines the importance of immanence and the univocity of Being to his system, and to philosophical systems in general. Hardt shows how Deleuze develops this idea through his close attention to the works of Spinoza. The plane of immanence can also be found in Bergson and Nietzsche. Beckett, in formulating his own system, drew in particular upon Schopenhauer, but also read Spinoza and Bergson. While Schopenhauer is considered to be an idealist, his own system owes a bit to Spinoza, whom he deforms to his own purposes; yet, clearly, a kind of univocity emerges through Schopenhauer.[8] Further, as hopefully will become clear when we examine Beckett's aesthetic methods more fully

---

[8] If not through his idealist point of departure, then through his descriptions of the 'thing in itself' as pure will, and through his notion of the artist's intuition of the Idea, which involves the demolition of the principle of individuation as the subject merges with the object to discover a Oneness or immanence which is the truly real (cf. Schopenhauer, 1995: 102).

below, Beckett did not follow any of these philosophical doctrines to the letter, instead developing his own consistency in following through his own artistic projects. That is, he in turn deforms Schopenhauer, mixing Schopenhauer's system with others (such as that of Bergson) which from a purely logical point of view might seem incompatible.

The identification of Beckett with Spinoza is one which Deleuze makes in 'The Exhausted', but in a peculiar kind of way, and one which, I feel, offers some insight into the strange identification of negation with affirmation which I have posited above. Deleuze sees Beckett's project as characterized by the problem of 'exhaustion', or, more specifically, 'the exhaustion of the possible'. For Deleuze the progression in Beckett is towards physical exhaustion, which runs parallel to mental exhaustion (just as the attributes of extension and thinking are parallel in Spinoza[9]); in addition there is the exhaustion of language (the medium through which these other exhaustions are to be accomplished) and the exhaustion of images and spaces (in those works where Beckett seeks to get around the particular problems posed by language: and these too are further, extra-linguistic, examples of Spinoza's parallelism of thinking and extension). Deleuze calls this exhaustion (a process of negation carried towards its limit) 'a relentless Spinozism' (1995: 3). Further however, this exhaustion involves a kind of exhaustion of modes or individuated things (here then, both Spinoza's modes and his attributes are being exhausted). In turn, this exhaustion of modes requires a merging again with the plane of immanence, the univocity of Being which is Spinoza's one substance. This occurs through a process of inclusive disjunction whereby the modes are at one and the same time finite or individuated *and* merging with the infinite substance within which they are no longer individuated (that is, there is a disjunction through which a mode is individuated, but that disjunction is inclusive so that it remains indistinguishable from the substance from which everything emerges). Alluding to Beckett's phrase from *Malone Dies*, 'everything divides . . . into itself', Deleuze states: 'The disjunction has become *inclusive*, everything divides, but within itself, and God, who is the ensemble of the possible, intermingles with Nothing, of which each thing is a modification' (1995: 4).

---

[9] There are three 'levels' in Spinoza's ontology. Firstly, there is Substance, the univocity of Being, a Oneness or pure immanence which is also called God or Nature. Secondly, there is the infinity of attributes which pertain to God (of which we only know two: thinking and extension). Thirdly, there are the modes or individuated things (such as you or I or this book, etc.) which always exist in both attributes. All individuated things, then, are modes of the attributes of the One Substance.

Here, then, with Beckett's pushing of negation to the absolute, we have an image of a thought which would be like the negative image of the Spinozian image. God, or Nature, who for Spinoza is Absolutely Everything, becomes, for the artist, Absolutely Nothing. I will discuss further below how strategies of inversion (a kind of perversion) seem to characterize Beckett's aesthetic project. Yet for the moment it is worth noting how exhaustion is not Beckett's only means of bringing to light the univocity of Being. Another key move, which finds its genesis, perhaps, in Beckett's reading of Schopenhauer, is Beckett's insistence on developing an art of non-relation.

The theme of creating an art which would definitively cut off all links, all points of relation between the subject and the object, was one which Beckett developed at some length in his aesthetic writings and his letters to friends from the thirties on (Beckett, 1983: 51–4; 118–45). It is outlined as clearly as anywhere in an unpublished letter which he wrote to Georges Duthuit, where he discusses the paintings of his friend Bram van Velde as an example of this art of non-relation:

What does [Bram] paint then, with so much fervour, if he is no longer in front of anything? . . . Whatever I say, I will appear to be locking him into a relation again. If I say that he paints the impossibility of painting, the deprivation of relation, of object, of subject, I appear to put him in relation with this impossibility, with this deprivation, in front of them. He is inside them, is this the same thing? He is them, rather, and they are he, in as full a manner as possible, and can there be relation in the indivisible? Full? Indivisible? Obviously not. It exists all the same. But in such a density (that is to say simplicity) of being, that only eruption can bring movement there, can overcome it, lifting up all as a whole.[10]

Here it becomes clear how the notion of non-relation necessarily involves the bringing to light of the univocity of Being. For the non-relation of the subject – artist – to the object, and the non-relation of the

---

[10] Beckett, 1949. My thanks to Dr James Knowlson, Dr Mary Bryden and the library staff at the University of Reading, and to Jérôme Lindon for permission to quote from this letter. My thanks to Dr Gay McAuley, Department of Performance Studies, University of Sydney, for checking over the translation of this letter. The original is as follows:

'Que peint-il donc, avec tant de mal, s'il n'est plus devant rien? Quoi que je dise, j'aurai l'air de l'enfermer à nouveau dans une relation. Si je dis qu'il peint l'impossibilité de peindre, la privation de rapport, d'objet, de sujet, j'ai l'air de le mettre en rapport avec cette impossibilité, avec cette privation, devant elles. Il est dedans, est-ce la même chose? Il les est, plutôt, et elles sont lui, d'une façon pleine, et peut-il y avoir des rapports dans l'indivisible? Pleine? Indivisible? Evidemment pas. Ca vit quand même. Mais dans une telle densité, c'est à dire simplicité, d'être, que seule l'éruption peut en avoir raison, y apporter le mouvement, en soulevant tout d'un bloc.

subject to itself,[11] is another process of negation through which all links are severed, a process which allows in the chaos (both in the microcosm of the mind of the so-called subject and the macrocosm of the so-called object which is the universe). That is, once all links are severed paradoxically all runs together becoming, following Beckett, 'indivisible'. As I alluded to above, the development of this aesthetic ideal seems to owe something to Beckett's reading of Schopenhauer. On a number of occasions in Knowlson's and Cronin's biographies of Beckett, we are told of Beckett's close attention to and admiration for Schopenhauer. It is worth quoting at length from Book 3 of Schopenhauer's *The World as Will and Idea*:

Raised by the power of the mind, a person relinquishes the usual way of looking at things, stops tracing, as the forms of the principle of sufficient reason prompt him to do, only their interrelatedness, the final goal of which is always a *relation* [my italics] to his own will. He ceases to consider the where, the when, the why, and the whither of things, and looks simply and solely at the *what*. He does not allow abstract thought, the concepts of the reason, to take possession of his consciousness, but, instead, gives the whole power of his mind to perception, immerses himself entirely in this . . . He *loses* himself in this object . . . i.e., he forgets his very individuality, his will, and continues to exist only as the pure subject, the clear mirror of the object. . . he can no longer separate the perceiver from the perception, but the two have become *one* [my italics] . . . If the subject has to such an extent passed out of all relation to something outside it, and the subject out of all relation to the will, then what is known is no longer the individual thing as such, but the *Idea*, the eternal form, the immediate objectivity of the will at this grade. (Schopenhauer, 1995: 102; Book 3, section 34)

A couple of things need to be said about this. Firstly, while the notion of non-relation, or the passing out of all relation, is already present in the passage cited, it is further underlined when one remembers that 'the principle of sufficient reason' (from which, for Schopenhauer, the person must disengage) is that principle which is essentially involved in the processes of relation or individuation that bring to light the (fabrication of) the ordered world of science and reason. That is, the principle of sufficient reason involves the perception of time, space and causation, and these, for Schopenhauer, are not objective co-ordinates existing in the world of matter, but subjective structures which exist in the mind and which we lay down over things. The artist, then, is put forward by Schopenhauer as the one most suited to seeing beyond these fictions of the mind, getting below the surface of these appearances to find the

[11] So that I ≠ I but, after Rimbaud – another antecedent shared by Beckett and Deleuze – *je est un autre* (I is an other).

essence which alone is real. The second point, which, necessarily follows from this, and is also apparent in the cited passage, is Schopenhauer's development of a kind of Platonism.[12] So, the question of how I understand Beckett's anti-Platonism is begged, and I will deal with this below.

Another point, which is not apparent in this passage, also occurs to me here. This is the correspondences between Beckett's thought and the thought of Bergson. Beckett gave a series of lectures which drew heavily on Bergson at Trinity College in the early 1930s (Cronin, 1996: 127); even had he not read Bergson carefully, his reading of Proust would have given him an introduction to many of Bergson's ideas. The notions of Habit, and spontaneous memory, which Bergson develops in *Matter and Memory*, are prominently displayed in Beckett's essay on Proust. In *Proust* Beckett intermingles or folds together in a peculiar way the ideas of these two thinkers, Bergson and Schopenhauer, in considering the possibility of pure perception.[13] Further, what Schopenhauer here calls the Idea (where all runs together) bears a strong family resemblance (however hidden it might be by the unfamiliar clothes it is now obliged to wear) to Spinoza's substance. Further, although I will not attempt to compare them point by point, it is hopefully clear enough how these notions expressed by Schopenhauer bear a striking resemblance to Beckett's aesthetic theories of non-relation which we have briefly encountered above and which I will describe in more detail below.

In comparing Beckett's non-relation and univocity of Being to that of Deleuze it might be tentatively suggested that Beckett seems to require a good deal more effort to uncover or accommodate his chaos. Subtraction, negation, exhaustion, presupposes such superhuman effort: after Beckett had finished writing his Trilogy and his early plays, his works both of fiction and drama became shorter and shorter, yet seemingly required more and more effort in composition. Further, this art, which is produced with difficulty, is full of consternation (though, as Beckett affirms, the consternation is 'behind' the form; see Shenker, 1956: 4). The style of Deleuze's writing, on the other hand, often strikes one as serene. This is not to suggest Deleuze necessarily found thinking or writing easy, just that the words themselves seem easy. So too, whereas,

---

[12] Though it is a deformed kind: the Idea or Form in Schopenhauer is not a pure quality as in Plato, but a kind of univocity which might admit no single pure quality because it contains all qualities – and because it is deformed it might already be considered a kind of anti-Platonism, a perversion of Plato.

[13] A process Bergson describes in *Matter and Memory* as involving the cutting of perception from time and causation, which leads, like Schopenhauer's Idea, to the merging of subject and object (Bergson, 1991: 31–40).

as we have seen, Beckett requires this great effort so that he might punch a hole through the surface (of words, of images) to reach the plane of immanence, achieving the plane through exhaustion or through the rare moment of pure perception, Deleuze seems to have little problem slipping between planes. The movement involved seems to be the same: Deleuze often uses Beckett as an example of the inclusive disjunction or the becoming through which one moves between planes, yet this movement is slow and laboured in Beckett whereas it does not always seem so in Deleuze and Guattari. In *A Thousand Plateaus*, for example, they describe the nature of the movement between the plane of organization and the plane of consistency: 'one continually passes from one to the other, by unnoticeable degrees and without being aware of it, or one becomes aware of it only afterward. Because one continually reconstitutes one plane atop another, or extricates one from the other' (Deleuze and Guattari, 1987: 269).

No doubt, the influence of Schopenhauer might also be implicated in Beckett's decision to adopt his principles of negation which produce, at their limit, the absolute of Nothingness as the univocity of Being; yet, this is also, perhaps, attributable to Beckett's debt to his literary antecedents, and Joyce in particular. Knowlson quotes Beckett:

> I realised that Joyce had gone as far as one could in the direction of knowing more, [being] in control of one's material. He was always adding to it; you only have to look at his proofs to see that. I realised that my own way was in impoverishment, in lack of knowledge and in taking away, in subtracting rather than adding. (1996: 352)

What we see here, perhaps, is a process of inversion; or a folding of thought whereby the opposite of an idea is played with to create new affects and percepts, that is, new sensations. A further example of this might be found in what I have called Beckett's anti-Platonism, which is another kind of thought he shares with Deleuze. Just as Beckett's univocity of Being (his chaos as nothing) both differs from and resembles Deleuze's affirmation of Being, Beckett's anti-Platonism differs from that of Deleuze; where they are in proximity, however, is that they both consider such a move away from the pure Form towards the real as it is experienced to be of the utmost importance.

BECKETT'S 'ANTI-PLATONISM'

Simply on a metaphorical level we might begin to find resonances between the reception of Beckett and the reception of Deleuze: the way both have written has at times been considered to be perverse (cf. Driver, 1961: 24; Cronin, 1996: 358). Yet one might trace a proximity less tentatively by attending to Beckett's aesthetic methods. I have mentioned above how Beckett's aesthetic method in some ways inverts that of Joyce, yet this reversing of terms is to be found also in the manner in which he distorts philosophy in order to create.

Before turning to a discussion of what, I feel, might properly be called anti-Platonism in Beckett, it is perhaps useful to list some examples of his perversion or inversion of philosophical thought. In a famous letter to Axel Kaun written in 1937, Beckett indicates how he would like to use philosophy in his work. His aim is to bore holes into the surface of words to find what is hidden beneath, 'be it something or nothing' (Beckett, 1983: 172), and this notion might be linked with his desire for an art of non-relation which, as we have seen, is linked to his notion of the univocity of Being. Yet later in the letter he talks of philosophy, suggesting that he would like to use its notions of strict methodology ironically, turning them against themselves.

On the way to this literature of the unword, which is so desirable to me, some form of Nominalist irony might be a necessary stage. But it is not enough for the game to lose some of its sacred seriousness. It should stop. Let us therefore act like the mad(?) mathematician who used a different principle of measurement at each step of his calculation. (Beckett, 1983: 173)

There is a commitment to impurity or perversity here. In terms of Platonic philosophy, perhaps implicit in Socrates' rejection of Rhetoric is the notion that it is not serious, as it does not rigorously trace through the causes of things. Firstly, to turn to another well-known example (cf. Murphy, 1994), Beckett's impurity and his ironic use of philosophers can be found in his use of Spinoza in *Murphy*. In the fifth book of the *Ethics*, Spinoza relates the third kind of knowledge to the intellectual love of God with which God loves himself (*Ethics*, Book 5, Prop. 35; 1992: 218). Beckett uses this phrase at the head of chapter 6 of *Murphy*, only he replaces the word 'God' with 'Murphy': he then proceeds to offer an ironic post-Cartesian treatise on Murphy, outlining theories on the relation between Murphy's mind and body. A couple of less well-known examples can be found in Schopenhauer. Firstly, in describing the *principium individuationis* (the principle through which things distinguish themselves from other things) in relation to the serene and ignorant egotistical will which divides itself from all others and sets itself up in conflict against the entire universe, Schopenhauer uses the metaphor of a man cast adrift in a boat on a boundless raging sea (Book 4, Section 63;

1995: 217); Beckett ends *Malone Dies* with a strikingly similar image, as Lemuel and the inmates of the lunatic asylum are cast adrift after murdering the philanthropists who had taken them out for a day trip, yet, rather than relating this to the *principium individuationis*, Beckett inverts the relation so that the men on the boat merge together and together merge into one with the sea and nearby mountains, passing into the plane of immanence. Secondly, in speaking of the sublime which allows one to pass to the Idea, Schopenhauer describes an artistic genius faced with a raging storm, who, confronting its terror without fear for his own safety, is able to pass to the other side and achieve true knowledge (Book 3, 40; 1995: 128). The passage bears a striking resemblance to the description Beckett offers of Krapp's 'vision' in *Krapp's Last Tape*, an episode which has erroneously been taken to be directly autobiographical (as Knowlson shows in his biography). With enormous enthusiasm, the voice of the younger Krapp describes confronting the raging storm and finding the blinding insight which is his vision; but the older Krapp, knowing that all this has led to nothing, cannot stand these romantic outpourings and quickly puts the tape to fast forward. There are, no doubt, many other examples.

We have seen, with the discussion of Schopenhauer above, how some notion of Form or Idea seems to persist in Beckett. He told the critic Lawrence Harvey that writing, for him, involved 'getting down below the surface' in an effort to find 'the authentic weakness within' (quoted in Knowlson, 1996: 492). Given that this seems to still speak of essences, how might this be considered anti-Platonic? In overturning Plato's opposition between essence and appearance, or the ideal and the real (as Beckett puts it), Beckett develops an essence of the impure. We find, especially in later plays, such as *Play* and *What Where*, for example, impotence and torture in essence; elsewhere there are so many sad passions in essence; failure and ignorance in essence; the essence, if you like, of the dirt under the fingernails; corruption and decay in pure form. Such a turn involves not just a simple inversion of essence and appearance but a process which involves one term passing into the other, just as the general passes into the particular in the indefinite, perverting the original Platonic purity.

In speaking of the eruption of involuntary memory into the present in *Proust*, Beckett suggests that the process involves the passing of the essence (held in the memory) into the appearance (present in matter), creating a bastard which he calls the 'ideal real': 'the experience is at once imaginative and empirical, at once an evocation and a direct perception, real without being merely actual, ideal without being merely abstract, the ideal real, the essential, the extra-temporal' (1987: 75). Such a bastard is found in different form in Beckett, whose characters have poor memories but who find other ways of breaking out of habit: through corporeal degeneration, for example, as in the second half of *Molloy*. It is a bastard which, for Proust (who developed many of his sensations of concepts through close study of Bergson), as much as for Beckett, is the offspring of an impure intercourse between literature and philosophy. In a passage which I have cited more fully above Beckett states, 'Poets are the sense, philosophers the intelligence of humanity' (1983: 24). He then repeats the Scholastic slogan 'Nothing is in the intellect that will not first have been in the senses' to suggest that philosophy (which is of the intellect) requires poetry (which is of the senses), or that 'poetry is a prime condition of philosophy and civiliza-tion' (24). That Beckett did not treat this relationship with the utmost seriousness, however, is illustrated in *Malone Dies*, where the Scholastic slogan is taught to a parrot who repeats it *ad absurdum* (Knowlson, 1996: 374). The ideal real, then, is the interpenetration of the so-called univer-sal and the particular; expressed in sensations which become sensations of concepts.[14]

MOVEMENT

In a footnote above I list a number of the occasions where Deleuze and Guattari and Deleuze make use of Beckett to illustrate concepts. Inter-estingly, many of these references to Beckett are related to movement: the stroll of the schizo; continuous variation; the rupture and the voyage. Indeed, it seems here that Beckett and Deleuze come together best, as 'movement' might in some ways be related to both the plane of immanence and to anti-Platonism; further, as it is aligned in Deleuze with becoming and with change in Beckett, it is through movement that the concept and the sensation most resemble one another.

As we have seen, Beckett was familiar with Bergson, and it is to Bergson that Deleuze turns in outlining the concept of the movement-image. Deleuze shows how in ancient times movement was conceived in relation to the fixed Ideas of Platonism, so that it consisted, in effect, of a movement from pose to pose. With the rise of modern science, however, the mechanical succession of instants replaced the movement

---

[14] I will define this terminology below.

from pose to pose so that movement came to be related, not to the privileged instant of the Idea, but to the indefinite instant of any-moments-whatever. In turn this allowed for the appearance or the production of the new, because, whereas the eternal Forms or Ideas suggest that a Whole can be constructed in which 'all is given' (and so nothing new can appear): 'When one relates movement to any-moments-whatevers, one must be capable of thinking the production of the new, that is, of the remarkable and singular, at any one of these moments' (Deleuze, 1986: 7). True movement of this sort contains change; the Whole is neither given or givable 'because it is Open, and because its nature is to change constantly' (9). This Whole is immanent existence, which elsewhere has been related to chaos over which a plane of immanence is thrown down.

In *What is Philosophy?* Deleuze and Guattari state: 'Chaos is defined not so much by its disorder as by the infinite speed with which every form taking shape in it vanishes . . . Chaos is an infinite speed of birth and disappearance' (1994: 118). Change, then, moving at infinite speed, constitutes the chaos from which all things are drawn and return. Change, coupled with movement, permeates much of Beckett's fiction. Molloy and Moran both set out on voyages which are also causing them to move closer to that state of exhaustion which will eventually transport them to the plane of immanence. Malone lies apparently still, but his bodily state and the state of his possessions continue to change as he moves closer to death; he helps himself arrive by passing the time with little narrative movements. *The Unnamable* seems to sit still, but is unsure, from one moment to the next, even of the state of his own body, or whether he has a body (although he does consider himself male); the stories he tells himself comprise a flux of the mind, offering a mental chaotic microcosm which opens into the macrocosm of the chaos of all Being.

Deleuze is careful to note, in 'The Exhausted', that Beckett attempts to exhaust 'sets' or ensembles rather than Wholes, as the Whole (that through which all is revealed, completed), as *The Unnamable* shows, is that which cannot be arrived at. Deleuze characterizes the Whole, approached through movement, by its openness, by the fact that it cannot be grasped, even as it is traversed. This openness, I would suggest, is reflected in two keywords in Beckett's texts: 'on' (as in 'I can't go on', 'I'll go on'; and the 'On!' of Pozzo in *Waiting for Godot*), a word imbued with movement and little else, and 'perhaps', 'Perhaps' (a word used 589 times in the Trilogy (cf. Barale and Rabinovitz); a word of

Openness and little else; which Beckett has called the keyword to his works (Driver. 1961: 23).

It is worth emphasizing that the 'ideal real' described above differs from the Platonic Idea in that it is not fixed; part of what remains real in this compound is movement. For example, the theatre piece *Play* seems to describe the essence of a sad passion, offering us an affect without name (but which might be approximated as a mixture of jealousy, impotence, guilt, and the pain of imperfect love), yet it remains in continuous movement, as the scene is repeated over and again, indefinitely, and the repetition brings change (as the lights continue to dim). There would be little difficulty in assembling numerous other examples of Beckett's on-going interest in change and the movements involved even in standing still, or lying down. For Deleuze, Beckett tries to achieve exhaustion so that the movement will stop, because without movement there is Nothing (and once Nothing has been achieved, the end, the merging with the infinite, has been reached at last).

DERRIDA AND BECKETT

I mentioned that Derrida approaches anti-Platonism from a somewhat different angle to Deleuze. It might be worth asking in passing and in a general sort of way from where these different 'angles' come: this sort of question is of the type which can get us into trouble as we attempt to take in too much information in a single glance, yet it is still worth asking, if only because it tells us something about how ideas move in series or through 'traditions'. In short, then, as we have seen, Deleuze considers himself to be working within a counter-tradition, one which affirms the univocity of Being as its ground or beginning (an ungrounded ground if, as in Deleuze's case, that Being is equated with an apparently ever-changing chaos over which the philosopher throws a 'plane of immanence'). Derrida, however, draws upon the work of Heidegger and Husserl on the one hand and the structuralist tradition founded by Saussure on the other; different traditions altogether (which Derrida opposes to one another, develops, and critiques) which could not conceive of their ground being in chaos (cf. Nancy, 1996). Still, like Deleuze, Derrida sees Platonism as a problem, something which must be overcome.

With Derrida, however, we see an altogether different strategy: he attacks Plato's dualisms (essence and appearance, or rhetoric and logic for example) from within, showing how the supposedly fixed terms, the supposedly fixed values are themselves constantly in a kind of move-ment. He indicates that rather than the two poles being fixed forever (one at good the other at bad, one at true the other at false), the terms within Plato's dualities can be seen to oscillate so that essence is con-founded with and requires appearance and vice versa. In simple terms, what we have is a play of meaning: certainty is replaced with ambiguity, one meaning with several.

Again, it is not so difficult to see how this approach might be related to Beckett, who, like Derrida (as we will see in the final chapter of this book) is deeply concerned with the problem of 'aporia'; deeply interest-ed in the play of language which always eludes us as we attempt to find an essence (whether it be the essence of self or any other essence). What is at stake here is not the complete obliteration of the boundaries between literature and philosophy but the simple need to recognize the *ground between* on to which both must necessarily stray or where, in fact, they are required to live. Once the homeland has been demolished by the wars driven by certainties and unquestionable truths, one is forced to live among the ruins, in the no-man's-land Beckett expresses as potently as any. Something of this point might be illustrated with a quotation from Samuel Butler's *Erewhon*, in which the Erewhonians, whom Butler so often disparages, seem to make ready sense in des-cribing the uses of 'unreason':

Life, they urge, would be intolerable if men were to be guided in all they did by reason and reason only. Reason betrays men into the drawing of hard and fast lines, and to the defining by language – language being like the sun, which rears and then scorches. Extremes are alone logical, but they are always absurd; the mean is illogical, but an illogical mean is better than the sheer absurdity of an extreme. There are no follies and no unreasonablenesses so great as those which can apparently be irrefagably defended by reason itself, and there is hardly an error into which men may not easily be led if they base their conduct upon reason only. (Butler, 1985: 187)

Although they are clearly quite different it is also clear that Butler, like Beckett, writes a literature of ideas. Indeed, the above lines from Butler call to mind others from Beckett's *The Unnamable*: 'and what is one to believe, that is not the point, to believe this or that, the point is to guess right, nothing more, they say, If it's not white it's very likely black, it must be admitted the method lacks subtlety, in view of the intermediate shades all equally worthy of a chance' (Beckett, 1958: 121).

It is clear, then, as I have suggested above, that Derrida might help us to understand how philosophy, because it too necessarily involves ambivalence and a play between fixed positions, cannot be strictly dissociated from literature. To quote Vincent Descombes:

> [Derrida] has not ceased to wage a campaign, certainly reprehensible in the eyes of tradition, in favour of equivocity. The metaphysical tongue is double; its words may always be shown to have two irreducible meanings (although not indeed 'opposed'). It is also deceptive, for it dissimulates its duplicity by retaining only one meaning, the 'right meaning', thereby claiming that the good is only good, that the true is all true and that meaning is full of meaning, etc. (Descombes, 1980: 140)

If Derrida shows us how philosophy requires rhetoric, then, how are we to turn this involvement around, so as to show, as we need to here, that literature might include philosophy within it? To do this it is necessary to return to Deleuze and Guattari, who offer a way in to thinking through the intermingling of these disciplines.

CONCEPTS OF SENSATIONS, SENSATIONS OF CONCEPTS

It might seem, at first glance, strange to attempt to consider the interrelation between literature and philosophy through reference to *What is Philosophy?*. Here, Deleuze and Guattari seem to spend a good deal of time isolating distinct 'kinds of thought': Philosophy, Science, and Art. These kinds of thought seem radically distinct: one might even consider them 'disciplines'; clearly, however, they are not disciplines in Foucault's sense (cf. Foucault, 1971); that is, they are not initially created through an order policed by rules of constraint and limitation. Rather, they are abstract kinds of thought which exist in the brain; that is, one assumes that we all more or less partake of these kinds of thought. Though we might and no doubt do develop one kind at the expense of the others, we are all capable of these kinds of thought that presuppose different kinds of questions about things. So then, when thinking 'philosophically', we might ask an abstract question of a thing – 'what/which one is it?' – and develop concepts in response to such questions. If thinking 'scientifically', we might ask – 'what does this thing do?' – and undertake partial observations so as to circumscribe how the thing functions. When thinking 'artistically', we might ask of this thing – 'how does it seem?'; 'how does it affect one?' – so as to perhaps create percepts and affects which are extracted from that thing. The kinds of thought, then, are, in an abstract sense, distinct, and they lead to differing forms of knowledge. Yet they all exist 'in the brain' and therefore they must, of necessity, also encounter one another. What interests me here, then, is the nature of this encounter. This interference is not described in great detail by Deleuze and Guattari, but they do touch upon it.

The three forms exist as three separate planes. The philosopher creates concepts and sets them in motion on the plane of immanence; the scientist lays down functions on the plane of reference or co-ordination by creating figures or undertaking partial observations; the artist creates affects and percepts or compounds of sensation on the plane of composition. These three forms of thought are understood as the three active responses of a human brain faced with the chaos of Being; active and necessarily on-going responses laying down planes on which their concepts, sensations, and functions are constantly in move-ment. These forms are distinguished from 'opinion', a reactive response which pretends that chaos can be tamed once and for all by insisting that concepts, functions, and sensations can be immobilized. The three forms not only define themselves against chaos then, they are also in constant conflict with opinion, which strives to limit their creation.

While the purity of the distinction between the three planes is stres-sed, Deleuze and Guattari also affirm that 'A rich tissue of correspon-dences can be established between the planes' (1994: 199). They con-clude that the 'three planes, along with their elements, are irreducible' (216), yet in drawing this conclusion they concede that there is of course interference; that is, having created the concepts which allow the distin-ction of these planes, they end by briefly sketching the question that now seems important to them, which concerns 'problems of interference between the planes that join up in the brain' (216).

In *What is Philosophy?* they go no further than to sketch the outlines of this interference. The first type is extrinsic: it involves one of the three (the philosopher for example) attempting to create a concept of a sensation or a function. In this case, what happens is that the concept ceases to behave like a concept; the 'interfering discipline must proceed with its own methods' (1994: 217). So the 'concept' of a sensation must in fact involve the creation not of a concept but of an affect, the philos-opher ceasing to be philosopher and becoming artist. The same would be true of the artist who attempted to create the sensation of a concept. This interference is a simple matter of planes being formed over planes. The planes do not merge. It is like a drop of oil resting on water.

There is a second 'intrinsic' type of interference. Here concepts (for example) leave their plane, the plane of immanence, and slip among 'the functions and partial observers, or among the sensations and aesthetic figures, on another plane'. This is a true subtle mixing that in turn produces mixed planes which 'are difficult to qualify' (1994: 217).

The final form of interferences 'cannot be localized'. Each kind of thought – science, art, philosophy – is also in relation with a negative of itself – non-science, non-art, non-philosophy. These negations are crucial to pedagogy (and Deleuze and Guattari have explained how in our time only pedagogy is capable of confronting opinion; 1994: 12): art has to teach non-art to feel, 'philosophy must teach us to conceive . . . science must teach us to know' (1994: 218), but this is not all. Each plane needs its own 'No', yet the No can only exist where the planes come into contact with chaos, rather than on the planes themselves. And this is where the third kind of interference occurs. In chaos the planes become indistinguishable, they cease *to be* as such. In this confusion: 'concepts, sensations, and functions become undecidable, at the same time as philosophy, art, and science become indiscernible, as if they shared the same shadow that extends itself across their different nature and constantly accompanies them' (218). What will, in large part, concern me in this book, then, is the nature of this interference with regard to literature and philosophy; that is, how Beckett might be said to produce 'sensations of concepts' which resonate with 'concepts of sensations' produced by philosophers.

THAT POETRY IS A PRIME CONDITION OF PHILOSOPHY

Before turning to a consideration of the interrelation between literature, philosophy and history, it is perhaps necessary to say more about the relation between literature and philosophy I am developing here, one which contends, following Beckett, that 'poetry is a prime condition of philosophy and civilization' (1983: 24). In a difficult passage from *What is Philosophy?* Deleuze and Guattari distinguish artistic or sensory becoming from philosophical or conceptual becoming. It might be useful to turn to this passage in order to further illustrate how philosophical concepts (of sensation) might be used to illustrate the compounds of sensations created by a writer such as Beckett.

Sensory becoming is the action by which something or someone is ceaselessly becoming-other (while continuing to be what they are), sunflower or Ahab, whereas conceptual becoming is the action by which the common event itself eludes what is. Conceptual becoming is heterogeneity grasped in an absolute form; sensory becoming is otherness caught in a matter of expression . . . [Artistic] universes are neither virtual or actual; they are possibles, the possible as aesthetic category . . . the existence of the possible, whereas events are the reality of the virtual, forms of a thought-Nature that survey every possible universe. (1994: 177)

Deleuze and Guattari affirm that concepts express events. Things might become clearer with an example. Yesterday, while sawing through a piece of wood, I bruised my hand. This could be understood in many ways. It comprises an event, the event of bruising, but there are many possible events of bruising. The concept of bruising, however, encompasses all the possible events of bruising. That is, the concept of bruising describes the virtual event of bruising: my grandfather's bruised toe, my bruised hand, my unborn great-grandson's bruised knee are all included under the concept of this virtual event. Thinking artistically rather than philosophically, however, I might write a short story about bruising, and, if I were an artist, I would hope to convey not so much the event, but to embody the virtual event in a possible world, and I would do this by creating a compound of sensations, the percepts and affects which combine to produce the sensations which one experiences in bruising a hand. If they should ever wish to discuss the virtual event of bruising conceptually, then, philosophers might perhaps quote my short story to illustrate this concept.[15] A critic might describe my method of composition, discover the actual event which inspired the story; or, perhaps, draw upon concepts of the sensation of bruising in order to interpret it.

We might better see how art and philosophy can be related through such an example. Art embodies the virtual event (the concept) in a possible world (by extracting it from the context of the actual world in which the artist lives and thereby creating the percept out of perception, the affect out of affection). The reality of art exists in possible worlds which are already free of the actual (and the causal chain of history) but are still related to the virtual (philosophical concepts) which they embody (rather than actualize). Because of this, I would argue, it is possible to use the concept (of a sensation) to relocate (that is, to interpret) the possible world.

A simple answer to the question of 'which criticism' would be: one which compares concepts, or virtual events, to the sensations or possible events which appear in Beckett's works. This might be termed a philosophical or aesthetic approach, but this is of little matter. What is important is that such an approach needs to establish the links which

---

[15] A scientist, considering the same phenomena would proceed very differently, describing the functions which go to produce the effects of bruising on soft tissue. An historian, on the other hand, would describe the particular event of the bruising of my hand on the 4 February 1997, drawing upon various opinions and perceptions to document this event.

would enable such comparison, links which would enable comparing philosophical concepts to literary sensations. To be more precise, one would be comparing the concepts of sensations which might appear in the work of a philosopher with the sensations of concepts which might appear in the work of a writer of fiction.

Haecceity, as the experience of immanence, for example, is a philosophical concept, but it might also be considered a special kind of sensation. It is a sensation which cannot be experienced;[16] it might, however, be 'apprehended'. This is a complex move to which I will attempt to do justice in chapter 2, below. Here, then, the apprehension of immanence described by Beckett might be understood as a sensation of a concept, while, on the other hand, the concept of 'haecceity' described by Deleuze and Guattari in *A Thousand Plateaus* (which I discuss in chapter 4, below) might be understood as an attempt to conceptually describe the sensation (or the apprehension) of immanence, and therefore it might be called a concept of a sensation.

My point is that the writer and philosophers might at times be said to approach similar ideas or sets of ideas from differing starting points. The philosophers often set out from the concept so as to describe a sensation, whereas, I would argue, Beckett often sets out from sensations which indicate or congeal about concepts which are concerned with change, with difference, with existence. Both the philosophers and the writer, then, oscillate between the boundaries set up between literature and philosophy, and, further, they encounter one another in this no-man's-land.

BEINGS OF SENSATION

For Deleuze and Guattari the blocs of sensation or compounds of sensation which artists create are also *beings* of sensation. The being of sensation, which is a complex of percepts and affects, is created from the juxtaposition or mixing of materials that vibrate in their mixture, or resonate through their relation (and such relations might be drawn closely together or might traverse the disjunction of unrelated series).[17]

---

[16] Because something needs to be experienced *by* someone or some other thing and immanence dissolves all the differentiation required for this kind of experience, as all things partake of the one thing which is immanence.

[17] On the 'asymmetrical synthesis of the sensible' involving three kinds of asymmetrical syntheses of forces ('Vibration', or Connective Synthesis; 'Resonance', or Conjunctive Synthesis; and 'Forced Movement', or Disjunctive Synthesis) which he identifies in Deleuze's aesthetics, and for an overview of Deleuze's aesthetic project, see Smith, 1996, especially pages 39–49).

While neither Deleuze and Guattari nor Daniel W. Smith, who has written an important article on Deleuze's aesthetics, dwell on this point, one might reflect on the implications of the notion of the *being* of sensation, implying, as it does, a separate existence. Is the existence separate because the work of art, once formed, no longer requires the human existence of the artist or depends upon the human existence of the individual viewer or reader for this existence, although it necessarily enters into complex relations with each of these individuals? To express this problem no doubt crudely: we all have perceptions and affections and opinions concerning the world (but these are necessarily and inseparably attached to our own existence, our own bodies and histories), what sets the artist apart is the manner in which the artist, drawing upon his or her experience or knowledge of the world, *extracts* percepts and affects from his or her own perceptions and affections, thereby creating not a set of opinions about the world but a compound of sensations which goes beyond simple opinion because it is detached from his or her own body, history and opinions. That is, the percepts and the affects differ from perception and affection in that the former exist independently of the individual (artist) while the latter cannot be separated from the individual around or within whom they exist.[18]

The artist, like anyone else, has opinions, but manages, through the sorcery of art, to leave these behind, offering us a bloc of sensations, which is something that stands up by itself. This, indeed, is why art can continue to exist long after the death of the artist and the death of the world in which the artist lived. The work, then, is sent out into the world by the artist, like a child, with its own body, a body comprised entirely of sensations that cannot be separated from the material form, be they words or paint or so on (either the sensation is realized in the material and does not exist outside the material, or the material passes into the sensation, becoming an aspect of that sensation; Deleuze and Guattari, 1994: 193).

Because it has a separate being, a separate existence, when the work encounters the reader it is not recreated or recomposed by that reader; rather, the reader enters into the compound of sensations which comprise the work's existence and affect that reader with new or previously unrecognized affects or percepts. We are drawn into the compound and we undergo the becoming which comprises the work. While the work requires both the writer and the reader, then, it still has a separate being

---

[18] Cf. Deleuze and Guattari, 1994: chapter 7.

(just as the child has a separate being from the parents and the others with which it interacts, although it could not exist if these parents and others did not exist).

The critic, then, cannot hope to fully explain or interpret any work, just as a biographer could not hope to fully explain or interpret any life. This, however, prevents neither works of literary criticism nor biographies from being written.

LITERATURE, PHILOSOPHY AND HISTORY:
THE PROBLEM-FIELD

We have just encountered the perhaps surprising notion that the blocs or compounds of sensation created by the writer are also beings with an existence which is separate both from that of the writer and that of the reader. This position, is, I feel, one which appeals to common sense: how else might we explain such things as the continuing relevance of the plays of Shakespeare, for example? The context of these plays changes with each performance, but, more strikingly, they have appealed to different peoples in different ages, few of whom will have had access to an adequate understanding of the Elizabethan England which was the context in which Shakespeare wrote. What better answer than that the plays have a being of their own, a being embodied in the sensations, the words, the character relations and the situations present in the plays. Nevertheless this notion of the being of sensations is undoubtedly controversial and provocative. Much criticism has explicitly attempted to tie the work either to the context of the writer (relying on the notion of authorial intention to limit possible interpretations of a text) or to the context of the reader (suggesting, for example, that the interpretations of readers are more important than any authorial intention, considering thereby that reading remakes or recreates any given work). The notion of the being of sensation, on the other hand, detaches the work from both the writer and the reader.

For my purposes, here, it will be necessary to consider one of the implications of this turn: that is, the relation of the work to history or historical milieux. As the being of sensation which is the work is separated from the author who sends it into the world, so too it must, in some sense, become detached from the history of the author. Writers who return to works they have written long before often feel dissatisfied, and at times, as with William Wordsworth (who reworked *The Prelude*), for example, or Samuel Butler (who added material to *Erewhon*), or

Samuel Beckett,[19] they have felt the need to revise the work of their younger selves. Clearly, the writers who wrote the original versions no longer exist when the revisions take place: critics are then left to argue over which of the versions is definitive. Once they are dead, of course, writers can do little to influence the fate of their works, their reputation is in the hands of new readers who might inhabit a world radically different to that in which the work was conceived. The work, of course, will always bear the marks of its conception and always bear the signature of its author (just as the child carries forth the image of the parents); my point is only that the duration of the work (the amount of time it continues to exist, to be read, to be printed) differs from that of the author, and the context in which it is received changes radically from the context in which it was conceived; so too, unless the writer (as some have been said to do) writes for 'all time', the intended audience will soon disappear. In this sense, then, the work detaches itself from the history within which the author must exist. It will have its own history, as it becomes more and less popular, as it appeals to a people, an age, and is overlooked by another.

Art preserves, but it preserves not the historical moment but a bloc of sensations (Deleuze and Guattari, 1994: 163–4). History is made up of perceptions, affections and opinions which are attached to people and peoples whereas art is formed from percepts and affects which the artist separates from the individual life to form beings of sensations. That is, rather than representing our world the work of art creates its own world which nevertheless opens into our world and speaks to it as we, readers in the world of history, enter into the compound of sensations offered by the work of art and are changed by it. So too, in embodying the virtual event through possible events the world of art brings to light these events, showing us *how it is* on an abstract level. Yet if art is not directly connected with the history of perceptions, affections and opinion, then neither is philosophy. The concept offers us the being of the event (which is virtual). The virtual event then, is not directly related to the particular events of *history*, yet it nevertheless describes them. Philosophy discusses the infinite: the *virtual* event which is timeless can nevertheless take the finite into account, while literature passes through the finite or particular to retrieve the infinite (Deleuze and Guattari, 1994: 197).

---

[19] With his revisions to *Godot, What Where* and other plays as director. Cf. Asmus, 1975, Chabert, 1980, Cluchey, 1984 and especially Knowlson, 1985, 1976, 1980.

'THE PROBLEM' AND HISTORY

Both, however, relate to history because their coming to light, their necessity, is determined by the particular historical problems from which they emerge. In fact literature and philosophy further come into contact insofar as they share, at the moment of their emergence, an historical milieu. Just as particular times and places foster certain kinds of art, so too particular times and places foster certain kinds of philosophy. Indeed, the relation of philosophy to its milieu and place is the major theme of chapter 4 of *What is Philosophy?*: 'Geophilosophy'. With regard to art, Deleuze and Guattari suggest that 'every sensation is a question', so too, concerning philosophy, every concept attempts to bring forth the event that expresses a problem. Therefore, developing a concept which corresponded to the event 'to die' would, in some sense, shed light on the problem offered by a writer who created a compound of sensations involved with the process of dying. The event, in effect, is that which comes to pass through the problem. Here philosophy comes into contact with history, as 'new concepts must relate to our problems, to our history, and above all, to our becomings' (1994: 27).

In philosophy, then, new problems are brought to light by the historical milieu as problems and types of becoming change with the times. So too, the artist discovers new sensations through the problems of his or her time and place: with Dostoyevsky's underground man, for example, we witness a bloc of sensations posing a problem which, according to Dostoyevsky, has specifically emerged in the historical time and place in which Dostoyevsky wrote.[20] It might be suggested that as much could be said of any true work of art. It is the problem, in effect, the problems of importance to one existing now and here, which links the work of art as much as the work of philosophy to history.

The event, as we have seen, the event of the bruise for example, is a matter of history as much as philosophy and literature. It is 'the problem' itself which ties art and philosophy and history together. Concepts are new events created to express the problems posed by current events (both philosophical and historical). In 'Geophilosophy' Deleuze and Guattari suggest that modern philosophy, the philosophy which they themselves practise, in confronting and critiquing capitalism becomes

[20] To quote from Dostoyevsky's author's note to *Notes from the Underground*: 'The author of the diary and diary itself are, of course, imaginary. Nevertheless it is clear that such persons as the writer of these notes not only may, but positively must, exist in our society, when we consider the circumstances in the midst of which our society is formed' (1992: 1).

'utopian'; a term which, following the references apparent in Samuel Butler's (anti-)utopia *Erewhon*, describes not only what is no-where but what is now-here. The term 'utopia', then, designates political philosophy: 'that conjunction of philosophy, or of the concept, with the present milieu' (Deleuze and Guattari, 1994: 100). The problems they pose are problems of the moment which therefore necessarily have political implications; that is, they comprise an attempt to come to terms with the contemporary world. So too, as Beckett's comments to Driver show,[21] in creating its sensations art must pose the problems of the moment; these might be 'universal' problems, but different universal problems occur at different times in history. The nineteenth century gave us Marx and Dickens, for example, and, at times at least, it might be argued that each was dealing with similar problems, Dickens's sensations posing the questions of history which Marx's concepts sought to express.

Michel Serres, a friend and contemporary of Deleuze, Derrida and Foucault, claims to be the first French philosopher to seriously consider the question of chaos. Interviewed by Bruno Latour in *Conversations on Science, Culture and Time* Michel Serres states:

My contemporaries will recognize themselves in what I have to say first. Here is the vital environment of those who were born, like me, around 1930: at age six, the war of 1936 in Spain; at age nine, the blitzkrieg of 1939, defeat and debacle; at age twelve, the split between the Resistance and the collaborators, the tragedy of the concentration camps and deportations; at age fourteen, Liberation and the settling of scores it brought with it in France; at age fifteen, Hiroshima. In short, from age nine to seventeen, when the body and sensitivity are being formed, it was the reign of hunger and rationing, death and bombings, a thousand crimes. We continued immediately with the colonial wars, in Indochina and then in Algeria . . . A written work, even an abstract one, cannot help remaining a distressed witness for a long time after such events, though it does not judge them . . . Weighing those early years in the balance, I can say that I only learned to disobey. All the events that took place around me only left me with the taste for disobedience. (1995: 2, 3, 20)

In his biography of Foucault, Didier Eribon quotes the following comments from Foucault:

the war arrived. Much more than the activities of family life, it was these events concerning the world which are the substance of our memory. I say 'our' because I am nearly sure that most boys and girls in France at this moment had the same experience. Our private life was really threatened. Maybe that is the

---

[21] Concerning the task of art now (to confront and accommodate the chaos in art).

reason why I am fascinated by history and the relationship between personal experience and those events of which we are a part. I think that is the nucleus of my theoretical desires. (Eribon, 1991: 10)

Further, in discussing the relations between the self and the 'unconscious' in *The Anti-Oedipus*, Deleuze and Guattari specifically turn from the supposed 'within' of the Freudian unconscious to the supposed 'without' of history:

The family does not engender its own ruptures. Families are filled with gaps and transected by breaks that are not familial: the Commune, the Dreyfus Affair, religion and atheism, the Spanish Civil War, the rise of fascism, Stalinism, the Vietnam War, May '68 – all these things form complexes of the unconscious, more effective than everlasting Oedipus. And the unconscious is indeed at issue here. If in fact there are structures, they do not exist in the mind, in the shadow of the fantastic phallus distributing the lacunae, the passages, and the articulations. Structures exist in the immediate impossible real. (Deleuze and Guattari, 1983: 97)

If the works of Beckett and philosophers such as Deleuze, Foucault, Serres, Derrida and Levinas have numerous and striking points of intersection, then it is partly because they have encountered or existed within the same non-discursive milieu (cf. Deleuze, 1989: 7–10), that time and place which produced the same series of problems, the same problem-field – the France, emerging from World War Two, of *'la guerre franco-française'*. That is to say they discuss the same problems because these were the social and intellectual problems inherent in the world they encountered. Each of their works, therefore, no matter how far they might seem to dissociate themselves from the political concerns of what was then the present, might be understood as differing attempts to come to terms with the same set of complex and contradictory problems (many of which we continue to encounter), as each, following the methods determined by the disciplines in which they worked, wrote not only (following Foucault) 'autobiographies', but 'histories of the present'.

This might further be exemplified with reference to the concept of the problem-field discussed by Deleuze in *Difference and Repetition*. Here the notion of problem-solving is related to societies, but it is also illuminating if related to texts which appear within those societies. In an article discussing the question of the rights of land ownership for Australian Aboriginals and Torres Strait Islanders as they are addressed in the Mabo decision of the Australian High Court, Paul Patton discusses Deleuze's notion of the problem-field around which structures are formed (Patton, 1995: 90). For Deleuze, events are themselves differences in that, like the present which repeats itself but is always a different present, the events which occur in our world are always different from one another. They are the things which happen in the world, the things which have happened and which are happening now, and it is this series of happenings which define who we are. Deleuze further considers that, like an animal adapting to a given environment, events happen around problems and it is the problems, if you like, which define the shape of a given society. The process is neatly summarized by Patton: 'The specific problems involved in a given form of society will determine the economic, juridical and political arrangements which constitute particular solutions, while the crucial events which mark the history of a society may be understood as the emergence of actual solutions to its problems, or the replacement of one set of solutions by another' (1995: 90).

We might arrive at a better explication of apparent similarities in the work of Beckett and the philosophers discussed in this book if we attend to this notion of the problem-field. That is, in short, the writers of fiction and philosophy, existing within the same problem-field (the same non-discursive milieu) write in response to common problems, drawing upon, as I will attempt to show, certain common antecedents, and thereby develop similar themes, similar responses.

This, then, might provide an explication of how works, apparently unrelated and belonging to different disciplinary traditions, resonate with one another within a given milieu. There was, in a sense, a problem-field which required a similar understanding of the nature of being in the world in post World War Two France; one which required an understanding of the nature of the decentred subject; one which had become aware of the fundamentally fascistic nature of judgements dependent on the concept of the unified subject. In consequence, against the political world of order, which chooses and generates black and white terms from which to choose, we find works which offer us a more inclusive world which reinserts the reality of human being in all its complexity into history (which, following Michel Serres, is no longer thought of as the simplistic uni-directional flow of a river, no longer as progress, but as the true, turbulent, chaotic flow, full of eddies and back-wash and sections otherwise released from the main current; Serres, 1995: 58–9).

There is another key component which serves to link together, in unexpected and continuously varying ways, the disciplines of literature, philosophy and history. In considering the manner in which the various internal elements within a work of art resonate and correspond, creating a compound of sensations from so many percepts and affects, Deleuze and Guattari briefly discuss the notion of 'counterpoint' in *What is Philosophy?* 'Counterpoint' is a concept which expresses the manner in which separate elements within a work influence and deform one another, resonating so as to produce the Refrain which constitutes the entire work (1994: 188). Earlier they had discussed how the displays of the bower bird creates a refrain which connects the bird's calls, gestures, and framing devices to the forest which opens to the cosmos in which it exists (184). The gestures, the calls, and the stage of leaves the bird constructs are separate elements, but the work of art the bird produces arrives through the collision of these elements in counterpoint, a compound into which the world itself is drawn.

It is clear, then, that the notion of counterpoint might be readily extended beyond the elements internal to the work of art. In 1988 I attended an excellent production of Shakespeare's *The Merchant of Venice* performed by the Royal Shakespeare Company at the Barbican in London and featuring Antony Sher in the role of Shylock. What struck me at the time was the manner in which the director skilfully made use of the fact that audiences can no longer watch this play and its Jewish lead character without thinking of the Holocaust. A 'purist', if we can imagine such a figure for the sake of argument, might claim that to allude to the Holocaust at all is to deform the play, as Shakespeare, of course, wrote hundreds of years before these historical events came to pass. Yet such an argument could change nothing in fact: no matter how hard one might try it is difficult to imagine a contemporary audience so ignorant of history as to not know of the Holocaust, and once one knows of the Holocaust it is impossible to watch a play which considers questions of anti-Semitism without these historical events being called to mind. Rather than fleeing from these associations, then, the director of this production underlined them through the setting, the programme to the production (which offered a history of Venice's Jewish ghetto at the time of the play's setting as well as a potted history of European anti-Semitism), and the emphasis given to key lines by the actors. What occurred, then, was a variation on Shakespeare's Refrain, as the play was allowed to enter into counterpoint with recent historical events as well as with the historical events known to Shakespeare. In short, rather than diminishing the play these new associations added resonance to the whole.

Clearly the director was not being overly original in 'modernizing' the historical contexts of the play: this is by now a well-worn method in Shakespearean productions. However, this does indicate, perhaps, something important about the nature of the relation between art and history: audiences are constantly contextualizing works by bringing them into relation with their own experiences and the historical milieux with which they are familiar. I would suggest that the reader, in effect, in contextualizing a work in this manner, is establishing new points of relation which enter into counterpoint with and add resonance to the compounds of sensations preserved by the work.

The same notion of counterpoint might be used to relate philosophy to art: new concepts, should the resonance be strong, might shed light on the sensations of existing works of art and enter into counterpoint with them, helping us to recognize aspects of the work we might previously have passed over. Works of literary criticism, if they attain a certain level of lucidity, might also enter into counterpoint with a work, influencing how audiences respond to that work (Esslin's development of the notion of the 'Theatre of the Absurd', for example, has surely influenced audiences and directors of Beckett's plays in this way). Counterpoint might also be used to explain the on-going importance of biographical and historical studies of literature. The effective biographer, like the effective literary historian, presents readers with materials which might enter into counterpoint with the work of art. Knowlson's uncovering of Beckett's strong interest in the visual arts is an example of a critic discovering a rich source of materials which might then enter into counterpoint with an artist's works (cf. Knowlson, 1996: 230–62).

To attempt to offer a fuzzy and generalized theory of genesis: most people would have little trouble in conceding that, in composing a work of art, the author will take other works of art, aspects of his or her own life experience, and historical events, and even, perhaps, philosophical concepts, transform them and place them in counterpoint with the being of sensations which is the work that author creates. The historical critic, and the biographer, and the critic who searches for allusions to other works in a work of art, might all be said to be unearthing materials which might be said to enter into counterpoint with the work under study. It is for this reason that, in Beckett studies, we owe a debt to James

Knowlson, Anthony Cronin, Lois Gordon and Deirdre Bair (who offer us materials of historical, artistic and biographical counterpoint) and to those other Beckett critics who will stand up over time (who might thereby add to our appreciation of Beckett by offering us critical and theoretical points of counterpoint).

In short, then, in addition to the arguments developed above, I feel that history and philosophy and literature might usefully be brought together around the notion of counterpoint. The writer writes in the midst of historical events, within a given milieu, drawing upon certain ideas and traditions, and the work created enters into counterpoint with these things. Later the work passes by new ideas, new historical events, encounters changed traditions, and, following the itinerary of its separate life, continues to enter into counterpoint with these things long after the writer who sent it into the world and the readers who first received it have passed away.

OBJECTIVES

Given that I have taken so long to come this far it is worth restating my objectives for the rest of this study. They are: to relate literature to philosophy by attempting to describe sensations of concepts in Beckett's Trilogy by relating them to concepts of sensations (by relating the possible events Beckett expresses to the virtual events expressed by the philosophers of difference); and to further relate these points of intersection by attempting to indicate historical problems which made the questions posed by the artist and expressed by the philosophers necessary.

I will look at each of the three novels of the trilogy in turn, identifying 'problems' (in the above-mentioned sense) in order to compare sensations and concepts. I will proceed either by attempting to describe concepts of sensations and sensations of concepts, or by comparing the virtual events described through philosophical concepts with the possible events embodied in literature, and, from time to time the actual events of history. In reading *Molloy*, as a way into the history of France of the forties, I will begin by examining the problem of surveillance and spectacle in Beckett and Foucault; then I will consider the problem of existence itself in Beckett, Deleuze and Guattari, Spinoza and Bergson. In reading *Malone Dies* I will consider the problem of ethics and morality; specifically focusing on the notion of judgement in Beckett and Deleuze and Guattari. Finally, in reading *The Unnamable* I will consider the difficulties of achieving justice; the aporia at the heart of the question of justice in Beckett, Levinas and Derrida. Existence, judgement, and justice, then, are the key problems I hope to encounter in this study, just as they have been key problems in recent French history and undoubtedly remain key problems for all of us everywhere here and now.

CHAPTER I

Molloy, surveillance, and secrets: Beckett and Foucault

LA GUERRE FRANCO-FRANÇAISE

To begin to test the kinds of interaction between literature, philosophy and history with regard to Beckett's Trilogy, it might be useful to juxtapose three texts: a work of literature (Samuel Beckett's *Molloy*), a work of philosophy attempting to describe the 'history of the present' (Michel Foucaults's *Discipline and Punish*) and an historical documentary film (Marcel Ophuls's *The Sorrow and the Pity*). I would begin by suggesting that all three enter into counterpoint around the historical events of what has come to be called *la guerre franco-française*, the French experience of the 1940s which included not only the period of Nazi occupation and the establishment of a French government at Vichy solicitous to the Nazis, but a virtual civil war fought along ideological lines which began in earnest on 16 June 1940 (when Marshal Pétain requested an armistice with the invading Germans), reached its peak in 1944, and continued after the Liberation of France in the form of a purge, or *épuration*, of those alleged to have collaborated with the Nazis (Rousso, 1991: 5).[1]

In *The Vichy Syndrome* the French historian Henry Rousso describes Marcel Ophuls's film *The Sorrow and the Pity*, released in 1969, as perhaps the first symptom of what was to be a new outbreak in France of cultural aftershocks from the French experience of the 1940s (Rousso, 1991: 100). The film ends with an American newsreel dating from 1944 in which the singer Maurice Chevalier flippantly denies rumours that he has been

---

[1] *The Sorrow and the Pity* directly treats this period of history; *Molloy*, completed between 1946 and 1947 in French, was written in the shadows cast by this period, which Beckett lived through as a member of the French Resistance and a refugee from the Gestapo; and *Discipline and Punish* is concerned with contemporary means of social ordering and control (the virtual events described by the concepts it develops of surveillance and spectacle, then, might be directly related to actual events of history during which such processes of control had been highlighted and pushed to their limit, as well as to possible events, described in a work of fiction which also concerns processes of social control).

killed in the purge and refutes in a more serious tone allegations that he had made a tour of Nazi Germany during the German occupation of France. He then goes on to sing, unaccompanied, a song with the following chorus:

> Let the whole world sigh or cry
> I'll be high in the sky
> Up on top of a rainbow,
> Sweeping the clouds away.
> ('*Sorrow and the Pity*', 1975: 173)

The closing scene gains resonance because we have heard Chevalier singing twice before in the film; on both occasions in propaganda newsreels made by the Vichy government. The contrast is further underlined by Ophuls as the second Chevalier song has been used to end part one of *The Sorrow and the Pity*. We have been directed towards a question, then, that we perhaps may not even wish to approach. A popular entertainer, a matinee idol, a veteran of the First World War and one of France's most beloved stars has been shown in blatant self-contradiction. Do we condemn him as a collaborator, or condemn the fact that he was, perhaps against his will, being used as a tool for propaganda, or do we shrug and say that, after all he was only a singer what else could he do but sing, no matter what the political climate?

This case highlights problems to do with judgement and the apportioning of blame and guilt, which are symptomatic of many of the cases shown in the film. It also highlights problems that arise when one state overturns another, which had been its enemy. Problems, in short, multiply. Yet what is the nature of these problems? Surprisingly, perhaps, I would suggest we might better come to understand their shape by repositioning a work of fiction, *Molloy*, into counterpoint with the historical period from which it emerged, and with a work of philosophy specifically concerned with questions of control and order.

In considering the functioning of order in *Discipline and Punish* Foucault develops a key dichotomy between the society of spectacle and the society of surveillance. A comparison between this text and *The Sorrow and the Pity*, however, underlines how this dichotomy is not neat: that is, spectacle has not passed completely away as societies turn to surveillance in their efforts to maintain order; rather, each seems involved in the other, so that the strange interrelation of these terms deeply affects the functioning of order. Further, I would suggest that *Molloy* shows us how this problem, the problem of the interrelation of these processes of ordering, might be more clearly defined, the question more subtly posed, thereby shedding light not only on Foucault's discoveries, but helping us to understand some of what is at stake in the otherwise apparently senseless events of the cruel period documented by *The Sorrow and the Pity*. As Rousso suggests;

The Sorrow and the Pity . . . disclosed a structural tension: the transmission of a history so full of conflict depends on an alchemy whose secret no one possesses – not the . . . [participants], not the historians, not the filmmakers. Nor can anyone claim exclusive possession of the truth. The truth is partial in both senses. History is not the mortar out of which an artificial unity can be created – unless the mortar is mixed with that express purpose in mind. *Sorrow* avoided just that. (1991: 114)

NEW INTERRELATIONSHIPS OF SPECTACLE AND SURVEILLANCE

If we open ourselves up to counterpoint, accepting for the moment the juxtaposition of these different texts attached to their separate disciplines, then Rousso's use of the words 'partial truth' above might cause bells to ring as we connect it with Foucault's description of the penal arithmetic which began in the Middle Ages, and carried through till the eighteenth century. Here the proofs used to establish the guilt of an accused were divided into categories such as full proof, semi-proof and distant clues. A full proof established guilt beyond doubt and led to execution, a semi-proof, however, meant that the accused was semi-guilty, and thus could undergo punishment (Foucault, 1991: 36, 42). Denunciation by a single eye-witness was enough to establish a semi-truth.

We might further equate this with the functioning of justice in France, both under Occupation and during the purge. In both cases denunciation was enough to justify arrest.[2] As well as this, in *The Sorrow and the Pity* we catch glimpses of a brutal world of punishment of the body strikingly similar to that world evoked by Foucault in *Discipline and Punish*. We are told of members of the French militia who confessed to plucking out the eyes of captured members of the resistance, placing live may bugs in their sockets and sowing up the eyelids ('*Sorrow and the*

---

[2] Lottman concludes, however, that there were significant differences between letters of denunciation under occupation and during the purge. The former were often anonymous, while Lottman shows that, officially, at least, under the purge the letters had to be signed, and states that these letters were generally treated with caution by the courts (Lottman, 1986: 77, 149).

Pity', 1975: 166–7). A former member of the Resistance describes the
torture of his wife at the hands of 'they': her nipples were torn off, she
was burned with a red-hot iron, and, he concludes, 'they buried her
without killing her first . . . one of the torturers himself told me that he
had pushed a broom handle into her vagina' (158). The horror of such
events does not pale beside Foucault's description of the execution of
Damiens, the regicide who was tortured and drawn and quartered
before what was left of his still living body was flung on to a pyre
(Foucault, 1991: 3–6).

In addition, in *The Sorrow and the Pity* we encounter something very like
the judicial torture (*la question*), of the eighteenth century and before,
which Foucault also describes at length. Here the accused, already
considered semi-guilty because of some semi-proof, is tortured in an
effort to extract a confession (1975: 38–42). In *The Sorrow and the Pity*,
Madam Solange tells us how she was arrested as a suspected collaborator – because of a letter of denunciation (161) – and tortured: 'he
plunged me into the tub. I held on . . . but they punched me on the chin
. . . I had to swallow water . . . the man . . . put his finger in my mouth. I
threw up . . . and he asked: "Well, do you confess or don't you?". . . . At
that moment I regretted not having done anything' (162–3). There are
also events recounted in *The Sorrow and the Pity* which remind us of the use
of punishment as a form of public edification, both under the occupation, where the Nazis rounded up and executed scores of people in
retribution for any casualties sustained at the hands of the Resistance,
and under the purge where, for example, women who had formed
relationships with Germans had their heads shaven before being subjected to public ridicule.

Here, then, we might begin to encounter some of the paradoxical
aspects of the relation between Foucault's dichotomy between the
society of spectacle and the society of surveillance. To clarify matters,
however, it is necessary to step back for a moment and trace through
Foucault's descriptions of the movement from the society of spectacle to
the society of surveillance in *Discipline and Punish*.

Foucault shows the disintegration of a number of codes leading to the
formation of the contemporary carceral network. The great spectacles
of torture used during the *ancien régime* as a means of training the
population against criminal activity are abandoned because the crowds
begin to feel too much sympathy for those tortured, because the state
appears too harsh in its penalties: the code has broken down, the
spectacles no longer signify that which they intend (Foucault, 1991:

58–69). Similarly, the spectacle of the chain gang is rendered ineffective by the irreverent attitude of the prisoners, who also manage to exceed the borders of the signifier 'convict' through the popular stories which circulate among the peasant class (the class they represent), glorifying their deeds. The chain gang is abandoned, new strategies have to be put in place to dislocate the empathy of the poor for the imprisoned (Foucault, 1991: 257–71).

In describing the society of surveillance, the new methods which emerged to take over the functions now inadequately performed by spectacle, the central image used in *Discipline and Punish* is Bentham's panopticon. In the nineteenth century the authorities exercising control over the excluded individual used two methods, that of branding and binary division (mad/sane; dangerous/harmless; normal/abnormal), and that of distribution in terms of difference; that is, of the type of coercion required in each case '(who he is; where he must be; how he is to be characterized; how he is to be recognized; how a constant surveillance is to be exercised over him in an individual way, etc.)' (199). Foucault goes on to conclude that 'All the mechanisms of power which, even today, are disposed around the abnormal individual, to brand him and to alter him, are composed of those two forms from which they distantly derive . . . Bentham's *Panopticon* is the architectural figure of this composition' (199–200).

The panopticon consists of a central observation tower surrounded by a circle or semicircle of cells. The structure allows the warder to view the inmate at all times. While the inmate is constantly aware of being watched, he/she can not see the authority in the tower who is watching. A lopsided and non-reciprocal power structure is then established which mirrors that between the judging transcendent God and Man (222). The major effect of the panopticon is 'to induce in the inmate a state of conscious and permanent visibility that assures the autonomous functioning of power' (201).

In our society, then, surveillance offers the dominant means of maintaining order. Yet, the examples taken from *The Sorrow and the Pity* underline the fact that torture and spectacle have not passed away in our time. How are we to understand this residue? What is left of the society of spectacle? What shadows does the medieval world cast upon our own? Clearly spectacle is no longer the same, and the passing of spectacle into surveillance is complex and produces strange effects, yet some of them, I feel, become apparent through a reading of *The Sorrow and the Pity* and *Molloy*.

PARADOXES OF ORDER: THE HIDDEN SPECTACLE,
THE OPEN SECRET

In short, I would suggest that the passing of spectacle into surveillance produces processes of paradox, indicated by oxymorons such as the 'hidden spectacle' and the 'open secret'. Further, these paradoxes seem to work through the interrelation of order and ignorance. What are the two defences most often used by those accused of war crimes? They are: (a) 'I was just obeying an order/the law' (cf. Lottman, 1986: 133–4, 269; Lacouture, 1991: 75–6); and (b) 'I did not know that this was going on.'

Perhaps rather than cynically sneering at these gestures, it might be more fruitful to attend to their shape and the hints at the nature of the structure of power they indicate. We are now used to the idea of secret wars. The Cold War was conducted in this way: so many spy novels and behind-the-scenes memoirs have been written recounting tales of es-pionage, of things going on in secret. World War Two already con-tained its secret wars within the declared wars: the French Resistance, for example, worked in secret, and the Gestapo provides the model for our notions of the secret police. Beckett's Resistance cell depended on secrecy for its survival and effectiveness, and, according to Bair and Knowlson, it was undone by a Gestapo spy in the shape of a supposed priest.[3] Members of the Resistance were tortured in secret, the deport-ation of the Jews and other 'enemies' of Fascism was undertaken in secret and, until the defeat of the Nazis, their fate was also successfully kept from most of those who lived through the war. The former spectacles of punishment, execution and torture, then, were still very much in existence, only now, paradoxically, they were being hidden away. The point I wish to make here is that, in order to be fought, secret wars require hierarchies built upon ignorance. The spy must be given his/her orders, his/her task, but it is dangerous for them to know too much; they must be kept in ignorance of everything other than that necessary to perform their tasks. Ignorance, then, is a key aspect within this system of order.

If, under oppressive regimes such as that experienced by the French during World War Two, the 'spectacles' have become 'hidden', it is also the case that they are necessarily somewhat poorly hidden. That is, the

---

[3] Cf. Bair, 1990: 336; Knowlson, 1996: 311–14. Gordon, 1996, however, disputes this claim, suggesting that the priest, Robert Alesch, only betrayed members of the Resistance in Lyons (see 142).

secret police function effectively through terror: in order to be effective, they must be feared. What goes on behind closed doors, then, the torture, the deportations, the executions, must also be readily accessible through rumour, at least. The hidden terror must become an open secret: people are expected to go in fear of a terror whose outlines they can only imagine, with their very ignorance exacerbating, rather than mitigating, the terror in which they are held. Further, however, this transformed 'spectacle', developing the medieval techniques we have inherited, now passes into surveillance through secrecy, for no one knows who might be an agent of the other side.

La guerre franco-française threw the workings of these disciplinary power structures into sharp relief. This supposition is based on the understanding, underlined throughout *The Sorrow and the Pity*, that in this time of civil war almost everyone not in power at a given moment could be seen, potentially, as an 'abnormal individual' and further, that anyone at all could be seen as a potential spy for the other side. The society had become one of fear and suspicion. In 1950–1 the American academic Laurence Wylie conducted a study of day to day life in the small village of Peyrane. This village, in the French Province of Vaucluse, is only a few miles from Roussillon, where Beckett spent the second half of World War Two hiding from the Gestapo after the betrayal of the Resistance cell for which he had worked in Paris.[4] Wylie describes the villagers' experience of the war as follows:

people had to buy on the black market . . . and that meant selling something on the black market . . . This meant a double violation of the law . . . to live in constant violation is uncomfortable. It leaves one vulnerable to attacks by *les autres*, that is, by all the other people of the village. By a simple denunciation any one of *les autres* may threaten disaster to your family. (1974: 28)

All this was taking place in a small village where people had lived all their lives, and Germans and Americans hardly even passed through this village during the war. Surely this is an example of the 'autonomous functioning of power'. It also gives an extreme example of the workings of our own society as Foucault sees it, a society of surveillance (Foucault, 1991: 209, 217), but one which, as *The Sorrow and the Pity* and *Molloy* teach us, also works through fear generated by the open secrets of the hidden spectacles of punishment.

---

[4] Cf. Bair, 1990: 340–66, Knowlson, 1996: 319–39, Cronin, 1996: 328–47, Gordon, 1996: 168–85.

CONSTERNATION – THE SECRET ORDER

It is worth turning to the possible events described in *Molloy* to shed some light on the virtual events described by Foucault and the actual events of *The Sorrow and the Pity*. In a well-known article by Israel Shenker, 'Moody Man of Letters', Beckett is quoted discussing the differences between his own works and those of Franz Kafka:

> The Kafka hero has a coherence of purpose. He's lost but he's not spiritually precarious, he's not falling to bits. My people seem to be falling to bits. Another difference. You notice how Kafka's form is classic, it goes on like a steamroller – almost serene. It seems to be threatened the whole time – but the consternation is in the form. In my work there is consternation behind the form, not in the form. (1956: 4)

What might Beckett mean by this notion of consternation 'behind' the form? If we are to consider in general terms the 'form' of *Molloy*, we might readily recognize that it is composed of two first-person narratives. The narratives, however, are apparently not undertaken freely – they both constitute reports which have been commissioned by some type of order – the nature of the order, however, and the purpose of the reports is never shown to us. We might guess that the one making the request is Youdi, but this is no answer: we have no real idea who Youdi is, and it seems likely that he is only a minor functionary, one rung in the hierarchy of power rather than the ultimate seat of power. Rather, the order remains hidden behind the forms it brings into being; we can only guess its shape which is hidden behind the reports and hidden from those who write the reports. That it is hidden is a cause for consternation. We are left with questions relating to the nature of this order, whereas, in Kafka, the order of 'bureaucracy' appears within the form of the narration. Kafka's characters are caught up within the machine of bureaucracy, they experience it from the inside; what happens is happening around them and directly to them. In *Molloy*, on the other hand, we encounter the paradox of the 'hidden spectacle'; or rather, we never encounter it, we merely sense its shadow, guess at its shape, which is never drawn out into the light of day (precisely because it is its nature to hide itself, to work through ignorance).

Foucault states that the 'turning of real lives into writing is no longer a procedure of heroization; it functions [now] as a procedure of objectification and subjection' (Foucault, 1991: 192). While the purpose of neither report is fully explained, it could be argued that they are meant as certificates of identification through which these abnormal individuals might be subjectified (Foucault, 1991: 199). It might be further argued that the process fails, as Molloy forgets too much and otherwise offers examples of his own dispersed subjectivity while Moran attempts to side-step the process by deliberately lying (as he suggests he has been all along through the well-known relation of the first and last sentences of his narrative).

In *Molloy*, while, as we shall see, at least in Moran's narrative, consciousness of surveillance is everywhere, there are only a few references to the 'hidden spectacle' described through those passages from *The Sorrow and the Pity* cited above. Most of them relate to Youdi, yet there is one direct reference to World War Two. Sending his son off to Hole because his leg has stiffened in the night, Moran flippantly asks, 'Who is the bicycle for, I said, Goering?' (Beckett, 1955: 196). Goering, of course, was responsible for both bringing the Gestapo into being and designing the infamous system of concentration and death camps; Moran's throw-away line implicitly links him with the Goering he is not (yet, may, perhaps resemble, in the eyes of his son). Earlier Molloy, who, though with his customary 'ataraxy', is conscious both of surveillance and the fate of those who fall foul of its exigencies into the open secret of society's terror and the anonymous 'they' who allow it to function, describes the techniques of survival:

Morning is the time to hide. They wake up, hale and hearty, their tongues hanging out for order, beauty and justice, baying for their due . . . towards noon things quiet down . . . Coming up to four or five of course there is the night-shift, the watchmen . . . you hug the walls, bowed down like a good boy, oozing with obsequiousness . . . the night purge is in the hands of technicians . . . the bulk of the population have no part in it . . . Day is the time for lynching, for sleep is sacred. (90)

Moran, on the other hand, works for the oppressive order as a spy, yet he claims to be ignorant of the fate of those he tracks down; it is not his province (187). Still, he clearly fears what will become of him if he disobeys orders: 'I was not going to expose myself to thunderbolts which might be fatal, simply because my son had the gripes' (162). The source of Moran's fear, his consternation (personified in the omniscient and omnipotent Godot-like Youdi,[5] and realized in the system for which

---

[5] In 'Interpreting *Molloy*' Fletcher refers to Deleuze's work on Sacher-Masoch in comparing this godlike figure to the father, Godot and Mr. Knott (Fletcher, 1970: 162). Thomas Trezise also compares Youdi to Knott, and Godot (Trezise, 1990: 46). Leslie Hill, like Linda Ben-Zvi and Alan Astro remarks that 'Youdi' is a derogatory French slang term for 'Jew' (Astro, 1990: 61; Ben-Zvi, 1986: 90; Hill, 1990: 98). None of these critics speculates as to the effect such a term used to designate one in power might have had on French readers who still would have had the unbelievable revelations surrounding the Holocaust ringing in their ears.

Moran works without understanding, and without knowing any others within that system but Gaber) is hidden from view.

DIFFERENCES BETWEEN MORAN AND MOLLOY: THE SECRET

A critical commonplace of Beckett studies has been to suggest that, throughout his narrative, Moran comes to resemble Molloy;[6] I feel, however, that much more might be brought to light through attending to their evident differences. Perhaps, with regard to the interrelation between spectacle and surveillance, the most important aspect of this difference might be seen through the different relations between order and ignorance that are established in each narrative.

Moran, as we have noted, obeys orders, indeed, he obeys orders to the very last (finishing the report that has been requested), but in doing so he is kept in ignorance. We have already touched on aspects of this ignorance; it goes to the very heart of the functioning of secrecy within institutions of power. Moran is only told the bare minimum he needs to know about any case and his descriptions of the role of the messenger who instantly forgets the message are well known. His only point of contact with the organization for which he works is Gaber, and Gaber, too, only works with Moran. He knows nothing of the fate of those he tracks down or the purpose of his assignments. Above all he knows nothing or next to nothing of Youdi, apart from what he is told by Gaber. For Moran, then, ignorance surrounds his orders. His obedience is the only area not composed of ignorance although he functions, for the system, through this ignorance. That is, ignorance is made a tool of order: Moran functions most effectively (as does the society as a whole) *because* he is kept in ignorance. Because of this, then, Moran can never really be sure that he is not continuing to obey orders, even once he begins to fall apart. Encountering Gaber towards the end of his narrative, he is concerned that Youdi might be angry that he has failed to carry out his orders, but Gaber tells Moran of Youdi's happiness, which seems connected in some way with Moran's plight (226). Moran is completely trapped, then, because as his ignorance is directly related to and is necessary to the order he follows, he cannot escape that order. Indeed, as I shall discuss below, Moran's power is totally dependent on

---

[6] The increasing resemblance between Moran and Molloy has been noted by a number of critics (see, for example, Cohn, 1973: 88–91; Kenner, 1973: 96–7; Fletcher, 1964: 149; 1970: 157–70; Doherty, 1971: 49–60; Ben-Zvi, 1986: 83–90; Alvarez, 1974: 54; Dettmar, 1990: 83; Rabinovitz, 1990: 31–67; Connor, 1988: 49–63; Trezise, 1990: 39–41).

what he knows, what he sees in spying on others, what he can verify. If he does move towards the 'vagrancy and freedom' he fears, it is not within his narrative, but promised in his assertion that he will no longer be the man he was and will now obey the voice in his head and move out to the garden. Yet within his narrative he never fully resembles Molloy: Moran still has his discipline, he still has his sense of order, his pride, his sense of self; ignorance, chaos, while it still surrounds and attacks him, has not yet completely driven order from his mind.

Through Molloy, on the other hand, we witness a surprisingly different interaction between order and ignorance. Rather than ignorance directly relating to and being necessary to the orders he is given, for Molloy orders pass into his own ignorance and disintegrate. That is, rather than ignorance being tamed and used as a tool by order, ignorance overcomes and dissolves that order. For the open secret to function effectively, both sides of the oxymoron must come into play: the secret must be open and hidden at the same time. With Molloy, however, through ignorance all becomes hidden and so the force of the power of oppressive order is nullified. He cannot follow orders; this is not necessarily because he does not want to, he is simply unable to. We see this when he first encounters the police: he cannot adequately answer the policeman's question as to what he is doing (25); at the station he fails to understand the sergeant (28–9); indeed, he has difficulty in understanding words altogether (40–1). There are orders he tries to follow: for example, the imperatives from within that tell him to go and see his mother (imperatives which underline the fact that his own freedom is partial), but due to his ignorance he is unable to follow these orders (it is others who finally deliver him to his mother's room). He too obeys the order to write a report, but he does so with indifference, he has no notion of its purpose or how to go about it or whether it is good or bad.

MOLLOY AND MORAN: SURVEILLANCE

If the differences between Molloy and Moran are apparent here with regard to the open secrets of order, they are also apparent with regard to surveillance and order. While Molloy is conscious of being watched, by the police, by Lousse (70–1),[7] by farmers, and so on, he does not enter

[7] Lousse is first called Loy by Molloy and the two names offer a range of interpretations. 'Loy' might refer to an Irish spade (reminding us that she buried her dog, would bury her parrot, and Molloy, if he let her: 49), or, alluding to 'Sansloy' from Spenser's *Faerie Queene*, might be taken to

into the rough game of surveillance; that is, he is watched, but he does not attempt to gain power by watching or spying in turn, nor, unlike Moran, does he recognize the supposed power of the one who watches him. This is not through decency; rather, Molloy is indifferent to and, as we have seen, ignorant of the workings of power.

The description of the society of surveillance, however, is most apparent in Moran's narrative. Unlike Molloy, Moran, at least at the commencement of his narrative, is very much part of society. And it is a society in which everyone is watching everyone else, the society of *les autres* described by Laurence Wylie.

To begin, the world Moran describes is middle-class and calm (126). The calm is soon shattered by the arrival of Gaber, Youdi's messenger, who instructs Moran to pursue Molloy. Subtly then, elements of hierarchical power are brought to our attention. In the two pages preceding Gaber's arrival Moran, to carefully choose a cliche, is master of all he surveys: he is the one who issues instructions to his son, to his cook; he watches over his bees, he imagines that he sees without being seen, but somehow Gaber sees him (127). Moran's illusion of power now begins to evaporate and we are made aware that the world he inhabits is one of continual surveillance. He catches a glimpse of his son spying on him from behind a bush and notes without satisfaction that, 'Peeping and prying were part of my profession. My son imitated me instinctively' (128). After his interview with Gaber he cannot locate his son, who he deduces has gone to church without him. But Moran is ever suspicious. He decides to ask Father Ambrose whether his son attended mass, and if he cannot help him, to ask the verger, who secretly notes all those who attend mass (130). Recognizing, perhaps, the apparently unchristian nature of such surveillance, Moran adds that 'It is only fair to say that Father Ambrose knew nothing of these manoeuvres, yes, anything in the nature of surveillance was hateful to the good Father Ambrose' (130–1). We soon learn, however, that Father Ambrose is not above surveillance as he questions Moran's son as to why Moran was absent from mass (136).

A moment from *The Sorrow and the Pity* brings to mind the conflation apparent here between religion, discipline, power and surveillance. Christian de la Maziere (who was a Fascist as a young man during the war and volunteered to serve in a French military unit fighting alongside the Nazis on the Eastern Front), asked what attracted him to fascism

mean 'law', that which seeks to hem in Molloy. Similarly, 'Lousse' is an obscure word meaning 'loose' or 'lust', referring, perhaps, to her love for Molloy, and negating, in a sense, the propriety of 'law'.

replies: 'The first impression we got from Nüremberg seemed to us a sort of birth, the birth of a new religion. I use the word "mass" now regularly because it really was like a mass. In every political ideology, there is a religious core' (1975: 149).

But the world of surveillance spreads beyond the confines of the church. Moran describes a meeting with an atheistic neighbour: 'A neighbour passed. A free-thinker. Well, well, he said, no worship today? He knew my habits, my Sunday habits I mean. Everyone knew them and the chief perhaps better than any, in spite of his remoteness' (133).

The purpose of surveillance is the desire to impose power through discipline and the model of this discipline is the judgement of an all-seeing, all-powerful God (whose omnipotence is inextricably linked with his omniscience). This is evident not just in the Sunday ritual, but in the moment-to-moment happenings in the household over which Moran rules with the severity of the God of the Old Testament. 'I like punctuality,' he states, 'all those whom my roof sheltered had to like it too' (133). Moran has a methodical mind and it is the progressive loss of this method and the gradual moving away from his disciplined approach that he seems to equate with the progressive dissolution of his body and mind.

As a final example for this list of the workings of surveillance in Moran's narrative we could turn to an episode with Moran and his cook, Martha. Martha also watches Moran, as Moran watches her, as he watches his son who watches him, as Youdi watches Moran. In this hierarchy Moran has some, though not absolute, power over those he observes. His power is mitigated by the extent to which they are able to watch him in turn and trick him with regard to their behaviour. The only absolute power is that of Youdi, who has this power because, like the operator of the panopticon, he sees without being seen, and seems to see all. In contrast, to exercise his own power Moran must remain vigilant and use his powers of deduction where his powers of surveillance let him down. But he fails to catch-out his cook, whom he suspects of an act of defiance. The scene is as follows: 'The stew was a great disappointment. Where are the onions? I cried. Gone to nothing, replied Martha. I rushed into the kitchen, to look for the onions I suspected her of having removed from the pot, because she knew how much I liked them. I even rummaged in the bin. She watched me mockingly' (139). The humour is augmented when we remember that the standard French rebuff hurled at someone considered a busybody, the equivalent in fact to 'mind your own business', is 'occupe-toi de tes oignons', which translates literally as 'mind your own onions'.

Clearly the world of surveillance Moran inhabits is an ordered hierarchical world, even if the nature of the hierarchy is hidden from view; such a world of hidden hierarchies still exists, no doubt, in the global economy for example, and its imagined shape is traced by contemporary paranoia (perhaps justified?), which appears in the modern mania for conspiracy theories.

If Molloy and Moran's narratives are different ways of responding to order, then we might recognize how Moran's narrative invites order in from the very beginning and attempts to evict it only after the greatest suffering and with a great deal of complaining and sentimentality. If ignorance is related to chaos then order successfully tames chaos much of the time in Moran's world, even as chaos disintegrates his body.

MOLLOY, IGNORANCE AND RESISTANCE

In Molloy's narrative, however, ignorance, chaos, has the upper hand. Molloy's narrative is short on physical events – the events themselves are often lost within sensations and meandering mental processes as his story lurches from one digression to the next in a free association of ideas (cf. 90 where his thoughts move from the day purge to night purge to sleep to beasts to zoos and children). In short, the significance of events dissolves before Molloy's experience of them. For Moran, the events of the ordered world drown out the sensations of the body. Moran tries to drive both emotion and abstract reflection out so that he can lean solidly on his opinions; but they fail him, falling into flitters in his hands, like his trusty umbrella. Molloy wonders whether Lousse's gardeners labour so hard merely to prevent change and Moran is a gardener of this type, only the garden overtakes him. Moran believes in a world of Platonic Forms, yet is forced to exist in a world of on-going change.

Opposed to the notions of surveillance and power in Beckett is the notion of freedom, and this notion is closely tied to questions of indiscipline, ignorance and failure. While neither Moran nor Molloy are truly free there is a difference of degree if not of nature in their relation to freedom. Moran does not want to be free if this means he must be removed from the comforts of society (181), whereas Molloy, while recognizing that his own freedom is limited, is more than happy with the small amount he is allowed given that he has no need for those comforts. Molloy states: 'I . . . loved the image of old Geulincx, dead young, who left me free, on the black boat of Ulysses, to crawl towards the East, along the deck. That is a great measure of freedom, for him who has not the pioneering spirit' (68). When *Molloy* was being translated into German the translator, Dr Franzen, wrote to Beckett requesting that he explain this particular passage. Beckett, who was not usually at all forthcoming when such requests were made, was on this occasion quite expansive. He wrote:

This passage is suggested (a) by a passage in the Ethics of Geulincx where he compares human freedom to that of a man, on board a boat carrying him irresistibly westward, free to move eastward within the limits of the boat itself, as far as the stern; and (b) by Ulysses' relation in Dante (Inf. 26) of his second voyage (a medieval tradition) to and beyond the Pillars of Hercules, his shipwreck and death . . . I imagine a member of the crew who does not share the adventurous spirit of Ulysses and is at least at liberty to crawl homewards . . . along the brief deck. (Beckett, 1984b)

Interestingly, the notion of opposing surveillance and order with ill-discipline and failure is also readily apparent in *Discipline and Punish* and *The Sorrow and the Pity*. In *The Sorrow and the Pity* two former members of the Resistance talk about their experience of the war. Marcel Faouche-Degliame states that 'The problems of everyday life no longer existed: we were very free.' Emmanuel d'Astier says, 'I think you could only have joined the Resistance if you were maladjusted.' Faouche-Degliame concludes: 'Free in the sense that, being outside organized society, all of society's objectives did not affect us very much, it simply didn't matter anymore' (1975: 118).

What is interesting about these comments is the notion of the type of freedom they convey: indiscipline, disorder. Tied to this idea of freedom is acceptance of the possibility or even inevitability of failure. Like Don Quixote or members of the Resistance such as Emmanuel d'Astier who states:

It's impossible to imagine a government minister, or a colonel, or an executive becoming a real partisan, a resister; if they're successful in their lives, then they'll be equally successful in dealing with Germans or Englishmen or Russians. But for all of us 'failures' – and I was a failure – well, we had the kind of Quixotic feelings that failures can always have. (118)

'Failure' has long been seen as one of the key ideas in Beckett's work.[8] Yet it is possible that the failure, linked with its freedom, comes about as

---

[8] Anecdotes concerning Beckett's affection for 'failure' and disdain for 'success' can be found in Bernold (1992a: 55–6) who recounts a conversation in which Beckett expressed his enthusiasm for the painter John Butler Yeats (father of William and Beckett's friend Jack), whom he admired because he had never finished anything, had botched his career, 'That's what one calls failure!'; and in Cioran, who recounts how Beckett turned his back angrily on a table of French literati debating which contemporary writers would come to be considered great (Cioran, 1992: 129–36).

much against the will of the one who fails as because of that will. Molloy opposes order, but his confusion shows that indiscipline as political opposition is not necessarily intentional.[9] The failure might be said to issue from the subject's resistance to subjectification. Foucault suggests that power should not be thought of as primarily destructive, but primarily creative. It produces the individual (Foucault, 1991: 194). It produces the soul (29). Yet if the subject comes into being through subjection to the order of secrets and surveillance, how can such a subject be free or freed, when, as Foucault concludes, 'The man described for us, whom we are invited to free, is already in himself the effect of a subjection much more profound than himself' (30). An answer might be that a type of freedom is to be found in that being which resists (even if unintentionally) subjectification. Moran wants to be who he is, but can only be 'freed' if he ceases to be a man, if he ceases to be Moran (240); Molloy, on the other hand, is familiar with the sensation of not being himself or anyone (56).

FREEDOM

The title of Beckett's first play, written in French just after *Molloy* and only recently published, is *Eleuthéria*, a Greek word meaning 'Freedom'. The protagonist Victor Krap, who wants nothing other than to not take part in society at all, is constantly harried by others who are scandalized by his behaviour (he comes, after all, from a good family), and demand that he explain his failure to act, his failure to take part. He cannot or will not. It is something he can only approach by negative definition. It is distance from others, the world, and the self, that Victor equates with freedom. He states:

(incoherently) You accept it when someone is beyond life, or when life is beyond you, and that people can refuse to compromise with life if they are prepared to pay the price and give up their liberty. He's abdicated, he's dead, he's mad, he's got faith, got cancer. Nothing wrong with that. But not to be one of you through being free, that's a disgrace and a scandal. (Beckett, 1996: 148)

To abandon society altogether and live 'far from it', with space under-

---

[9] This might disturb the revolutionary, but revolutionary ideals are no more immutable than anything else. In addition, it is possible that they appear as much through necessity, rather than through pure will. One is reminded of Sartre's assertion in *Saint Genet* that Genet, because he was a revolutionary through and through, chose to be homosexual. Genet shrugged at this idea, affirming that he had no choice in the matter, but rather had always been homosexual. Cf. White, 1993: 38.

stood here as intimately tied to perception (or rather want of it, as perception is tied to the self-surveillance of the fixed subject), as a means of achieving freedom is scandalous. The most visible of those who attempt to live in such a way, those who achieve such distance from our society while still living among us, are called bums, or vagabonds.

Molloy lives as a vagabond and as such attracts the attention not only of the police but of Welfare groups, who Foucault also mentions as serving a function of surveillance and discipline within society (1991: 212). Foucault cites numerous examples of laws enacted specifically as a means of incarcerating vagabonds who were seen as living dangerously outside society and therefore outside the law (88, 122, 210, 289–90).[10] The most telling example of the equation of vagabondage with freedom in *Discipline and Punish* is the case of Béasse, a child of thirteen, charged with vagabondage and sentenced to two years in prison in 1840. Foucault quotes from an account of the trial:

'The judge: . . . What is your station in life? . . . [Béasse]: I don't work for anybody. I've worked for myself for a long time now . . . – It would be better for you to be put into a good house, as an apprentice and learn a trade, – Oh, a good house, an apprenticeship, it's too much trouble. And anyway the bourgeois . . . always grumbling, no freedom. – Does not your father wish to reclaim you? – Haven't got no father. – And your mother? – No mother neither, no parents, no friends, free and independent.' (290–1)

The allusion to work and family in relation to propriety and property might remind us of the Vichy motto, 'Travail, Famille, Patrie', or perhaps the signs which hung at the gates of the entrance to Auschwitz and other Jewish extermination camps, stating, *'Arbeit macht frei'*, or 'work makes one free'. Foucault discusses how work was considered a purifying ethic reforming the morally corrupt whose sins were seen to stem from idleness (121–2). Such ill-discipline, such idleness, might also be linked to the subculture called *'zazou'* that existed in Paris during the Occupation.

Les zazous were a collection of upper middle-class French teenagers who listened to American swing. At a time when the French were being told their defeat in the war stemmed from decadence, a loss of the great values (such as work, family, etc.) and the influence of foreigners, and that they now must clean up their collective act; at a time, moreover,

---

[10] In an interview published in *Le Nouvel Observateur*, 25 May 1970, concerning his involvement with the Black Panthers, 'Genet was careful to deny that he was a revolutionary; he preferred the term "vagabond"' (White, 1993: 620).

when the Gestapo patrolled the streets and the best way to stay out of trouble was to blend in with everyone else, *les zazous* went out of their way to look and behave differently, with a difference that could only be considered decadent and foreign. They might be seen, in defiantly claiming their freedom to be different, to have constituted a kind of resistance. Perhaps the most striking example of their tongue-in-cheek defiance came when French Jews were ordered to prominently display a yellow Star of David with the word 'Juif' at all times. Some *zazous* made and openly wore yellows stars of their own. And in the centre they had written the word 'swing' (Thoumieux-Rioux, 1993: 32–9).

Such resistance involves not only indiscipline and disorder, but the short-circuiting of the panoptic machine and the society of secrecy. Instead of fearing the gaze of the society of surveillance *les zazous* welcome it, instead of hiding they ask to be seen, to be noticed, so that they might thumb their noses. This is the kind of resistance without ideology which questions our notions of what is political. Just as those notions are questioned by the type of freedom achieved through failure and the subversion of power through humour expressed in the works of Samuel Beckett. Early in the novel a policeman suspects Molloy of vagrancy and demands to see his papers:

Your papers! he cried. Ah my papers. Now the only papers I carry with me are bits of newspaper, to wipe myself, you understand, when I have a stool. Oh I don't say I wipe myself every time I have a stool, no, but I like to be in a position to do so, if I have to. Nothing strange about that, it seems to me. In a panic I took this paper from my pocket and thrust it under his nose. (Beckett, 1955: 26)

CHAPTER 2

Perception and apprehension: Bergson, Foucault, Deleuze and Guattari and Beckett

TWO PLANES IN 'MOLLOY': ORDER AND CHAOS

We are now ready to attempt to compare certain of the sensations Beckett creates in *Molloy* with concepts of sensations in an effort to better recognize the kinds of existence Beckett expresses. As has already been discussed, *Molloy* is broken into two parts, two 'relations' or reports. If we are to turn from the problem of the imposition of order, which was discussed in the previous chapter, to the problem itself of being in the world, it might be claimed that each part is primarily concerned with a different kind of being: the narrative of Molloy, a vagabond existing 'outside' society, might be read as an attempt to express a kind of existence outside order, an existence within disorder or chaos; the narrative of Moran, the bourgeois spy, on the other hand, might be read as an attempt to express a kind of existence within order, the ruled and regulated society. It is, of course, much more complicated than this, as the society of order reaches into Molloy's world and affects his being, just as disorder reaches into Moran's world and affects his; yet I will argue throughout that the world Beckett expresses presupposes two 'planes' or possibilities of existence, two planes which interpenetrate and are confused with one another but which nevertheless remain distinct.

As a point of departure, however, I might begin by referring to a joke in *Molloy* which I have not seen mentioned before. Moran begins his narrative in his garden. When Gaber arrives, he asks his son to fetch some beer and the brand of beer he drinks is 'Wallenstein' (Beckett, 1955: 132, 133). To the best of my knowledge no such brand exists. There was, however, a famous Austrian soldier of that name (1583–1634), and Schiller has kept his name alive in writing a dramatic trilogy based on Wallenstein's life. The first of these plays is 'Wallenstein's Lager'. There is, no doubt, in Beckett's reference here, a multilingual pun at play: 'lager' in both German and English refers to beer. In German, however, it also refers to 'camp', and this is the sense carried in Schiller's usage. Now, a military camp or fort is an outpost, the outpost of an order inhabiting hostile territory; and military orders strike out from camps in the attempt to subjugate such hostile territory. Moran's realm, then, might be read as the realm of order, an outpost or camp from which he strikes out in an effort to subjugate another realm, the realm of disorder or chaos which is inhabited by Molloy.

Movements between the realms of order and disorder, I feel, are embodied in the possible events of *Molloy*; in describing these finite events, however, Beckett is able to recapture the infinite, so that these movements might be seen not only to be particular to the characters Moran and Molloy, but in some sense generally applicable. That is, they describe an 'ideal real', passing into an indefinite, one which is, thereby, of on-going relevance to all of us, as we continue to exist between these realms of order and stability on the one hand, and disorder, change and disintegration on the other.

THE MOLAR AND THE MOLECULAR

In a footnote to the first chapter of *Discipline and Punish*, Michel Foucault acknowledges the influence of Deleuze and Guattari, who were then working on part one of 'Capitalism and Schizophrenia', *The Anti-Oedipus* (Foucault, 1991: 309). An aspect of this influence might be identified with reference to the Deleuzo-Guattarian concepts of the molar and molecular as they are described in *The Anti-Oedipus*.[1] The terminology is borrowed from physics and does not involve metaphor so much as matter.[2] In crude form these opposed terms are identified with the social (molar) and desire (molecular) (Deleuze and Guattari, 1983: 183). The molar concerns institutions, society writ large; the molar discourse is the discourse of history books as they are generally written, involving political parties, trade unions, religious, ethnic or ideological groupings for example, but organizations smaller indeed than these, schools, the

[1] While a number of Beckett critics have referred to the work of Deleuze, especially *Différence et répétition* (cf. Connor, 1988; Trezise, 1990; Locatelli, 1990; and Fletcher, 1970, who refers to Deleuze's essay on Sacher-Masoch), only Mary Bryden has given a sustained reading of the work of Deleuze and Guattari (although Watson, 1991 briefly touches upon their concepts of the body without organs and desire; see 94–5) in her book *Women in Samuel Beckett's Prose and Drama* (see especially the chapter 'Beckett/Deleuze/Guattari: Gender in Process', 58–69). André Bernold has also spoken and written on Deleuze and Beckett (see Bernold, 1992b; 1992a: 85–6).

[2] See Deleuze and Guattari, 1983: 283: 'the body without organs and its intensities are not metaphors, but matter itself'. The 'intensities' here refer to the molar and the molecular, which Deleuze and Guattari refer to as 'the two sides of the body without organs' (281).

family, (including the particular manifestations which comprise *your* school and *your* family). The molar aggregate is not only to be understood in abstract terms, it concerns the real interaction of real bodies insofar as these contribute to the production of larger bodies which are molar. These molar bodies interrelate in forming still larger molar bodies; think for example of the institutions which go together to form a state. In *A Thousand Plateaus* the molar is considered arborescent in structure, hierarchical (1987: 505). On the other hand, the molecular is concerned with multiplicities, unstable entities constantly undergoing processes of formation and transformation, constantly in flux. Yet the two poles are inextricably linked. Desiring-machines, which are composed of molecular multiplicities, 'never exist independently of the historical molar aggregates, of the macroscopic social formations that they constitute statistically' (1983: 183). The molecular is considered rhizomatic in structure, non-hierarchical, revolutionary in *A Thousand Plateaus* (1987: 505). The whole is molar, the multiplicity is molecular (1983: 69). The fixed human subject is a molar manifestation (1983: 287); there is no fixed subject in desire (identified with the molecular): desire lacks a subject (26).

An isomorphism might be recognized between important conceptual pairings in Bergson, Spinoza, Foucault and Deleuze and Guattari: Spinoza's distinction (of types of existence) between the absolutely infinite substance, and the finite modes; Bergson's distinction between 'concrete extensity' and 'homogeneous space'; and Deleuze and Guattari's distinctions between the molar and molecular and those subsequently developed (in *A Thousand Plateaus*) between (i) the strata and the plane of consistency and (ii) the plan(e)[3] of organization and the plane of consistency. We might add to this list Schopenhauer's Idea or 'thing in itself' (which seems to resemble, as I discussed in the introduction, Spinoza's substance and so Bergson's concrete extensity and Deleuze and Guattari's plane of consistency) and his understanding of the principle of sufficient reason and the *principium individuationis* (which resembles the production of homogeneous space in Bergson, which distinguishes individuals in the manner of Deleuze and Guattari's plan(e) of organization and Spinoza's modes). Further, I hope to show in this chapter how Beckettian distinctions between non-relation (substance) and relation (modes) and disorder (substance) and order (modes) might be added to this list.

---

[3] See Massumi's note on this translation (Deleuze and Guattari, 1983: xvii).

In *The Anti-Oedipus* Deleuze and Guattari state that, 'The body without organs is the immanent substance, in the most Spinozist sense of the word' (1983: 327). Their description of the relation between the body without organs and the molar and molecular is complex. As noted (in footnote 2) above, to an extent they are considered to constitute the two sides of the body without organs. On the other hand, however, the schizophrenic – which is in turn related to desire, the molecular (277, 286) – is shown to have a privileged relation to the body without organs,[4] while the social machine – related to the paranoiac, the molar – is in certain senses opposed to it.[5] Read in this way the molecular level (through its proximity with the BwO) might be compared with Spinoza's substance, and through extrapolation the molar might be compared with Spinoza's modes. The identification becomes at once clearer and more obscure in *A Thousand Plateaus* with the introduction of the new conceptual pairings, the strata/plane of consistency, plan(e) of organization/plane of consistency. While these pairings are more readily comparable to Spinoza's distinction between substance and modes,[6] the distinction between the molar and molecular now becomes largely subordinate to them. The molar and molecular are described as together partaking of the strata which are concerned with formed matter (whether atomic or organic), while the plane of consistency is concerned with the phylum, or unformed matter, the chaos from which the world (of the strata) is created (1987: 502–3). In such a description the former might be compared with modes, the latter with substance. To highlight this comparison it is the plane of consistency which is now identified with the body without organs (507). In plateau ten the plan(e) of organization replaces the strata in opposition to the plane of consistency in order to facilitate the discussion of the formation of individuals. The

---

[4] 'the schizophrenic table is a body without organs' (1983: 8).

[5] 'The social machine or socius . . . is never a projection . . . of the body without organs' (1983: 33).

[6] It is never, however, completely possible to perfectly identify Deleuze and Guattari's concepts with those of Spinoza. Spinoza's substance is a metaphysical entity; it is absolutely indivisible univocal Being while the molecular level is composed of multiplicities. To completely identify the two would involve a naive materialist reading of *The Ethics*, one which Spinoza specifically disallows in Part 1, Props. 12 and 13. Through recourse to the concept of the BwO, however, Deleuze and Guattari do identify a proximity; this proximity is clearer in relation to the plane of consistency which, like Bergson's concrete extensity, is conceptualized not as composed of multiplicities but as indivisible, unformed matter. The identification with the metaphysical substance then, is still incomplete, as Deleuze and Guattari and Bergson are describing the physical, and the precise nature of the causal relation between Spinoza's metaphysical Nature (substance, *natura naturans*, or naturing nature) and physical nature (modes, *natura naturata*, or natured nature) is one of the most controversial points of *The Ethics*. For an aspect of Deleuze's response to this problem, see Deleuze, 1988b: 92–3.

former is the plane which constitutes fixed subjects, the latter constitutes a different conceptualization of an individual called haecceities (506–8).[7] However, to complicate these identifications further, this opposition might be related not only to mode/substance but to the description of the molar and molecular given in *The Anti-Oedipus* whereby the molar is seen to be the level on which subjects are produced and the molecular is said to constitute multiplicities or assemblages of elements similar to the haecceity type: 'Yes, all becomings are molecular: the flower, or stone one becomes are molecular collectivities, haecceities, not molar sub-jects, objects, or form that we know from the outside and recognize from experience, through science, or by habit' (1983: 1987: 275).[8]

Added to the isomorphism of Spinoza's and Deleuze and Guattari's concepts there is that with Bergson's opposition (described in *Matter and Memory*) between concrete extensity (which most resembles the 'un-formed matter' or phylum of the plane of consistency and so the molecular of *The Anti-Oedipus* and Spinoza's substance) and homogene-ous space (the level on which objects and subjects are identified, re-sembling the strata, the molar of *The Anti-Oedipus*, the plan(e) of organiz-ation and Spinoza's modes). A further, partial comparison might be made between the concepts of the molar, the strata, the plan(e) of organization, and Foucault's descriptions of the institutions of discipline in *Discipline and Punish*. Much of the following discussion depends upon the isomorphism of these concepts and how they might be related to the planes of order and chaos in *Molloy*.

INCLUSIVE DISJUNCTION

In *The Anti-Oedipus* Deleuze and Guattari conceive of the molar and the molecular as polarities (1983: 277–83) and describe one aspect of the relation between the two in terms of a kind of oscillation, which they term 'inclusive disjunction'.[9] 'Inclusive disjunction' is a concept

---

[7] A fuller discussion of these distinctions is given in chapter 4 below.
[8] The reference to 'habit' calls to mind, as we shall see below, the work of Bergson.
[9] Leslie Hill uses Beckett's concept – developed in 'Dante . . . Bruno . Vico . . Joyce' (Beckett, 1983: 19–33) – of the 'coincidence of contraries' in a very similar way to how I use 'inclusive disjunction' here. Hill's reading is extremely interesting and an important contribution to Beckett studies. I feel, however, that the Deleuzo-Guattarian conceptual framework provides a superior means of describing what is at stake here. Firstly, because the concept described by Beckett describes an 'identification' (Beckett, 1983: 21). The inclusive disjunction, however, 'does not reduce two contraries to an identity of the same; [it] affirms their distance as that which relates the two as different'. The *difference* is important. This is not to say that Hill does not do justice to the notion of difference in his reading of identified contraries (on the contrary).

Deleuze has turned to again in his recent essay discussing the work of Samuel Beckett (Deleuze, 1995) yet, already, in *The Anti-Oedipus*, they acknowledge Beckett in describing its functioning:

The schizophrenic is dead *or* alive, not both at once, but each of the two as the terminal point of a distance over which he glides. He is child *or* parent, not both, but the one at the end of the other, like the two ends of a stick in a nondecomposable space. This is the meaning of the disjunctions where Beckett records his characters and the events that befall them: *everything divides, but into itself* . . . [The schizophrenic] does not reduce two contraries to an identity of the same; he affirms their distance as that which relates the two as different . . . The disjunction, being now inclusive, does not closet itself inside its own terms. On the contrary it is nonrestrictive. 'I was then no longer that sealed jar to which I owed my being so well preserved, but a wall gave way'[10]– an event that will liberate a space where Molloy and Moran no longer designate persons, but singularities flocking from all sides, evanescent agents of production. (76–7)

The inclusive disjunction is required to complicate a simple opposition between the molar and molecular:

There are fundamentally two poles; but we would not be satisfied if we had to present them merely as the duality of the molar formations and the molecular formations, since there is not one molecular formation that is not by itself an investment of a molar formation. There are no desiring-machines that exist outside the social machines that they form on a large scale; and no social machines without the desiring-machines that inhabit them on a small scale . . . everywhere there exist the molecular *and* the molar: their disjunction is a relation of included disjunction, which varies only according to the two directions of subordination, according as the molecular phenomena are subordinated to the large aggregates, or on the contrary subordinate them to themselves. (340–1)

Elsewhere in *The Anti-Oedipus*, however, Deleuze and Guattari work with this dualism, opposing the paranoiac (aligned with the fascistic molar bodies) to the schizophrenic (aligned with the revolutionary molecular bodies). It is a contradiction they readily acknowledge and it will appear again in slightly different form in *A Thousand Plateaus*, when they discuss the relation between the plane of consistency and the plan(e) of organization (1987: 262).[11] A consequence of this contradiction is that the importance of perception is underlined. The gaze, perception, might be regarded as being of central importance not only to

[10] This quote is taken from *Molloy* by Beckett (65). I have modified the translation; replacing Lane, Hurley and Seem's translation of Beckett's French version with Beckett's own translation.
[11] This relation is discussed in chapter 4 below.

Discipline and Punish, and Beckett's *Molloy* in particular, but to notions of freedom and the nature of the individual in general.[12]

The project of describing the relation between the molar and the molecular, which is not only a project undertaken by Deleuze and Guattari (and, according to their reading, at work in Beckett's fiction) but also, as he asserts in an interview, by Foucault (1980: 124), is one which serves to show that the molar which produces fixed subjects is not all-powerful. The description alone of the relation between the molar and molecular could only have the effect of giving alternatives to the single, molar perspective. They might provide a counter-memory with which to oppose the histories of institutions, for example, or a description of the complex interactions between institutions and individuals, an interaction that is complex because it is not simply monodirectional, not simply a one-way street involving the repression of individuals by institutions.

AFFECTS AND BEING AFFECTED

It might be argued that *Discipline and Punish* does not simply describe how the molar institutions of discipline produce subjects (which would leave us with little more than despairing images of an inescapable process of subjection); but rather that it describes how molar bodies *affect* molecular bodies. The affect described is crucial in that it de-creases the affected body's ability to receive other affects, which amounts to reducing that body's power to act. Spinoza has described a body's power to act in terms of its ability to affect and to be affected: a powerful body is a body that can be affected in many ways. If you build up one of the body's faculties to the detriment of other of its faculties, you are not increasing your power but decreasing it. If you work obsessively on increasing the size of your muscles, for example, and that obsession serves to weaken other of your faculties, you would not become stronger, you would become weaker (cf. Lloyd, 1996: 91). *Discipline and Punish* is about repression, it provides a description of processes through which a body's ability to be affected is reduced; it shows how bodies are trained, exercised, so that they do not act, but simply react, through habit, duty, a sense of right and wrong. But this description itself constitutes a counter-memory, a change of perspec-tive. In showing how an individual's power to affect and be affected are

---

[12] Iser mentions the importance of perception in *Molloy*, but he does so in developing (briefly) an opposition between consciousness and self-consciousness which is not what I hope to do here. See Iser, 1974: 166–7.

strictly controlled by molar institutions, Foucault may succeed in putting the habit out of joint, to cause us to question the strictness of our routines. This in turn might amount to a modification of codes whereby we begin to doubt the justness between the relation of two terms (as for example the relation between an individual designated as a delinquent and a prison term as a viable means of correction). Yet we are not provided with a step-by-step plan of action; rather it is the intellectual's role to provide us with a 'topological and geological survey of the battlefield' (Foucault, 1980: 62).

This overview, however, as a counter-narrative, might itself undermine the faith of individuals in the code, facilitating a line of flight, a revolutionary tendency initiated on the molecular plane (cf. Deleuze and Guattari, 1983: 281–3). Such revolutionary tendencies are those to which Deleuze and Guattari refer when they speak of molecular phenomena subordinating the molar to themselves. Examples of such revolutionary moments appear in *Discipline and Punish*, thereby affirming that the power relation is not monodirectional, from the molar to the molecular.

BECKETT'S 'PROUST', BERGSON, FOUCAULT AND HABIT

A similar revolutionary movement can be recognized in the concept of 'involuntary memory' which Beckett describes in his reading of Proust.[13] The individual is characteristically a creature of habit. Such might be considered a disciplined individual who has been successfully subjectified by the molar institutions. 'Habit is a compromise effected between the individual and his environment, or between the individual and his own organic eccentricities, the guarantee of a dull inviolability' (Beckett, 1987: 18–19). The description of habit is similar to Henri Bergson's descriptions of the effectively functioning mature human being in *Matter and Memory*. For Bergson habit involves the diminution of the intake of sensory data, it involves choice, something is learned by heart, a ready-made response to a given situation is adopted which removes the need for the being to respond to the cacophony of questions which are constantly posed by pure sensory perception and thus allows action to

---

[13] A number of critics have referred to *Proust* as 'the preliminary to Beckett's works' (see, for example, Jacobsen and Mueller, 1969: 60; Rosen, 1976: 173; Fletcher, 1967: 19). I will be referring exclusively here to Beckett's essay, not how it relates to Proust's work. For detailed readings which examine this question, see in particular Zurbrugg, 1988, and Pilling, 1993. While Bergson has been mentioned from time to time (by critics such as Connor, 1988, and Pilling, 1976), little work has been done to date relating his ideas to Beckett's works.

take place (Bergson, 1991: 44–5). For Bergson habit allows the individual to act, to live:

> our whole life is passed among a limited number of objects, which pass more or less often before our eyes: each of them, as it is perceived, provokes on our part movements, at least nascent, whereby we adapt ourselves to it. These movements, as they recur, contrive a mechanism for themselves, grow into a habit and determine in us attitudes which automatically follow our perception of things. (84)

Both Beckett and Bergson oppose a similar kind of memory to habit: one which Beckett (extracting his concepts from his reading of Proust and Bergson) terms 'involuntary', and Bergson calls 'spontaneous' (Bergson, 1991: 83–5; Beckett, 1987: 28–30). For Bergson part of the purpose of habit is to inhibit spontaneous memory. Habit is developed through training, experience or education: consequently spontaneous memory is most apparent in children and savages, because they are ill-disciplined:

> The extraordinary development of spontaneous memory in most children is due to the fact that they have not yet persuaded their memory to remain bound up with their conduct. They usually follow the impression of the moment, and as with them action does not bow to the suggestions of memory, so neither are their recollections limited to the necessities of action. (1991: 153–4)

When the molar wishes to act upon the individual and render him/her docile, then, it does so through training, exercise, education (cf. Foucault, 1991); that is, it does so by creating habit. The ideal of transparent punitive codes proposed in the eighteenth century which Foucault describes would have functioned through habit: an effect (such and such a punishment) is, ideally, eternally and forcefully linked to a cause (such and such a crime) in order to educate the population so that they might master the habit of obeying the law (98, 106, 110–14). For the artist, however, as he is represented by Proust's narrator as described by Beckett, involuntary memory which erupts into the present and puts habit out of joint is equated with the revolutionary reappearance of pure sensation into the numbness of everyday existence. That is, it is one of the ways in which the molecular might exceed the molar, overflowing its borders. Beckett quotes Proust: 'If there were no such thing as Habit, Life would of necessity appear delicious to all those whom Death would threaten at every moment, that is to say, all Mankind' (1987: 29).

It might be further argued that this overflowing of sensation equates to an increase in the body's ability to be affected. And indeed, Bergson links perception, affection, and the power to act, though in promoting an opposite point of view:

[The body] does not merely reflect action received from without; it struggles, and thus absorbs part of this action. Here is the source of affection . . . Perception, understood as we understand it, measures our possible action upon things, and thereby, inversely, the possible action of things upon us. The greater the body's power of action (symbolized by a higher degree of complexity in the nervous system), the wider is the field that perception embraces. (1991: 56)

With regard to action, the power to act, when Bergson speaks of perception he is talking of *conscious* perception, which is antithetical to the pure sensation experienced at the moment of involuntary or spontaneous memory. Bergson concludes that to 'perceive all the influences from all the points of all bodies would be to descend to the condition of a material object. Conscious perception signifies choice, and consciousness mainly consists in this practical discernment' (49). Such pure sensation, however, descending to 'the condition of a material object', resembles not only Molloy's state from time to time but the being of the unformed matter of the body without organs on the plane of consistency, described by Deleuze and Guattari.

If Bergson's conclusions with regard to the *value* of the proper functioning of the human being differ from those of Foucault, Deleuze and Guattari and Beckett, his understanding of *how* that being functions seems to be in accord with theirs. Indeed his system constitutes a major influence on Deleuze (see Hardt, 1993) and was well known to Foucault (Eribon, 1991: 38) and to Beckett who, in his youth, lectured at Trinity College, Dublin on Bergson (Pilling, 1976: 7; Cronin, 1996: 127). Similarly Bergson (Hardt, 1993: 130, n. 3), Foucault (Eribon, 1991: 38), Deleuze (Hardt, 1993: 56–111), Schopenhauer[14] and Beckett (Pilling, 1992: 2–3) were all close readers of Spinoza.

MOLLOY: ESCAPING HABIT

In *Molloy* the molecular assault on the disciplined molar individual Moran is of central concern. In *Proust* the mind is shown spilling over

[14] Schopenhauer refers favourably to Spinoza throughout *The World as Will and Idea*. See in particular Book 3, paragraph 34 (part of which I have cited in the introduction above), where he refers to the opening to the Idea as being precisely that which 'was in Spinoza's mind when he wrote: "The mind is eternal insofar as it understands under the aspect of eternity" (*Ethics*, V. 31, note)'; that is, the mind is eternal insofar as it understands itself as an aspect of the one substance, God or Nature, which, Schopenhauer understands as being equivalent to the revelation of the Idea.

into the body through involuntary memory, putting habit out of joint, and thereby transporting Proust's narrator beyond the mundaneness of the plan(e) of organization (a molar plane) to a plane of overwhelmingly intense pure sensation, a plane which, though formed from a world which is past, is in a sense more immanent than the present world of habit and manners because it is a world in which everything, all sensation, is experienced at once (Beckett, 1987: 35–45).

In *Molloy*, on the contrary, it is the body which spills over into the mind: against the afflatus of Proust's aesthetic vision of recuperation Beckett posits a corporeal degeneration. Moran changes physically, and the physical changes (most manifest in the stiffening of one of his legs) produce corresponding affects in his mental state. The degeneration of the mind and body run parallel, and together they constitute a molecular metamorphosis which ends in prising Moran from his comfortable existence within the molar institutions. He was religious, a disciplinarian father, a good worker understanding both his station and his duty, with a well-kept house in a respectable community in which he was readily accepted; he ends with no belief in God (against whom he blasphemes), no interest in his son (whom he is about to abandon), unemployed and without interest in further work, allowing his house and property to run down, largely outside the community, on the verge of vagabondage.

MORAN'S CORPOREAL DEGENERATION

In accordance with these changes Moran begins to *feel* more. The first hint of his physical malaise comes immediately after his orders concerning Molloy. Instead of setting his mind firmly to the external task, as is his habit, a task which involves thorough planning and discipline, he allows his mind to wander, turning inward and inventing a Molloy who bears little relation to the facts at his disposal; the molecular acting on the molar:

That a man like me, so meticulous and calm in the main, so patiently turned towards the outer world as towards the lesser evil, creature of his house, of his garden, of his few poor possessions, discharging faithfully and ably a revolting function, reining back his thoughts within the limits of the calculable so great is his horror of fancy, that a man so contrived, for I was a contrivance, should let himself be haunted and possessed by chimeras, this ought to have seemed strange to me and been a warning to me to have a care, in my own interest. (Beckett, 1955: 156)

He feels an acute pain in one of his legs, which, it later becomes apparent, is the first warning that it is about to stiffen (163). He becomes uncharacteristically sentimental; towards his maid Martha, and his son (165–6). He strikes his son violently and joins in the general tears after the event (173–4). His behaviour becomes increasingly erratic, increasingly less well planned. Clearly Moran moves away from habit, the existence neatly set out in time and space that was his (that existence we are trained to adopt by the molar institutions of the plan(e) of organization) towards pure sensation that equates with immanent existence, the plane of consistency. Bergson would maintain that this would decrease Moran's power of action (and indeed it does, within the ordered world at least). For Beckett, however, Moran's dissolution, his movement towards vagabondage is, as we have seen in the previous chapter, like the vagabondage Foucault describes in *Discipline and Punish*, a movement towards freedom. He is, if all unwittingly, kicking clear of the institutions which have enslaved him, following a process Deleuze and Guattari term a line of flight or escape, a process instigated on the molecular level which consequently involves a turning from a world of analogy or resemblance to Forms and towards a world of real existence, a process which might, in consequence, give one the impression that one is casting off the trappings of the properly subjectified self and approaching, perhaps, the essence of self which it would be assumed lies underneath:

Physically speaking it seemed to me I was now becoming rapidly unrecognizable. And when I passed my hands over my face . . . the face my hands felt was not my face any more, and the hands my face felt were my hands no longer. And yet the gist of the sensation was the same . . . And to tell the truth I not only knew who I was, but I had a sharper and clearer sense of my identity than ever before, in spite of its deep lesions and the wounds with which it was covered. (233–4)

What we witness here are sensations of change: Beckett shows us how change or becoming is intimately tied up with sensations and suffering. The artist, that is, adds to our understanding of the process expressed conceptually by the philosophers by showing us the pain and decay involved in each move.

These processes of metamorphosis are closely allied to the opposition between conscious perception and pure sensation. In Beckett's *Proust*, as in *Molloy*, pure sensation is all-encompassing, relating to all the senses; it is the return of the immanent cacophony of sensory stimulation. By a

process of metonymy we are in the habit of discussing conscious perception through reference to the gaze. *Discipline and Punish*, insofar as it
illuminates a reading of *Molloy*, might best be read paying strict attention
to the gaze.

Discipline and Punish addresses itself to non-reciprocal power structures, the molar acting on and affecting (with an affect that selectively
reduces other affects) the individual. Insofar as Foucault overtly deals
with the gaze (which is central to the structure of the book) it is a
monodirectional gaze. Power, indeed, is, as we have seen in the previous
chapter, intimately connected with the gaze. More specifically, power is
connected with the control over the gaze. The gaze of the panopticon
represents the gaze of power, the sovereign or the state. The single gaze
of the state – or its representative, and all who enter into the panoptic
machine in order to view the subjects under surveillance become its
representatives regardless of their intentions (1991: 202) – monitors and
corrects the many, who have no gaze, or no ability to regard the state in
response.

In the society of spectacle the process of subjectification was dependent on forcing the crowd to adopt a given interpretation; once the
counter-narratives intervened this process ceased to function properly.
The onus had been on each member of the crowd to perceive. With the
society of surveillance, however, the crowd understands that it *is being
perceived* (Foucault, 1991: 202–3). The gaze no longer involves a conscious
perception (which must perceive adequately), but a consciousness of
being perceived. The crowd (which, despite its size, can be more a
molecular assemblage than a molar aggregate) is divided into molar
subjects who understand that their behaviour is perpetually under
observation.

OVERCOMING SURVEILLANCE: 'MOLLOY' AND THE LINE
OF FLIGHT

With the emergence of surveillance, then, a more fool-proof system
seems to have been devised: the subjectification through surveillance
Foucault describes seems more difficult to escape than subjectification
through spectacle. The question then becomes, by what processes might
the strict borders imposed by subjectification through surveillance be
exceeded? For Deleuze and Guattari, as for Foucault, it is not a matter
of devising a concrete plan of action and implementing it. For the
former escape is a matter of the more or less unavoidable metamorpho-

sis of molecular bodies. An analogy might be found in the struggles of medical science against bacteria. Scientists discover penicillin with which to destroy bacteria, but the bacteria are in constant flux, constantly undergoing metamorphosis. In consequence, it has been predicted that all antibiotics may cease to be effective in the near future as highly resistant strains continue to appear. Similarly there is no such thing as a water-tight molar system which might contain completely and forever the molecular; the molecular might always overflow, leak away, following a line of flight like liquid through a hole in a cup.

Molloy, as has been noted by Deleuze and Guattari, describes a process of escape, and this escape is an escape from the supposedly fool-proof society of surveillance. The being experiencing the inclusive disjunction between order and disintegration exceeds the limits set on the disciplined body. The oscillation might be identified as being between the human being of conscious perception and the will, the molar subject (and even the vagabond, as Foucault has shown, is not outside the carceral network), and the being of pure sensation and desire, that being which has become what Bergson describes as no better than a material object, the being of immanent existence in whom the gaze of conscious perception gives way to pure sound, pure sensation, pure light:

And there was another noise, that of my life become the life of this garden as it rode the earth of deeps and wildernesses. Yes, there were times when I forgot not only who I was, but that I was, forgot to be. Then I was no longer that sealed jar to which I owed my being so well preserved, but a wall gave way and I filled with roots and tame stems for example. Stakes long since dead and ready for burning, the recess of night and the imminence of dawn, and then the labour of the planet rolling eager into winter . . . But that did not happen to me often, mostly I stayed in my jar which knew neither seasons nor gardens. (Beckett, 1955: 65)

This is Molloy expressing the sensation of what, conceptually, might be called an 'inclusive disjunction' of conscious perception *and* pure sensation. He is a vagabond but even he spends most of his time in his jar, consciously perceiving the world which is the world of selective perception, the world of the plan(e) of organization, only moving from time to time over to the plane of consistency, the molecular plane, where the particles of his body mingle with the Spinozian univocal being which is all Being.

Molloy is a narrative which describes instability, metamorphosis, which challenges the notion that a body can be fixed forever as a subject through subjectification brought to bear by subjection. It describes Molloy's journey, which begins as a quest for his mother and proceeds through degeneration to a point of stasis when he ends in a ditch, a stasis from which he is already called by his rescuers (66). Both in his narrative and that of Moran there are conflicting movements of time and space, as the characters oscillate between the molar and molecular.

I have discussed the differences between Molloy and Moran in the previous chapter, but there are also resemblances. Both Molloy and Moran go forward through time and space with increasing difficulty: a small space seems enormous and takes an inordinate amount of time to traverse. So Molloy crawls through his forest, so Moran, struggling forward, bent double, takes a year to return from a journey out which has taken less than a week. In another sense time and space cease to have meaning, Molloy barely ever refers to time and has no real concept of space, he is never sure where he is in relation to his own town, and as for the region which is his, it seems to him endless (88). For Moran, too, time and space begin to dissolve. But in yet another sense things are going faster; Molloy's degeneration starts to positively gallop, everything begins to shut down with extreme rapidity once he leaves the seaside and enters the forest, and Moran's flight from his old life continues faster and faster: 'I shall go faster, all will go faster. They will be happy days. I shall learn. All there was to sell I have sold. But I had heavy debts. I have been a man long enough, I shall not put up with any more, I shall not try any more. I shall never light this lamp again. I am going to blow it out and go into the garden' (240). While Moran here speaks of choice, the story he has described has shown how the initial escape which has brought him down this line of flight, the molecular escape which has swept he and Molloy along, was not a matter of choice, not a matter of conscious decision. On the contrary, it was the very antithesis of conscious decision and this is precisely the point.

PERCEPTION AND APPREHENSION

The crucial opposition here is between the gaze, the conscious perception of the will, and the unconscious perception of pure sensation and desire. In *Matter and Memory* Bergson describes the functioning of conscious perception:

the perceiving mind . . . marks out divisions in the continuity of the extended . . . But . . . to divide the real in this manner, we must first persuade ourselves that the real is divisible at will . . . we must throw . . . beneath concrete extensity, a network, of which the meshes may be altered to any shape whatsoever and become as small as we please: this substratum which is merely conceived, this wholly ideal diagram of arbitrary and infinite divisibility, is homogeneous space. (1991: 209–10)

Bergson here follows Spinoza in affirming that Being is univocal, that all bodies are elements that are part of the greater body which is everything that exists. Nature in its uninterpreted state, then, is not divided, it is conscious perception which divides extensity (in reality all runs together so there is no space, everything is the one body), thereby inventing or conceiving of 'space' through selection; through ignoring most of the sensory data with which we are constantly being bombarded. At the same time the memory (which is not the spontaneous memory mentioned above but a selective, utilitarian memory that helps to form perception – remembering how to walk, who you are, etc.; the memory of habit) conceives of time, coalescing the discontinuous discrete moments which are present existence in its naked state into a continuity which extends from the immediate future back into the past (Bergson, 1991: 210). To consciously perceive then, is to *fix*; the process of achieving conscious perception which comes to us through instinct in part, but also in large part (since it involves conception, the imagination) through culture, is the process of achieving identity, consciousness, the process of subjectification: 'In short, then, to perceive consists in condensing enormous periods of an infinitely diluted existence into a few more differentiated moments of an intenser life, and in thus summing up a very long history. To perceive means to immobilize' (208).

By means of better identifying the two forms of perception, conscious and 'unconscious', it might be best to follow Bergson in calling the first simply 'perception' and to borrow the term 'apprehension', which Beckett uses in his essay 'Dante . . . Bruno . Vico . . Joyce' (Beckett, 1983: 27–8) to describe the inclusive perception (involving the switching off of everyday conscious perception) required of the reader of Joyce's *Work in Progress* (*Finnegans Wake*), to describe the second.

APPREHENSION

Having come this far in gathering a number of philosophical concepts around the question of the being of order and disorder, it is worth tracing through the possible events expressed in *Molloy* to better consider the interactions between the two planes. At least in terms of appearances, as we have seen, Molloy is largely identified with the realm of disorder at the outset of his narrative whereas Moran is largely identified with the realm of order. Beckett's novel, however, shows us how the interaction between these two realms is never simple or neat, but involves a complex mixing or overlapping of one realm with the other.

In the much quoted *Three Dialogues with Georges Duthuit*, Beckett discusses his aesthetic ideal of an art in an absence of relation.[15]

The analysis of the relation between the artist and his occasion, a relation always regarded as indispensable, does not seem to have been very productive . . . van Velde is the first to desist from this estheticised automatism, the first to submit wholly to the incoercible absence of relation, in the absence of terms or, if you like, in the presence of unavailable terms, the first to admit that to be an artist is to fail. (Beckett, 1987: 124–5)

In producing such an art himself, I would suggest that, in *Molloy*, Beckett adopts two approaches, and that both of these involve apprehension. These might also be said to be examples of a type of inclusive disjunction as the two modes of apprehension seem antithetical to one another, polarities, and yet each involves the other. The first polarity of apprehension, or pure sensation, is the apprehension of a single object alone, divorced from its world or any world. The second polarity is the apprehension of everything at once, like that experienced by Proust's narrator through involuntary memory, a stumbling on to the plane of consistency.[16]

The first form of apprehension, like the second form, attacks the world of perception of the molar individual, because it involves the dislocation of habit and thereby allows the sensations repressed by perception to surge back, momentarily returning that fixed molar subject to the molecular being in continual flux (which it has never ceased to be). It also involves, however, the inclusive disjunction, perception *and* apprehension. That is, perception *of a certain type*, can open the way to apprehension. Beckett describes the process in *Proust*: 'when the object is

[15] On this point see Dearlove and Adorno's respective essays on *Endgame*.
[16] Molloy's experience might be equated with Murphy's. The inclusive disjunction, the switching between planes, seems similar to that which James Acheson describes – introducing St Augustine's concept of 'Chaos' and highlighting the concepts of the 'virtual' and 'actual' which Beckett uses in *Murphy* and which might be identified, as indeed they are by Brian Massumi (Deleuze and Guattari, 1987: xvii) with, respectively, the plane of consistency and the plane of organization: 'Zone three . . . is in darkness: it consists of virtual rising into actual and actual falling into virtual in "a perpetual coming together and falling asunder of forms" ([Beckett] *Murphy*: 79) reminiscent of St Augustine's Chaos. Transposing himself in imagination to this last zone, Murphy has the sensation not of being free, but of being caught up in the actual/virtual flux as a "mote in the dark of absolute freedom" ([Beckett]*Murphy*: 79)' (Acheson, 1993: 79). Connor also discusses this aspect of *Murphy* in relating Murphy to Malone (Connor, 1988: 66).

perceived as particular and unique and not merely the member of a family, when it appears independent of any general notion and detached from the sanity of cause, isolated and inexplicable in the light of ignorance, then and then only may it be a source of enchantment' (1987: 22–3). This example might remind us of the manner of extracting the Idea as described by Schopenhauer in a passage (quoted in the introduction, above) from *The World as Will and Idea*. Further, as we have seen with reference to Bergson, perception involves the ability to extract objects from a background noise, but this selection always involves a context. With the aid of memory (habit) the individual who perceives gives the object a continuity in time and a place among all the other perceived objects in space. What allows the perceiving individual to act is the fact that he or she distinguishes (or constructs) this context in which everything has its place, in which nothing is surprising or new, in which, as Bergson says, the objects and more importantly the response to them are 'ready-made' (1991: 45). The type of perception opening to apprehension which Beckett is talking of here, however, involves the kind of radical decontextualization of an object that his sometime chess partner Marcel Duchamp brought to bear in producing his famous 'ready-mades'.[17]

When an object is apprehended it is cut from the causal chains of which, by necessity, it is a part. Following Spinoza, although on one plane everything emerges from the infinite substance of God (the univocal Being), on another plane all finite modes or things are caused by other finite modes[18]. An object detached from context then, through apprehension, is an impossible object. For, as Bergson suggests: 'does not the fiction of an isolated material object imply a kind of absurdity, since this object borrows its physical properties from the relations which it maintains with all others, and owes of its determinations, and consequently, its very existence, to the place which it occupies in the universe as a whole?' (1991: 24). In divorcing the object from all context, the being who apprehends breaks with what is possible, and therefore the plane on which things can be realized or made possible, the molar plan(e) of organization (cf. Deleuze, 1992: 57–79). The being divorces it from all relation, including (and above all) that relation between the individual who apprehends and the object apprehended.

The expression of such apprehension appears in a well-known example from Molloy's narrative. He has taken a number of pieces of

[17] On Beckett and Duchamp, see Prinz, 1987. [18] Spinoza, *Ethics*, Props. 15–18, and 28, Part 1.

silver with him on leaving Lousse's house; among them a small, uniden-
tifiable object (1995: 85).[19] Molloy says he could never bring himself to
sell this object, which haunted him:

And from time to time I took it from my pocket and gazed upon it, with an
astonished and affectionate gaze, if I had not been incapable of affection. But
for a certain time I think it inspired me with a kind of veneration, for there was
no doubt in my mind that it was not an object of virtue, but that it had a most
specific function always to be hidden from me. I could therefore puzzle over it
endlessly without the least risk. For to know nothing is nothing, not to want to
know anything likewise, but to be beyond knowing anything, to know you are
beyond knowing anything, that is when peace enters in, to the soul of the
incurious seeker. (85–6)

The apprehension of a specific object, unknowable and impossible, is,
as Molloy lets on here, a quasi-religious experience, emptying the body
of all conscious thought, of all perception, thereby allowing the medita-
tor entry to the plane of consistency. Through another inclusive disjunction then, the first kind of apprehension (the isolation of a singular
object) opens the way to the second kind of apprehension (sensation in
the absence of all choice) admitting all possibility and so having done
with the possible, renouncing all possible action, for: 'Our representation of matter is the measure of our possible action upon bodies: it
results from the discarding of what has no interest for our needs, or
more generally, for our functions' (Bergson, 1991: 38). The renunci-
ation of this perception, then, involves the abandonment of all possible
relation, dissolving one's own identity in merging with all Being. For,
following Spinoza, 'matter is the same everywhere, and its parts are not
distinguished one from the other except insofar as we conceive matter
to be affected in various ways, whence its parts are distinguished one
from the other modally but not in reality' (Ethics, Part 1, Prop. 15, note;
13–16).

Another example of this first type of apprehension is to be found in
Moran's description of the contemplation of his bees. On his long
voyage home he reflects on his observations of his bees. An apparent
difference between Molloy's sensation of apprehension (which recurs for
him, one assumes, with other objects, as he is constantly forgetting the
names of things) and that of Moran is that, at first at least, Moran's joy
seems to come from the contemplation of order. He seems interested in

---

[19] David Hayman identifies it as a knife-holder (1970: 129), yet Moran is shown playing with a knife-
rest in his narrative (106), so perhaps this term is to be preferred.

meticulous scientific categorization. It becomes clear at last, however, how it is not so much the order, but rather its dissolution into a final ignorance which brings him peace: 'And I said, with rapture, Here is something I can study all my life, and never understand. And all during this long journey home, when I racked my mind for a little joy in store, the thought of my bees and their dance was the nearest thing to comfort' (1995: 232).

With the first form of apprehension we have an example of inclusive disjunction. The enchantment Beckett speaks of in *Proust*, the peace Molloy discovers and the nearest thing to comfort Moran describes come about initially through the act of perception. Something is isolated, or rather, something isolates itself. But this isolation goes further, becomes true isolation, as all possibility of comprehension is removed. Comprehension here referring to the process of contextualization, the process of assimilating a thing or phenomenon to a ready-made world-view, a view we have been trained to perceive by molar institutions. This further, impossible isolation involves the formation of the plane of apprehension over the plane of perception. Molloy speaks of ignorance in quasi-religious terms because, as in Schopenhauer, it involves an opening to the infinite, to the true concatenation of things which is pure concatenation, which excludes all possibility of 'comprehension' (where that consists of isolating a few modal causes to explain a few modal effects). Excludes, that is, the possibility of comprehension brought about through the relation of one readily distinguished thing to another: such ignorance involves having done with that type of relation, is the description of the true absence of relation. The process of meditating on the obscure object or the language of the bees, then, involves inclusive disjunction: it is perception *and* apprehension, highlighting, if one interprets the move conceptually, the oscillation of the molar and molecular.

THE SUBORDINATION OF PERCEPTION TO APREHENSION

The second form of apprehension also involves the subordination of perception. Molloy's narrative is full of examples of impaired perception. From the point of view of the molar institutions, this would be equated with the impaired functioning of an individual. From another point of view, however, Molloy's gaze or world-view might be conceived of as better emphasizing the inclusive disjunction, 'perception *and* apprehension'. To repeat an earlier citation from *The Anti-Oedipus*: 'everywhere there exist the molecular *and* the molar: their disjunction is a relation of included disjunction, which varies only according to the two directions of subordination, according as the molecular phenomena are subordinated to the large aggregates, or on the contrary subordinate them to themselves' (Deleuze and Guattari, 1983: 340–1). Molloy's perception is impaired because it has become subordinated to apprehension. In this, as we shall see, his direction of subordination differs from that of Moran. Molloy has difficulty in relating one thing to another thing, has difficulty perceiving. He – like the stranger Moran meets in part 2 (1955: 200) – has lived 'far from words' (41), he has difficulty remembering his name, his town, his station, has difficulty relating his own being to these instruments of subjectification. He relates his story, but the words with which he relates seem far from the experience he must attempt to relate, far from the actuality of the impossible experience that does not involve relation (119).

Words accumulate like metal filings around the molar polarity and flee from the molecular. It is in their nature to hang together, to mean, as it is in the nature of perceived things to relate one to the other, 'For all things hang together, by the operation of the Holy Ghost, as the saying is' (Beckett, 1955: 54). Words are the names of things, and as Bergson has shown, we learn to isolate things, divide them off from the pure, indivisible, extensity which is reality. And this is done, as Foucault has shown, through the proper disciplining, the proper training of our senses. They are trained to perceive: the world we think we describe may merely be that which we have been taught to see, our experience of reality equating to a grading of our comprehension of the lessons we have learnt by heart – the process of learning by heart being the figure Bergson uses to describe the training of memory, the trained memory constituting habit (1991: 79–90). To quote Molloy:

I had been living so far from words so long . . . And even my sense of identity was wrapped in a namelessness often hard to penetrate . . . And so on for all the other things which made merry with my senses. Yes, even then, when already all was fading, waves and particles, there could be no things but nameless things, no names but thingless names. I say that now, but after all what do I know now about then, now when the icy words hail down upon me, the icy meanings, and the world dies too, foully named. All I know is what the words know, and the dead things, and that makes a handsome little sum, with a beginning, a middle and an end as in the well-built phrase and the long sonata of the dead. And truly it little matters what I say, this or that or any other thing. Saying is inventing. Wrong, very rightly wrong. You invent nothing, you think you are inventing, you think you are escaping, and all you do is stammer out your lesson, the remnants of a pensum one day got by heart and long forgotten, life without tears, as it is wept. (Beckett, 1955: 41–2)

Here Beckett expresses the sensations which occur in exhausting or having done with language (paradoxically through language). Still, we are required not only to enter into the compound of sensations expressed here, but also to reflect. To consider, for example, how speech might be understood to involve the reciting of a pensum. Such an idea might be grasped conceptually through a concept expressing the manner in which order imposes sense (through a concept such as the 'order-word' described by Deleuze and Guattari, for example; 1987: 75–110); to bring to light this process through sensations, however, tying them to possible events and to an individual's experience of being, would be a really difficult process. All the same, this is what Beckett attempts, as we shall see, later, in *The Unnamable*.

Molloy, though such a thing is impossible to imagine on the molar level, fails to relate. He watches the full moon moving across a window at night and wonders if it could be the same moon he had seen two nights before, which was new, then realizes it could not have been a moon at all as his are moonless nights (56). In Lousse's house the room about him is in constant flux, and he is constantly endowing it with new properties, and this is all because he 'sees darkly' (58). That is to say, he perceives ill, all he sees is ill-seen, all he says ill-said. He is out of sync with the molar, the plan(e) of organization, though he is well aware of its existence, happy even to concede its priority. If things are so unstable, it is not their fault, they obey strict laws, it is his fault, it is not they which are outside order (the order of time and space) it is he: 'that there were natural causes to all these things I am willing to concede . . . It was I who was not natural enough to enter into that order of things, and appreciate its niceties' (58–9). What is involved is a failure of perception, rather than a failure of sensory perception. That is, pure sensation is felt, there is apprehension, but no *thing* is perceived. It is a failure of comprehension, a disobedience to orders, 'the words I heard, and heard distinctly, having quite a sensitive ear, were heard a first time, then a second, and often even a third, as pure sounds, free of all meaning' (66). It is the subordination of perception to apprehension, the opening towards Being in the absence of relation, univocal Being, the Idea of Schopenhauer, that which the artist encounters in the obscure object, that which the artist fails to express in apprehending, 'the incoercible absence of relation' (Beckett, 1987: 125):

And my eye too, the seeing one, must have been ill-connected with the [thing before me] for I found it hard to name what was mirrored there, often quite distinctly. And without going so far as to say that I saw the world upside down . . . it is certain I saw it in a way inordinately formal, though I was far from being an aesthete, or an artist. (67)

While Foucault is right in suggesting that there is no outside the carceral network insofar as it is that molar network which creates the subject who comes to consciousness inside the world which has extracted him/her from the background noise of Being, there is always the molecular level which that individual never leaves. While it would take a molecular assemblage greater than the individual (a crowd for example, or a class) to bring about a revolution which would radically affect the molar institutions, the molecular level will always affect the molar subject, opening lines of flight through which the individual might escape the tyranny of subjectification. To quote Molloy:

Yes it sometimes happens and will sometimes happen again that I forget who I am and strut before my eyes, like a stranger. Then I see the sky different from what it is and the earth too takes on false colours . . . I vanish happy in that alien light, which must have once been mine, I am willing to believe it, then the anguish of return, I won't say where, I can't, to absence perhaps, you must return, that's all I know. (56)

He must return, for, as Deleuze and Guattari affirm, it is a case of the molar *and* the molecular, of inclusive disjunction; there cannot be one without the other. While in the case of Molloy, the molar phenomena are subordinated to the molecular phenomena, he is still subject to the return of those molar phenomena, their incursions on to the plane of consistency. So he is called back to himself by the police. So, while he enters the forest where his perception becomes increasingly weak and his physical degeneration proceeds at a gallop, where he seems farther than ever from the molar aggregates, he continues to move, however slowly, and eventually leaves the forest again, perception bursting through as if rushing to his rescue, when, in fact, it might just as easily be conceived as rushing to recapture one who is nothing less than a fugitive, to contain him at last. So a detective is dispatched on the fugitive's trail, so he is contained in his mother's room, forced to relate his story, forced, that is, to relate, constrained to perceive:

at this painful juncture, which I had vaguely foreseen, but not in all its bitterness, I heard a voice telling me not to fret, that help was coming. Literally . . . I lapsed down to the bottom of the ditch. It must have been spring, a morning in spring. I thought I heard birds, skylarks perhaps. I had not heard a bird for a long time. How was it I had not heard any in the forest? Nor seen any. It had not seemed strange to me . . . I did not fret, other scenes of my life came back to me. There seemed to be rain, then sunshine, turn about. Real spring weather. I longed to go back into the forest. Oh not a real longing. Molloy could stay, where he happened to be. (123–4)

THE INCOERCIBLE ABSENCE OF RELATION

There is clearly a difference in styles between the narrative of Molloy and that of Moran. To simplify this difference, it might be suggested that Moran is more concerned to relate events, those things which happened to him. Even when he describes his thoughts, they seem an attempt to reconstruct his thoughts of the moment. That is, Moran's narrative seems an attempt to describe or represent what happened to him during the Molloy case; he attempts to report, or to relate; in short, even when he lies it is through a deliberately inconsistent relation. In Molloy's narrative, on the other hand, there is a poverty of events. Molloy's relation is not only interrupted by constant uncertainty as to his percepts (about A and C, or the moon, for example), but also by flights of thought as he wanders among the 'ruins' of ideas. While Moran wishes to be concerned with the concrete, then, Molloy is constantly diverging into abstractions which dissolve into confusion.

It is interesting to contrast the idea of the former Moran as a practical soul, turned to the outer world as to the lesser evil, with that of the former Molloy, who studied all sorts of abstract systems of knowledge. While recounting his stay at Lousse's house, Molloy tells us of his academic career. He began by studying the gods, if you like, through astronomy, then moved to the earth, with geology, then the study of the cultural habits of people, through anthropology, and then to the mental states of people through psychiatry. So, he moved from the heavens to the earth, ending with 'Man', but this was not the end of his studies. His final port of call was 'magic'. That is, he moved from sciences which work through relation to an art which requires the absence of relation. (52)

To begin, then, Moran[20] tells us he writes a report, while Molloy suggests he merely writes pages which are taken away at the end of each week. The former suggests a goal potentially achievable in time and space, a molar project, the latter involves a purely immanent process of writing, announcing no goal, no notion of achievement, a molecular

[20] In Beckett's French version of *Molloy*, the word used for 'report' is 'rapport' (Beckett, 1988b: 125), which translates literally into English as 'relation'. Alan Astro notes that 'Moran' is an anagram for 'roman' (the French word for novel): a relation *par excellence*.

process. Against the Molloy who from time to time forgets to be, the Moran we are initially presented with is 'a solid in the midst of other solids' (147), a fixed subject who can both relate and be related to. In relating his story Moran tells us that he becomes again what he was at the time of the narrative, so that what he was ignorant of then but is no longer ignorant of, the sequence of events, again occurs to him as if he was going through it for the first time. His relation, he suggests, is near perfect: 'I am far more he who finds than he who tells what he has found' (182). Molloy, however, suggests that his relation is far more invention and elaboration than a strict chronicle of the truth. Unlike Moran, who perceives and describes his perceptions, Molloy apprehends, and it is only in vainly attempting to relate these apprehensions that he translates them into perceptions:

And every time I say, I said this, or, I said that . . . and then a fine phrase more or less clear and simple, or find myself compelled to attribute to others intelligible words, or hear my own voice uttering to others more or less articulate sounds, I am merely complying with the convention that demands you either lie or hold your peace. For what really happened was quite different . . . In reality I said nothing at all, but I heard a murmur, something gone wrong with the silence. (118–19)

As Moran's narrative begins, the reader is also called upon to relate. We might be tempted to relate Molloy's shambles (28) to Moran's slaughterhouse (130), Moran's gong (158) to Molloy's (120–1), but the desire to relate is frustrated: Moran travels for a number of days to reach Molloy's country, so how could the gong Molloy hears be Moran's, and how could the shambles be the same when Moran tells us the two of them live in different towns?[21] The frustration of attempts to relate will, though this is not initially clear, become characteristic of Moran's narrative. Things will increasingly refuse to relate to one another, or rather, the incoercible absence of relation will increasingly rise to the surface, obliterating the former world of Moran with its perceived order.

APPREHENSION SUBORDINATED PERCEPTION

That the world of Jacques Moran as he first appears has been the world of perception is clear from the examples given in the previous chapter

---

[21] The abortive nature of such relations is characteristic of much of Beckett's work of this period; in particular *Waiting for Godot*. It is discussed with regard to the examples I list here by Connor, 1988: 50–1, and has been most elegantly summed up with regard to another form of relation (intertextual) by Hugh Kenner (1973: 97–8).

which display the prevalence of surveillance in and around his household. He is a spy who takes delight in his ability to relate: he catches his son out swapping his best stamps into the book of duplicates (148) for example, relating the haste of young Jacques in closing his books and his guilty look to a previously noted propensity to gloat over his best stamps to arrive at this insight.

Yet if his ability to perceive is highly developed, his ability to apprehend is correspondingly weak. With regard to sound, for example, he notes, 'I have an extremely sensitive ear. Yet I have no ear for music' (175). This is in contrast with Molloy who, as we have seen, has difficulty perceiving words but is stopped in his tracks by music to which he longs to listen (26). Music which, in a well-known letter to Axel Kaun, Beckett praises for its ability to tear at and dissolve its own surface, the surface of relation, so as to uncover the silence beneath, the silence of non-relation, the silence of apprehension like that encountered by Molloy in his forest, who hears no birds, a silence like that Beckett hoped to display in his fiction: 'I know there are people, sensitive and intelligent people, for whom there is no lack of silence. I cannot but assume that they are hard of hearing. For in the forest of symbols, which aren't any, the little birds of interpretation, which isn't any, are never silent' (Beckett, 1983: 172).

While Moran begins as one unable to apprehend because he is too ready to perceive, his narrative involves, as we have already touched on above, a process of metamorphosis. Apprehension and perception exist in inclusive disjunction, as do relation and non-relation (as we are only able to recognize non-relation through a process of relation), yet as with the molar and molecular, to which each grouping pertains, the direction of subordination varies. Molloy does not seem to seek to give us a report, he writes his narrative page by page and professes ignorance of the purpose of his writing, yet even as it tears the surface of words in sabotaging the world of order by relating ill the process of perceiving ill, it still constitutes a relation. Things hold together, more or less, despite everything, fragile links might be asked to traverse unfathomable gulfs, but traverse them they do. It too is an inclusive disjunction, relation *and* non-relation. So Moran, who is proud of his ability to perceive, who begins by perceiving well, finds that the direction of subordination between perception and apprehension begins to change as his body begins to degenerate. He stops perceiving and begins to apprehend.

THE DIRECTION OF SUBORDINATION

Apprehension is not unknown to Moran, he has experienced it before, yet unlike Bergson who sees perception as a fabrication laid over the reality of apprehension, for Moran apprehension is an illusion and perception is the real:

The blood drains from my head, the noise of things bursting, merging, avoiding one another, assails me on all sides, my eyes search in vain for two things alike, each pinpoint of skin screams a different message, I drown in the spray of phenomena. It is at the mercy of these sensations, *which happily I know to be illusory* [my italics], that I have to live and work. It is thanks to them I find myself a meaning. So he whom a sudden pain awakes. He stiffens, ceases to breathe, waits, says, It's a bad dream, or, It's a touch of neuralgia, breathes again, sleeps again, still trembling. (151–2)

Moran denies the reality of the chaos of apprehension as if it were a bad dream with no real effects. Yet he is only fooling himself: his nightmares are coming true. The swamping of perception by apprehension is exhilarating because frightening: after Proust (Beckett, 1987: 29), perhaps, it is a matter of life appearing delicious because death threatens at every moment. Indeed the analogy Moran draws between this startling eruption of apprehension which swamps perception, of the plane of consistency which swamps the plan(e) of organization, and the feelings of one awoken by a sudden pain, relates directly to his own situation when his leg begins to stiffen (189). The pain, the metamorphosis, has broken the surface of habit; it is the portion of death which rests in pain, in change, in physical degeneration, which has brought about this break. It is a matter which leads to both the apprehension of pure sensation and the apprehension of one in fear.

The oscillation involved in the relation of inclusive disjunction between perception and apprehension is further underlined by Moran's suggestion that in order to find Molloy it is necessary to leave the plan(e) of organization, of perception (perhaps because it is a plan(e) Molloy visits so rarely) and enter the plane of consistency, of apprehension. Moran seems to suggest he might descend into apprehension in order to extract the necessary perception. It is a process directly opposite to that of perceiving the obscure object in order to apprehend. Here one apprehends, takes on board all sensation in the hope that the object to be perceived will announce itself from among the spray of phenomena to which it belongs. The subsequent passage follows immediately on from that just quoted above:

And yet it is not unpleasant, before setting to work, to steep oneself again in this slow and massive world, where all things move with the ponderous sullenness of oxen, patiently through the immemorial ways, and where of course no investigation would be possible. But . . it was only by transferring it to this atmosphere, how shall I say, of finality without end, why not, that I could venture to consider the work I had on hand. For where Molloy could not be, nor Moran either for that matter, there Moran could bend over Molloy. And though this examination prove unprofitable and of no utility for the execution of my orders, I should nevertheless have established a kind of connection, and one not necessarily false. For the falsity of the terms does not necessarily imply that of the relation, so far as I know. (152)

The falsity of the terms in the process of imagining Molloy that Moran undertakes becomes quickly apparent: the Molloy he imagines bears little resemblance to the Molloy who has presented himself to us in the first half of the novel.[22] The relation however, as Moran suggests, does not seem quite so false. The relation seems to be that of the hunter, inhabiting the plan(e) of organization, seeking a quarry on the plane of consistency (even though the existence of such a quarry on such a plane let alone the idea of a hunter removing himself, as himself, to that plane is impossible).[23] While the relation itself is impossible, the relation of the impossibility of this relation is a just relation. It describes, to use the term loosely, a cross-dimensional pursuit, involving not the pressing of the fisherman's face into water in order to better mark his fish, but rather the becoming water of the fisherman in quest of a fish more water than fish.

[22] I am in disagreement, then, with Ruby Cohn, Thomas Trezise and Alan Astro who all remark how accurate Moran's imaginings of Molloy are (Cohn, 1973: 87; Trezise, 1990: 51–2; Astro, 1990: 66). Trezise makes some good points in this passage concerning Moran's process of metamorphosis, yet his claims of complete identification are not backed up by the novel, especially not by this passage where Moran imagines Molloy. How for example can we relate the following descriptions to Molloy as he describes himself in part one: 'He was massive and hulking, to the point of misshapenness. And, without being black, of a dark colour.' Molloy is certainly not 'massive and hulking', he seems rather of delicate constitution and weak, and as for his colour, this is never commented upon. 'He was forever on the move. I had never seen him rest.' How unlike Molloy! Molloy spends an unspecified amount of time at Lousse's house, and rests continually: resting is one of the things he does most often. And so on as the passage continues. As for the list: 'uproar, bulk, rage, suffocation, effort unceasing, frenzied and vain' which Trezise (52) particularly highlights with regard to Molloy resembling Moran, it is difficult to see how more inappropriate adjectives (except perhaps 'vain') could be found to describe Molloy; a model of indifference.

[23] I think then, that Ludovic Janvier (and Alan Astro who agrees with Janvier (1990: 62), gets things back to front when he suggests that an 'immanence' called Moran, pursues (and misses) a 'transcendence' called Molloy (1966: 52). On the contrary, I feel that it is Moran who should be considered strongly linked to transcendent world-views (the world of the judging Christian God) and Molloy to a world-view which is overwhelmingly immanent (the world of Spinoza's atheistic, pantheistic God, God or Nature, the absolutely infinite and indivisible univocal substance).

Moran is relating in hindsight, and he is no stranger to justification; submerging his self in the plane of consistency may not be the conscious decision he seems to wish to make us believe it is. Even if it were, however, it becomes apparent that he is mistaken in his estimation that he would still be able to perceive in some manner on that plane where perception ceases to exist. That the parallel degeneration of Moran's mind and body constitute a molecular metamorphosis has been noted above. Such a metamorphosis involves not only a change in the direction of subordination of molar over molecular to its inverse, but also of perception over apprehension to its inverse. Moran, whose job it is to perceive, begins to apprehend. The forest of symbols cease to be any, the little birds of interpretation are no longer. These things, which are never silent, are no longer heard. Moran begins to hear the silence; that is, to apprehend. It is a state of which he has long been aware, but had placed neatly into relation with his own self-assurance. Silence, with its spiritual connotations, is seen as a thing among others, mastering it a skill among the many he possesses. Just as Moran is over-confident in believing he can control apprehension, such silence, he believes, is also open to mastery:

> Not one person in a hundred knows how to be silent and listen, no, nor even to conceive what such a thing means. Yet only then can you detect, beyond the fatuous clamour, the silence of which the universe is made. I desired this advantage for my son. And that he should hold aloof from those who pride themselves on their eagle gaze. (166)

Yet he increasingly finds it is not so easily controlled. The molecular metamorphosis he is undergoing, which drags him increasingly into apprehension, is a line of flight he can only follow, leading him away from the subject he has been made towards the self he may be. Having sent his son to purchase a bicycle, Moran, now unable to sit or walk any distance because of his stiff leg, lies alone in his shelter in the woods, apprehension swamping his perceptions: 'I surrendered myself to the beauties of the scene, I gazed at the trees, the fields, the sky, the birds, and I listened attentively to the sounds, faint and clear, borne to me on the air. For an instant I fancied I heard the silence mentioned, if I am not mistaken, above' (199). He still would have us believe he is in charge of the situation, master of his destiny. Assured of the certainty of his own self, the goals he has set. But he is unable to focus on the project at hand, he sees it only dimly, and even the subject he once was, fixed and stable, has begun to quaver with instability, admitting the flux from which it has been fabricated:

I tried again to remember what I was to do with Molloy when I found him. I dragged myself down to the stream. I lay down and looked at my reflection, then I washed my face and hands. I waited for my image to come back, I watched it as it trembled towards an ever increasing likeness. Now and then a drop, falling from my face, shattered it again. (199)

In short, Moran, the fixed subject, begins to decay, revealing his true being, which partakes perhaps of that Being described by Bergson as the real or by Schopenhauer as the 'thing in itself': undivided extensity, the univocity of Being (Bergson, 1991: 209–10). Moran feels he is drawing towards his true self like the sands towards the wave, or the turd towards the flush (223). Like Molloy he feels a partition begin to give way: 'I seemed to see myself ageing as swiftly as a day-fly. But the idea of ageing was not exactly the one which offered itself to me. And what I saw was more like a crumbling, a frenzied collapsing of all that had always protected me from all I was condemned to be' (203). The metamorphosis he experiences bears a striking resemblance to the process of becoming described by Deleuze and Guattari in *A Thousand Plateaus*. The becoming which is a molecular process, a process which exceeds the model, the Idea of the subject. The model or Form is always molar (Deleuze and Guattari, 1987: 286), while the becoming is a proximity, a zone of indiscernibility, 'To become is not to achieve a form (identification, imitation, Mimesis), but to find the zone of vicinity, of indiscernibility or indifferentiation so that one can no longer distinguish oneself from *a* woman, from *an* animal, from *a* molecule' (Deleuze, 1993a: 10). This is metamorphosis as Moran experiences it. It is a moving into the indefinite where he is no longer so readily identifiable as Moran, but becomes a man resembling all others (in the manner that A resembles C, 'they looked alike, but no more than others do' (10)), once stripped bare of his pretensions and shown in all his comic insignificance and tragic vulnerability. It is a process of becoming which amounts not only to the molecular exceeding the strict limits of the molar model, but to apprehension exceeding perception:

it was like a kind of clawing towards a light and countenance I could not name, that I had once known and long denied. But what words can describe this sensation at first all darkness and bulk, with a noise like the grinding of stones, then suddenly as soft as flowing water, smooth at first, and scarcely paler than its escorting ripples, then little by little a face, with holes for the eyes and mouth and other wounds, and nothing to show if it was a man's face or a woman's face, a young face or an old face, or if its calm too was not an effect of the water trembling between it and the light. (203–4)

SHAKING THE FOUNDATIONS

As we have seen in the previous chapter, towards the end of *Discipline and Punish* Foucault shows us the child vagabond Béasse. He appears as an example of disorder, and disorder, its very existence within the society of discipline, of surveillance, presents that society with apprehension in the face of the possibility of its own death. Order is brought into existence from disorder. It is the disorder that has priority, the disorder which is the real from which we contrive our order, just as Bergson describes the selectivity of perception extracting time and homogeneous space from an indivisible extensity existing as a succession of instants (1991: 209–10), just as Deleuze and Guattari describe the fabrication of the plan(e) of organization over the plane of consistency (1987: 262), or the plane of immanence over chaos (cf. Deleuze and Guattari, 1994). Foucault equates Béasse's disorder with liberty, he displays 'An indiscipline that is the indiscipline of native, immediate liberty' (1991: 292). What is this disorder, this indiscipline, this freedom, other than an example of a (molecularly instigated) line of flight from the model prescribed by (molar) institutions. Béasse calls the values of the society of surveillance into question. These values are judgements, a selection from the real, they are perceptions. Béasse opposes the negations of judgement with his affirmations of life: 'All the illegalities that the court defined as offences the accused reformulated as the affirmation of a living force: the lack of home as vagabondage, the lack of a master as independence, the lack of work as freedom, the lack of a time-table as the fullness of days and nights' (290). In mapping an overview of the battlefield as it currently stands Foucault directs us to the weakness of the molar aggregate which forms the society of surveillance. To the gaze of the sovereign can be opposed the innumerable gazes of the ill-disciplined, whether they look directly back at that sovereign or at anything whatsoever; the sovereign is not the sun to which, or from which, all eyes turn, and this is enough to shake the foundations of the panopticon, there is always the possibility that one subjected to it will not comprehend how it is supposed to work, lessons can be badly learnt, habits forgotten, as the unnamable states: 'My inability to absorb, my genius for forgetting, are more than they reckoned with. Dear incomprehension, it's thanks to you I'll be myself, in the end' (Beckett, 1958: 51).

In the final chapter of *Discipline and Punish* Foucault suggests that the date of the completion of the carceral system, that system which is at the centre of the society of surveillance which is our society, is 'the 22 January 1840, the date of the official opening of Mettray' (293). Mettray was a famous French prison farm for delinquent youth. If Foucault did not have to enter into a detailed description of Mettray, if Mettray was so well known to his French readers, it would have been to a degree at least because of the writings of Jean Genet. Foucault could hardly have brought Mettray to mind without thinking of Genet, who was a good friend of his at this time (Eribon, 1991: 238–42; White, 1992: 652–63). Such a choice would have to involve some irony. Taking Mettray as a metonym of the carceral edifice would have to carry with it the suggestion of an edifice built on foundations which, if not unsound in themselves, are subject to the vagaries of geology and the weather, the possibility of shifts which, even though slight, are more than capable of undermining the most solid of structures. Mettray trained Jean Genet! Mettray subjectified Jean Genet! Genet the 'vagabond', the perpetual revolutionary. Genet who delighted in describing his own morality, a counter-morality to that of the society of Mettray, that of the molar institutions, inverting the values they named 'Good' and 'Evil' (cf. Genet, 1991: 193; White, 1993: 121, 181, 321, 433), just as Béasse opposed their negations with affirmations. If a Genet might be the product of the archetypal institution of discipline, of subjectification, then it is evident that the society of surveillance can never hope to build a water-tight order, and that which is not water-tight will always be subject to molecular leakage, trickling away in a line of flight.

The process of molecular leakage we have been tracing in *Molloy* concerns the human individual, the molecular multiplicity that goes to form a life. Revolutions require larger assemblages, but such assemblages are built upon counter-narratives, counter-memory. While, as Foucault displays, the molar institutions (in affecting the molecular assemblages) *effect* the subjectified individual, the molecular Being of which that individual never ceases to partake never ceases to *affect* both that individual and those molar institutions. Molecular assemblages larger than the individual, those of a generation, a crowd, a class, a planet, can and do affect the molar institutions to the extent that the latter are forced to modify or face extinction. The most famous recent example of this phenomenon in France, that which influenced a generation of intellectuals including Deleuze and Guattari and Foucault, was May '68. As we have seen, in *Discipline and Punish* Foucault describes the manner in which such radical affects have been brought to bear. It takes only apparently small lines of flight to undermine the edifice, to begin a sequence of events which might bring the whole thing crashing down, like the trickle of water which announces the imminent collapse of the dam. With the society of spectacle it consisted of a few counter-narratives; convicts seeing themselves, and being seen by their class as heroes, for example. Foucault indicates a similar process elsewhere in beginning an essay on Maurice Blanchot: 'In ancient times, this simple assertion was enough to shake the foundations of Greek truth: "I lie"' (Foucault, 1990: 9).[24]

This might bring to mind the famous last lines of *Molloy*, the conclusion of Moran's relation which announce themselves as relating to the first lines of his narrative. In effect Moran is saying, 'I lie, I have been lying from the very beginning, you will therefore be incapable, in the absence of any other evidence, of deciding what is true.'[25] In effect his final comments undermine all possible relation. Through the inclusive disjunction, relation *and* non-relation, they affirm the incoercible absence of relation. The reader who stumbles in, like a seeker into a forest of symbols (which it is understood, never cease to raise their voices) listening to the birds of interpretation in a quest for meaning, finds instead the disorder, the silence of an absence of relation, which cannot perhaps be perceived, can only be faced with apprehension:

It is midnight. The rain is beating on the windows. (125)

Then I went back into the house and wrote, It is midnight. The rain is beating on the windows. It was not midnight. It was not raining. (241)

[24] Connor and Trezise also refer to the paradox of the Cretan liar; Trezise drawing attention to the famous passage I cite below (Trezise, 1990: 102, n. 33) while Connor, speaking in relation to *Malone Dies*, draws attention to 'a restless alternation between the linguistic and metalinguistic levels' (1988: 70).

[25] For an interesting discussion of this paradox (using different concepts to those I have described here) see Raymond Federman's essay, 'Beckettian Paradox: Who is Telling the Truth?'

CHAPTER 3

Crisis with the moral order in post World War Two France

'MALONE DIES' AND 'MOLLOY'

The structure of *Malone Dies* clearly differs from that of *Molloy*. Rather than two narrators ostensibly telling stories about themselves in relation to society as in *Molloy*, in *Malone Dies* there is a single narrator ostensibly outside society telling stories about others. Similarities, however, remain, as, rather than passing beyond the theme of the interpenetration of order and chaos, Malone's stories multiply and complicate this theme. Rather than simply allowing him to move beyond the self, the stories Malone tells seem to both extinguish and multiply that self, and while on the one hand they seem to carry him further from society and its order, on the other they nevertheless return him to that society which he seems long ago to have left[1]. Further, while, as we have seen, the structure of *Molloy* brings to light the interpenetration of order and chaos, the structure of *Malone Dies* offers us a new series of dichotomies, which are all, nevertheless, clearly related to order and chaos.

The difference in structure between the two novels might loosely be considered to involve a moving from a so-called external to a so called internal world. That is, while *Molloy*, to speak no doubt too generally, might be considered to show us two narrators facing an external order (in preparing their reports or non-reports of their relation or non-relation to that external order), *Malone Dies* offers us a single narrator who (while still not completely divorced from the world in the manner of the unnamable) is beginning to turn inward and face a set of internal contradictions: 'All my senses are trained full on me, me. Dark and silent and stale, I am no prey for them' (Beckett, 1956: 9). The internal contradictions Malone faces, however, resonate with the external contradictions we are now

---

[1] For example, once the woman and hand no longer tend Malone 'they' appear, first as a idea and finally in the shape of the intruder who is conflated by Malone with all those people he has ever seen.

familiar with from *Molloy*; for if in *Molloy* we see order (of the world and of
the self) in inclusive disjunction with chaos (of the world and of the self),
in *Malone Dies* we see chaos and order in inclusive disjunction within the
self. Yet the world does not disappear; on the one hand it is apparently
passing away, yet on the other it has also clearly already passed into the
self as Malone's stories bring back the world and its trivia.

To begin to unravel some of this complexity, which I will treat in
more detail in the next chapter, it is worth listing a series of dichotomies
which are all isomorphic with the dichotomy of order and chaos in
Malone Dies: life (order) and death (chaos); the wholeness of the self
(order) and decomposition of the self (chaos); the light (order) and the
dark (chaos); play (order) and earnestness (chaos). As with *Molloy*, one
might add to this series Beckett's aesthetic dichotomy of relation (order)
and non-relation (chaos), and, as I shall argue more fully in the next
chapter, also add the dichotomy of transcendental judgement (the
ordering process, with Good and Evil as stable points of reference) and
immanent ethics (a more fluid or chaotic process, with good and bad as
variable terms). Each term in this series exists in inclusive disjunction
with its opposite; yet the direction of subordination in *Malone Dies*
predominantly involves order passing into chaos; as Malone's process of
death and decomposition continues; as the light fades and the darkness
descends.

Interestingly this decomposition also seems to involve the multiplica-
tion of terms: while Molloy and Moran apparently speak of themselves,
Malone at first describes Sapo and his two worlds (the Saposcats and the
Lamberts), then Macmann, then Macmann and Moll, then Macmann
and Lemuel and finally the six inmates: Lemuel, Macmann, the giant,
the young one, the thin one, and the Saxon. This should not surprise us
because when, in dying, something which is whole begins to pass away,
it does so through a process of that whole passing again into multiplicity:
your body dies and your particles disperse. Importantly, however, as we
shall see, this kind of dispersal also has important implications for the
process of judgement, because to judge one needs stable terms of
relation. The decomposing self, then, throws into sharp relief the way in
which we must inevitably exceed systems of judgement.

As we have seen and as I will again attempt to illustrate below, order
operates by causing chaos to pass into that order. With regard to the self,
this process might be termed 'subjectification': one is educated and
disciplined by order so that chaos is driven out and through this process
the self, which is alarmingly dispersed in the infant, becomes whole. So

the light (of language, knowledge) appears and consumes the dark (of confused and unknowable sensations); play dissolves earnestness and drives it out; relation banishes non-relation. As this ordering process occurs judgement (where the stable terms 'Good' and 'Evil' are related to you and your thoughts and actions which are considered to be comprised of equally stable terms) drives out your immanent understanding of what is good for you and what is bad for you and you therefore live for the reward to come and so stop living in the moment. *Malone Dies*, however, in one way reverses this process, as chaos passes into order and dissolves it, the dark consumes the light, earnestness the play, non-relation dissolves relation and judgement is driven out by immanent, ethical existence. In yet another way, it might be said that the artist, here represented by Malone (who represents not only artists but all of us), can also bring into existence. That is, the artist can make form (just as Malone invents his stories) as a response to the chaos (in a manner similar to that described by Deleuze and Guattari in *What is Philosophy?*), laying down form over the chaos. This differs from the above-mentioned oppressive order, however, because it involves bringing into existence, or creation, through the affirmation of one's being, rather than through the subjectification and oppression of other beings brought about by judgement. Creation, then, which is aligned with existence, is opposed to oppression, brought about by judgements which seek to circumscribe, contain, or fix existence in place.[2]

JUDGEMENT: ORDER THROUGH SUBJECTIFICATION

To better recognize the radical gesture involved in the full descriptions of death and decomposition (with order being overcome by chaos, judgement by ethical existence), in *Malone Dies* it is useful to place the work in counterpoint again with the France from which it emerged in the late forties. The question of judgement, of what might comprise an adequate morality, or better still an ethics, was one which was seen to require an urgent solution in post World War Two France. Elkaîm-Sartre has noted how Jean-Paul Sartre, at the conclusion of *Being and Nothingness* talks of the need for an ethics and promises to dedicate a future work to this problem: his *Notebooks for an Ethics* were eventually published posthumously (Elkaîm-Sartre, 1992: xxiii). I would suggest that in post World War Two France apparently random applications of

---

[2] On this point see Beckett's comments to Charles Juliet, which I quote later in this chapter (Juliet, 1986a: 27–8).

judgements and justices established the problem of ethics as a territory which had to be traversed.

This sociohistorical counterpoint, however, could be made still more forceful with a reflection on the nature of subjectification and its role in promoting order and judgement (order which is always maintained through judgement, and judgement which can only be effectively applied to stable subjects). During the Vichy regime, the National Revolution expressed a desire to put an end to chaos, the very real chaos apparent in France's humiliating defeat.

I feel that the sociohistorical importance of subjectification and its role of driving out chaos can be examined in two ways; ways which will also serve to establish how an opposition to it was necessitated by the very failings of overly oppressive attempts to subjectify. That is, in too forcefully attempting to create order, regimes often merely succeed in repressing chaos which either returns later in more aggressive form (just as the revolution, however late, answers oppression) or is in effect created by the very gestures thought to impose order (just as those who claim to 'cleanse' countries tend to leave piles of rotting corpses).

Firstly, the idea of imposing social order through subjectification might be addressed by examining the differing notions of education under the Third Republic and under Vichy which overturned this Republic. The idea that education is important to the formation of subjects or citizens is by no means controversial; indeed, to illustrate this point I need only draw upon a well-known schoolbook of French history: Pierre Miquel's *Histoire de la France*.

The republican education reformers led by Jules Ferry in the 1890s saw the Second Empire with its return to aristocratic values as decadent, because administrative power was being distributed according to social position rather than according to talent, and this was a state of affairs which they considered had led to the country being governed badly. In response Ferry endeavoured to lessen the role of the Catholic church in providing education, in part because the church strongly promoted monarchist values: indeed part of the purpose of the Catholic education system might be argued to have been the 'production' of monarchists. The republicans, wanted education 'for all' so as to be able to reach the formerly illiterate, and thereby better disseminate republican values. Educating all French citizens to republican values – and the very concept of 'citizens' as equal and free individuals (opposed to the monarchist 'subjects' existing in a hierarchy) was a republican value – would serve to bury the monarchist threat to the Republic and, ideally, allow people to seek promotion according to ability rather than station/ class. The republican education system, it was thought, would end the perceived chaos engendered by the mismanagement stemming from the monarchist system of privilege (Miquel, 1976: 426–8, 438–41).

On the other hand, the National Revolution of Vichy which succeeded the Third Republic considered that the republican education system instituted by Ferry promoted individualism above all else and thereby bred a selfishness which divided the nation and so promoted a new kind of chaos. They proposed a return to traditional religious education which would inform people of their duty and their place and encourage them to know and keep that place: a return to a church-based education system, then, would allow a return to the harmony of 'natural' (immutable and derived from the perceived order of God) hierarchical order, opposed to the chaos of 'every man for himself' promoted by the Third Republic. Clearly, each of these political poles (and Vichy might be seen in many ways to embody monarchist ideals which the nineteenth century had failed to extinguish) blamed the other for chaos and saw itself as embodying order. Just as clearly, however, neither was able to extinguish the chaos, which reappeared in spite of the stable subjects their systems of education sought to produce (Griffiths, 1970: 254–65; Miquel, 1976: 504–39).

These points can be further clarified by examining the general positioning of the subject in society in relation to the *mots d'ordre* or slogans of each state form. The famous slogan of the Republic is 'Liberté, Egalité, Fraternité', while that of Vichy's National Revolution was 'Travail, Famille, Patrie'. The first slogan promotes an individual-centred notion of subjectification (the self positioned in relation to his [*sic*] own freedom), while the second promotes the social identification of the individual (the self positioned in relation to his/her position in society); the first implies a contract, an order through reason (cf. Rousseau's *The Social Contract*), the second a more medieval ideal of a 'natural' order, overseen in the end by God mediated through 'the king' or chief of state; an order through duty and position. Clearly then, the notion of order here, both for the Third Republic and the National Revolution, involved or required as its first task the subjectification of the individual, and in both cases subjectification led to judgement. You would be judged by both in accordance with how well you had learnt your lessons. That is, you would be judged in terms of your own recognition of your station in society by the National Revolution and in terms of your 'merit' (or academic 'success') by the Third Republic. Further, you would be

judged on your 'affiliations' in the virtual civil war of the 1940s by both
the National Revolution and the returned Republic under the purge.
That is, each system judged the subject you had become: and a successful subject is judged by the extent to which he/she contributes to or
subscribes to the values of that system currently in power.

What we witness in the France of *la guerre franco-française* is the evident
failure of both systems of order. The attempt to impose order led at best
to the confusions and ineffectualness of the Third Republic and at worst
to the sometimes astounding oppressions under Vichy and the more or
less bloody purge. Order is imposed through judgement and in effect
through violent, chaotic, oppression (and the paradox of order appearing through chaos, a return of the inclusive disjunction which has
already been discussed at length, is significant). In all cases ordering
proceeds firstly through the judgement of each individual. Have they
been properly subjectified? Are they truly French subjects/citizens? If
not, they must be cast out, excluded or somehow reintegrated.

What opposition could there be to such oppressive subjectification?
For Beckett, in *Malone Dies*, the answer is already apparent: the completely subjectified individual is a myth, chaos has never been driven
out, the subject itself in life as much as art is always unstable, decentred,
the subject itself is as much chaos as order, dark as much as light,
undergoing the oscillation of inclusive disjunction, an oscillation which
will end at last, however, as the dark descends and the self disperses.

These ideas might be tied in to Beckett through brief reference to
Malone Dies, paying attention to the contrast between the Saposcats
(good bourgeois citizens who believe in progress through education, as
promoted by the Third Republic) and the Lamberts (good peasants,
working the land as the French had for centuries, a family with a marked
hierarchy and knowledge of place as Big Lambert lords it over his family
like a king by divine right).[3] The theme of education is apparent with
both families: the Saposcats have faith in Sapo's schooling and Big
Lambert 'educates' his family through his stories and harsh judgements.
There are also two different kinds of order: the 'natural' (monarchist)
order of the Lamberts and the 'rational' (republican) order of the
Saposcats. But compromising both conceptions of order is Sapo, the
decentred subject, who exceeds both poles in failing to be properly
subjectified. We also find echoes of this in *Molloy* and *The Unnamable*,

---

[3] Whether these peasants are Irish or French has been a matter of some debate and I discuss this
question more fully in the next chapter, indicating there why I think they might be read as being
French.

where the forgetfulness of the protagonists, the fact that they fail to learn or understand their lessons, is what allows them to find a kind of freedom in the face of such oppression (Beckett, 1958: 51).

In the unpublished letter Beckett wrote to Georges Duthuit in 1949, Beckett discusses the paintings of his friend Bram van Velde as an example of the art of non-relation. Beckett takes the notion of 'relation' as a point of departure, suggesting that by relation we have come to understand not only that between, 'the artist and what proposes itself to him from outside, but also and above all those which, within him, assure him of the lines of flight and recoil, of variations of tension, and give to him, among other benefits, that of feeling himself many (at the lowest estimate) while all the time remaining (of course) one.'[4] Before going on to suggest that Bram van Velde makes use of neither of these two types of relation in his paintings, Beckett, expressing little enthusiasm for a tiresome job and admitting that he is probably only talking about himself, goes on to specify what he means by the relation of 'self in self':

Let's suppose it's a question of the happy knack of existing under various guises, which somehow verify one another, or are verified one after the other by the one charged with this task and who . . . from time to time indulges in a small autological get together, with a greedy sucking noise.
   Tenebrated in this way . . . the artist can wallow in so-called non-figurative painting in complete tranquillity, assured of never being short of themes, of always being in front of himself, and with as much variety as if he had never renounced strolling along the banks of the Seine. (Beckett, 1949)[5]

In describing his non-relational art, Beckett turns first to what might be considered a problem concerning the concept of subjectivity. He disparages here the artist who feels he or she can be many and yet

[4] Beckett, 1949. The original reads as follows: 'Par rapport nous entendons, naturellement, non seulement celui, primaire, entre l'artiste et ce que le dehors lui propose, mais aussi et surtout ceux qui, en-dedans de lui, lui assurent des lignes de fuite et de recul et des changements de tension et lui dispensent, entre autres bienfaits, celui de se sentir plusieurs (au bas mot), tout en restant (bien entendu) unique.'

[5] The original reads as follows: 'Mettons qu'il s'agisse de l'agréable faculté d'exister sous diverses espèces, dont en quelque sorte les unes constatent les autres, ou qui se font constater à tour de rôle par celle préposée à cet office et qui . . . se livre de temps en temps à une petite séance d'autologie, avec un bruit goulu de succion. / Ainsi ténébré . . . l'artiste peut se rouler dans la peinture dite non-figurative en toute tranquillité, avec l'assurance de n'être jamais à court de thèmes, d'être toujours devant lui-même et avec autant de variété que s'il n'avait jamais renoncé à flâner aux bords de la Seine.'

remain one (a position which requires an understanding of the expressive artist of relation as a unified and stable self with all order guaranteed by the truth of this self). The ordered artist of relation Beckett describes is *whole*, an integral being who makes images or meaning by reflecting on diverse materials or by taking on diverse personas while remaining, at bottom, the same. The artist of non-relation, on the other hand, recognizes that the multifarious nature of his or her own self and the percepts and affects extracted from that self cannot be so easily unified, that the subject or the (non-)expressions that pass through it (as expression comes from outside rather than originating with the self[6]) cannot be unified into, or underwritten by, a stable entity. The artist of non-relation constitutes a self in dispersion, exemplifying what has come to be called the 'decentred' subject. Against the order and tranquillity of the artist of expression who unifies (through totalization) and is unified, we have the chaos and apprehension of the decentred subject of non-relational art who recognizes that heterogeneous materials and experience can never be completely given as a whole.

The narrator in Beckett's *Enough* assures us that 'The art of combining is not my fault. It's a curse from above. For the rest I would suggest not guilty' (Beckett, 1984a: 140). Beckett's use of the legalistic metaphor might be taken to suggest that the identification between relation and comprehension could be extended to include notions of judgement. Further, it is judgement which imposes order, and to function effectively judgements require that there be fixed subjects, because in order to be judged a term must be stable.

We must forcefully underline this series of concepts then: relation (of a signifier to a signified; a signifier to a signifier and so on) enables comprehension (the production of meaning, the making of sense), which in turn enables (and partly comprises) judgement (of the fixed subject), which in turn produces order (which was considered to have been disturbed by the action requiring judgement). Testing the stability of these posited identifications and eventually mapping an alternative to them will comprise some of what chapters 3 and 4 hope to achieve in considering how *Malone Dies*, offering us a portrait of a decomposing subject, explains how such processes of judgement can never adequately define or contain a life; shows us how, that is, life passes beyond judgement.

---

[6] This theme will be examined in more depth in chapters 5 and 6, below.

CRISIS WITH THE MORAL ORDER

To understand the peculiar kind of resistance mounted to ideologically sponsored moral orders or systems of judgement by a number of post-war French writers and philosophers, we perhaps need to recognize how the social orders of the forties and beyond themselves seemed to generate atrocity. That is, certain ideas of 'order' themselves came to be seen as the cause of problems of injustice rather than a solution to problems of injustice; the laws themselves, rather than bringing forth justice, seemed, through their overly rigid judgements, to produce injustice. It might be suggested that these writers encountered the same problems, that they became acutely aware of these problems and that their works thereby bore traces of their outlines.

As we have seen, like most histories that of the French is no stranger to atrocity. In his letter to Duthuit, Beckett talks of the artist renouncing the Seine, but perhaps he does not do this altogether. The Seine might just as well be looked at in contemplation of death as love. Indeed a man described in Beckett's late play, *Ohio Impromptu* seems to be contemplating both. Beckett's paternal forebears were French Huguenots, who moved to Ireland in the seventeenth century for 'economic and religious freedom' (Bair, 1990: 2). On the night of 23 August 1572, the infamous night of Saint Bartholomew, 3,000 Huguenots were strangled and their bodies tossed into the Seine (Miquel, 1976: 170). More recently the river has carried the bodies of those slaughtered both under Nazi Occupation and in the purge following Liberation. But to understand the workings of injustice through order it is perhaps worth moving to a time well after the purge, under the Republic of de Gaulle, rather than the much vilified Vichy regime. For although these events take place after the composition of *Malone Dies*, they still show us, perhaps more clearly, the shape of a problem which, coming into sharp relief during *la guerre franco-française*, still remains visible in France and elsewhere today.

On 17 October 1961 the French police chief Maurice Papon incited his men to the massacre of an estimated 200 Algerians, who, in the midst of the Algerian War, were attempting a peaceful march into Paris in moral support of the FLN (the Algerian revolutionary army) and in defiance of curfews. In a film recounting the events, *Drowning by Bullets*, Claude Bordé, a former editor of the weekly *France Observateur*, describes how three or four policemen came into the offices of the newspaper in a state of distress: 'They said they'd seen in the police headquarters courtyard about fifty Algerians killed, their bodies thrown into the

Seine.' While dozens of other demonstrators were being killed all over Paris, the police corralled hundreds into the central courtyard of police headquarters on the Ile de la Cité late at night. One survivor, Idir Belkagem, states: 'The Police told us: "It's your last day on earth. Pray, because you won't ever be seeing your family again. We brought you here to be eliminated, pure and simple, every single one of you."' Another survivor, Cherhabil Hachemi, describes his ordeal: 'They beat us with truncheons . . . they had cords attached to the ends. They put the cords around people's necks. They did it to me, but by reflex I had lowered my chin and it stayed there. Then they began to garrotte people' (*Drowning by Bullets*).

Besides detailing the massacre itself, the film investigates how the events had been surrounded by silence. Official reports listed the death toll at two. Although the government exercised its power of censorship to keep more accurate reports from circulating widely, it is apparent that, while Jean-Paul Sartre and other autonomous leftists attended demonstrations condemning racial violence (without knowing the full extent of the massacre), the powerful official left wing, and in particular the French Communist Party and the union movement, knew of the massacre and made no effort to protest. Jean Louis Peninou, editor of the daily newspaper *Libération*, details the silence:

The big parties of the left and the union leaders didn't react out of fear of being associated with the enemy. It was a tacit wartime reaction. For them, an Algerian demonstrator was not a worker but a potential enemy. There wasn't one hour's strike! Over one hundred workers killed in Paris and not even an hour's strike. (*Drowning by Bullets*)

The silence was near complete, so much so that the events have only recently begun to be commemorated. This atrocity illuminates two points whereby the questions of judgement and the moral code come to a point of crisis. A crisis which I would suggest had already been heavily underscored by *la guerre franco-française*.

Firstly, it highlights the fact that the police, that is to say the system of justice – for the actions of the police in October 1961 were backed up by the judiciary who dismissed all complaints filed against the police (*Drowning by Bullets*) – are capable of committing atrocities in the name of the law. Furthermore, it again highlights the fact that, depending on the government of the day and the system of morality they embrace, the law itself can be engineered to generate atrocities. Another film, *The Architecture of Doom*, argues that Hitler's Nazi party constructed a morality around an aesthetics: Good was identified with 'Beautiful' and Evil with 'Ugly'. Other examples of the shadings of this dichotomy were healthy/ sick, normal/depraved, progressive/backward, and notions of racial superiority with its dichotomy Aryan/Jew. According to this formula, in an era of rampant nationalism and absolute faith in the continuing progress and superiority of Western culture, the Fatherland was identified with Good. Following the simple formula of triumphalist and expansionist nationalism, the equation (whose mechanism of calculation has always been the law) demanded the promotion of the Good and the suppression of Evil.

René Bousquet, assassinated in June 1993, was, as the former General Secretary of Police for the Vichy government, responsible for ordering the rounding up of Jews for deportation (to extermination in Nazi camps) during World War Two. As a means of justifying his actions Bousquet always maintained that he only ordered the incarceration and deportation of 'foreign' Jews (that is, those Jews who had recently fled to France to escape persecution and those who had been stripped of their French citizenship) as a way of saving French Jews; or those of Jewish extraction born in France, who were, on the whole, not deported (Raffy, 1993: 28–33). A statistic often quoted after the war was that only five per cent of Jews of French citizenship died at the hands of the Nazis (*Sorrow and the Pity*: 139);[7] while this is accurate, of the 76,000 foreign Jews (and Jews who had been stripped of French citizenship) captured by the French police and delivered to the Nazis, only 2,500 survived (Rousso, 1992: 100). According to the nationalist-based morality of the times, then, Bousquet, who was not a Fascist (Raffy, 1993: 28–33; see also Husson, 1992), had a simple choice, if not between Good and Evil then at least between Good and not-Good. Good was *La patrie*, France, and the outsider was not-Good: the foreigner whom many blamed for France's humiliating defeat. According to the moral code, then, in sacrificing the foreigner to save the French citizen, Bousquet had acted with absolute propriety. In no sense could he be said to have acted in bad faith: with regard to the nationalistic moral code to which he was referring (and it was by no means his own private code) the explication of his actions is implicit in his judgement.

The name of René Bousquet is probably now reviled for many reasons. One is because we are less likely to accept the validity of a moral code based on nationalistic or racial dichotomies. Yet to couch the

[7] On the portrayal of the treatment of Jews in France in post-war French history, see Poznanski, 1992.

problem of Bousquet in more radical terms, it could be claimed that what is objectionable about his trade-off is the notion of judgement itself. 'Judgement' requires the support of a coherent moral code. If the moral code on which Bousquet based his judgement is now thoroughly discredited, we, in retrospect, fail to see how he could judge at all. During the war the French police were used by those in power to 'control' those 'opposed to the state' (composed of the occupying Nazis and Vichy). After the war, once power was taken from the partisans and vested again in a central government, the same police were used to round up those said to have collaborated, and the same judiciary used to try them. Further, other arms of the state not generally considered to be involved with questions of justice or judgement might also be implicated: France's national railway company, the SNCF, collaborated in the transportation of the Jews out of France and France's post and telecommunications network, the PTT, was responsible for listening in on all phone calls and opening all letters sent into 'the free zone' of Vichy France as a means of uncovering activities judged to be against the national interest (Lefêbre, 1993). While individuals from the police or judiciary and other state institutions were purged for individual acts of collaboration the institutions themselves which had sanctioned and, indeed, generated the atrocities at times required by this collaboration, maintained continuity (Lottman, 1986: 34, 66, 184, 194–202, 290; Mazey and Wright, 1992; Delarue, 1992). Maurice Papon, who, like Bousquet, was belatedly accused of crimes against humanity for his role (as General Secretary of the prefecture of Gironde) in the deportation of Jews from France during the war, after the war became the chief commissioner of the Paris police and, as we have seen, using this position instigated the massacre of 200 Algerian supporters of the FLN, in Paris on 17 October 1961. Papon was later to become Minister of the Budget in the cabinet of Raymond Barre under the presidency of Valéry Giscard d'Estaing (Lottman, 1986: 288). Having served his nation, and, like Bousquet, having had the foresight to ally himself with members of the Resistance to establish his patriotic credentials when things began to turn sour for the Nazis, Papon's brilliant career was uninterrupted by his personal complicity in the war crimes of World War Two. It was only very recently that his complicity in war crimes from a different war, that with Algeria, even begun to be mentioned, and this tardiness might again be explained by the fact that Papon was, in fact, serving the interests of the state and acting in accordance with its moral code (*Drowning By Bullets*; Etchegoin, 1994: 50).

As a first point of crisis for the moral order then, it would have been evident to many who lived through *la guerre franco-française* that the moral code of the state was the same moral code that sanctioned and generated atrocities. There had been an apparent complete reversal of system of government from Fascist to non-Fascist, yet under both of these systems it was the French national interest which was presented as the transcendental Good against which a more fluid Evil might be defined. The leaders of the Vichy government which collaborated with the Nazis, Pétain and Laval, and de Gaulle, who resisted them from London and later became president of France (and was president when Papon instigated the massacre of Algerians) all appealed to the notion of *La France*, to the unchallengeable good of the French nation state to justify the actions of their governments (cf. Rousso; 1991, 1992; Griffiths, 1970; and Lacouture, 1990, 1991).[8]

In these terms a major difference between the Vichy regime and the Fourth and Fifth Republics was the answer to the question of what it was that was in and against the national interest, although in each case this answer was, at least structurally, the same. What was said to be against the national interest was that which was against the ideological interests of the state as formulated by those administrations. Undeniably it was the nation that was Good, but that nation was in reality identified with the state. Under both these systems that Good was used by the police and judiciary to attack with impunity what was seen to be Evil. With the swift reversals of the Occupation and the Liberation and again with the atrocities of the Algerian War it became evident that the notion of moral code itself was in crisis, that the state-based moral code itself was problematic, a symptom of, rather than a cure for, the maladies of society. As to how all this, the production of chaos by orders, might have affected indivuals who lived through this period of history, Michel Serres, at least, is on record as saying: 'I only learned to disobey' (1995: 20).

The second point of crisis circled about the notion of a viable political opposition within the existing polarized political system. The failure of the big parties of the left to condemn the massacre of 17 October demonstrated that they too were locked into a similar, equally problematic moral code. It is well known that the PCF, acting on orders from Moscow which followed on from Stalin's signing of a non-aggression pact with Hitler, condemned the war France had entered against

---

[8] These claims are illustrated more fully in chapter 5, below.

Germany as a bourgeois war which had nothing to do with the interests of its constituent, the worker. The PCF did not join the Resistance against Nazi occupation until Hitler invaded the Soviet Union in 1941 (see Lacouture, 1990: 373; and Bourgeois and Martelli, 1993).

While the PCF had claimed that the transcendental Good on which it based its own moral code was the interests of the proletariat, with the opening of Communist archives in the former Soviet Union much evidence has surfaced to suggest that the true centre of the moral code of the PCF rested with the Soviet state. From the thirties onwards each person applying to be a member of the French Communist Party was required to fill in a 74- to 76-item questionnaire designed to test ideological strengths and weaknesses. In a system of unprecedented multinational surveillance all of these questionnaires, along with minutes from each cell meeting, were dispatched to Moscow for assessment. In this way Moscow was able to hand-pick the leaders of the PCF and to *intervene* to determine the direction of the party. Elements of the leadership of the French party resided, at various times, in Moscow, and answered at all times to Moscow. Furthermore, the PCF was financed by the Soviet Union (Bourgeois, 1993: 4–9; Jauvert, 1993: 50–4). In effect, if unbeknownst to most of its members, the PCF was little more than an arm of the Soviet state. Its moral code was not centred on the interests of the proletariat then, but on the interests of that Soviet state. Few would now claim that the Soviet state's interests, while themselves disguised as the proletarian interests, amounted to much more than its own perpetuation, an anchor point which was able to justify, under Stalin in particular, some of the most astounding atrocities of the twentieth century.

It should be noted that the moral code based on the transcendental notion of Good (identified here with the fatherland or the party) and Evil (any opposition to that state or party) bears structural similarities to those codes propagated by organized religions. The Good/Evil paradigm is fundamentally religious (cf. Deleuze, 1993a: 156–69). Clearly Beckett was aware of the hypocrisies of both nationalism and communism and scornful of the moral codes they propagated. In Four Novellas Beckett finds time to satirize both the patriot and the doctrinal Communist, outlining in each case the connection with religion. In *First Love* the narrator describes the Irish patriot: 'Wherever nauseated time has dropped a nice fat turd you will find our patriots, sniffing it up on all fours, their faces on fire. Elysium of the roofless' (Beckett, 1984a: 8–9). In *The End*, one of Beckett's vagabonds, who is quickly heading towards death and has taken to begging, sees a Communist on a street corner:

He was bellowing so loud that snatches of his discourse reached my ears. Union . . . brothers . . . Marx . . . capital . . . bread and butter . . . love. It was all Greek to me . . . All of a sudden he turned and pointed at me, as at an exhibit. Look at this down and out, he vociferated, this leftover . . . Take a good look at this living corpse. You may say it's his own fault. Ask him if it's his own fault. The voice, Ask him yourself. Then he bent forward and took me to task . . . Do you hear me, you crucified bastard! cried the orator . . . He must have been a religious fanatic, I could find no other explanation. (Beckett, 1984a: 65–6)

Such overt reference to politics is not common in Beckett. Yet aspects of his work in the Trilogy and in particular his rejection of judgements based on the Good/Evil, Black/White dichotomies of the moral code might be seen as a response to the moral crisis that became apparent after World War Two. In *The Unnamable*, Beckett's narrator asks: 'and what is one to believe, that is not the point, to believe this or that, the point is to guess right, nothing more, they say, If it's not white it's very likely black, it must be admitted the method lacks subtlety, in view of the intermediate shades all equally worthy of a chance' (Beckett, 1958: 121).

Further, when questioned by Charles Juliet as to the necessity for the writer to think in terms of morality Beckett stated:

What you say is true, but moral values are not accessible. Nor can one define them. To define them it would be necessary to pronounce a value judgement, which cannot be done. This is why I've never been in agreement with this notion of the theatre of the absurd, because there is a value judgement there. One can no longer even speak of the true. It is this which causes an aspect of the distress. Paradoxically, it's through form that the artist can find a kind of way out, by giving form to the unformed. It is perhaps only at this level that there can be an underlying affirmation. (Juliet, 1986a: 27–8)

Faced with chaos, then, one cannot judge, but one can, paradoxically, bring into existence, making form out of chaos. This is an extremely difficult intellectual turn, one which, like Beckett's insistence on impossibility in the *Three Dialogues*, seems to take us to an impasse. Something of what is involved in this impasse, can, however, be described conceptually, if through concepts which are thoroughly paradoxical (and therefore apparently 'illogical' or anti-Platonic), and this is what I will attempt to express in the next chapter.

We have seen how both the nationalist-based moral code used to justify the ruling power of the French state and the party-based moral code used to justify the official political opposition to that state were becoming increasingly suspect, for while necessary as a mechanism for generating judgements, such judgements appeared more a means of maintaining and enforcing (oppressive) power than of providing justice.[9] The need for some sort of alternative was increasingly felt, a need, to echo Deleuze invoking Artaud, to have done with judgement.[10]

Considered in counterpoint, the French experience of *la guerre franco-française* and the post-war period, which I have discussed here, and *Malone Dies*, which I will discuss in more detail below, show that orders, and the systems of judgement on which they depend, are neither rational (as the republicans might have claimed) or natural (as Vichy might have claimed). For while existence in all its frailty and imperfection might be considered 'necessary', 'the real', 'the essential', human orders and judgements are contingent – matters of accident which say nothing about one's true being (much as they might menace or affect it). That is, one might be condemned or murdered by this or that order, but there where one is sent, beyond life, exiled from order, bears no natural or rational relation to the human order that dispatched you. Rather, it so far exceeds and overflows that order on all sides that that contingent order itself will of necessity pass away (into the plane of consistency which is the chaos where all forms and orders appear and disappear at infinite speed).

Yet what we, also of necessity, must always face now and here is not so much the problem of death as the problem of life. So we must exist amongst orders, but that does not mean we must surrender our souls to this or that order; rather, life at times requires us to disobey, to pass beyond judgements towards the reality of our being and that ethical existence which will allow us to live fully, so that, following Malone, 'My story ended I'll be living yet' (115).

[9] In support of this idea, see Michel Foucault, in 'Intellectuals and Power: A Conversation Between Michel Foucault and Gilles Deleuze' (Foucault, 1977). In particular the following quote from Foucault: 'What is fascinating about prisons is that, for once, power doesn't hide or mask itself; it reveals itself as tyranny pursued into the tiniest details; it is cynical and at the same time pure and entirely "justified" because its practice can be totally formulated within the framework of morality. Its brutal tyranny consequently appears as the serene domination of Good over Evil, of order over disorder.'

[10] Cf. Deleuze's essay, 'Pour en finir avec le jugement', which alludes to Antonin Artaud's radio play *Pour en finir avec le jugement de dieu* (Deleuze, 1993a: 160; Artaud, 1976).

CHAPTER 4

Towards an ethics: Spinoza, Deleuze and Guattari and Beckett

ETHICS AND MORALITY

As a first step towards an ethics – that which might overthrow the system of judgement – we might underline how 'comprehension' is not synonymous with 'understanding'. Deleuze deals with the problem of defining an ethics in *Spinoza: Practical Philosophy*:

> . . . all that one needs in order to moralize is to fail to understand. It is clear that we have only to misunderstand a law for it to appear to us in the form of a moral 'You must' . . . Adam does not understand the rule of the relation of his body with the fruit, so he interprets God's word as a prohibition. (Deleuze, 1988b: 23)

A series of identifications might be proposed: comprehension (in the narrow sense I mean it here) involves the relation of one imagined (that is, inadequately understood) stable term (such as 'this fruit') to another (such as 'prohibition') and such relation (distinct from the adequately understood relation of one body to another) makes judgement possible. Comprehension of this kind, then, that comprehension which is based on the relation of supposedly stable terms and leads to judgement, does not set out from knowledge but from ignorance; furthermore, it also functions as a means of obscuring understanding, as a means of keeping us in ignorance:

> Law, whether moral or social, does not provide us with any knowledge; it makes nothing known. At worst, it prevents the formation of knowledge (the law of the tyrant). At best, it prepares for knowledge and makes it possible (the law of Abraham or of Christ). Between these two extremes, it takes the place of knowledge in those who, because of their mode of existence, are incapable of knowledge (the law of Moses). (Deleuze, 1988b: 24)

Knowledge should under no circumstances be confused with obedience to a command, to a moral code which prescribes what is Good and what is Evil; rather, knowledge bears a direct relation to ethics, it is knowledge which determines the difference between good and bad (Deleuze, 1988b: 24–5).

Spinoza overturns the traditional philosophical notion that the mind has primacy over the body and replaces it with the thesis of parallelism, which maintains that there is no such primacy; that 'an action in the mind is necessarily an action in the body as well, and what is a passion in the body is necessarily a passion in the mind'. The practical significance of this move is that it reverses the traditional principle on which morality was founded, through which consciousness (or the mind) was given the task of mastering the passions (or the body) (Deleuze, 1988b: 18). Deleuze quotes Spinoza: 'we neither strive for, nor will, neither want, nor desire anything because we judge it to be good; on the contrary, we judge something to be good because we strive for it, will it, want it, and desire it' (Deleuze, 1988b: 20–1). It is not a matter of referring to a moral code first, which specifies an action as Good or Evil, and then acting on that advice (formulated after all through a comprehension whose nature it is to affirm and propagate ignorance); rather it is simply a matter of seeking to be joined with that object which agrees with your nature and avoiding that object which disagrees with your nature (20–1).

In the Garden of Eden, God tells Adam, 'Thou shalt not eat of the fruit' and Adam interprets this as a prohibition, as a moral precept; he must not eat the apple because the apple is Evil, because it has been judged to be Evil by God. Deleuze however, suggests that these words refer to 'a fruit that, as such, will poison Adam if he eats it'. That is, the fruit will not agree with Adam's nature and so he should avoid it, but 'because Adam is ignorant of causes, he thinks that God morally forbids him something, whereas God only reveals the natural consequence of ingesting the fruit'. There is no Good or Evil, but there is good and bad. When a body that agrees with our nature is joined with us it increases our power (*puissance*)[1] and this is good. The paradigm for this is food. When a body that does not agree with our nature, the paradigm for this being poison, is joined with us, this decreases our power and is bad. 'Hence good and bad have a primary, objective meaning, but one that is relative and partial: that which agrees with our nature or does not agree with it' (22; see also 30–43).

In consequence good and bad have a secondary, subjective and modal meaning which qualifies two types of existence. Firstly, there is

---

[1] Cf. Brian Massumi's textual note to *A Thousand Plateaus* concerning the use of the English word 'power'. It is generally used to translate both '*puissance*' and '*pouvoir*' (Deleuze and Guattari, 1987, xvii).

the case of the good individual (also called free or rational or strong), who within the limits of his power tries to increase his power by seeking to organize his encounters so that he might 'combine his relation with relations that are compatible with his, and thereby . . . increase his power. For goodness is a matter of dynamism, power, and the composition of powers.' Secondly, there is the case of the bad (or servile, weak, or foolish) individual, 'who lives haphazardly, who is content to undergo the effects of his encounters', but complains whenever the effect is unpleasant:

For by lending oneself in this way to whatever encounter in whatever circumstance, believing that with a lot of violence or a little guile, one will always extricate oneself, how can one fail to have more bad encounters than good? How can one keep from destroying oneself through guilt, and others through resentment, spreading one's own powerlessness and enslavement everywhere, one's own sickness, indigestions and poisons? In the end, one is unable even to encounter oneself. (23)

'In this way', Deleuze continues, 'Ethics, which is to say, a typology of immanent modes of existence, replaces Morality, which always refers existence to transcendent values.' As we have hinted at above, with reference to the religious structure of the moral code, 'Morality is the judgement of God, the system of Judgement.' But, Deleuze suggests, 'Ethics overthrows the system of judgement' (23).

If a crisis with the notion of the moral code itself had become apparent due to the swift reversals of what the state designated as 'Good' and 'Evil' in *la guerre franco-française*, then Deleuze through Spinoza and Nietzsche provides us with an alternative, an ethics adaptable to an age of chaos, an age when, according to Beckett, 'one can't even say what is true', and where 'one can never know enough, but not to judge' (Juliet, 1986b: 16; Bernold, 1992a: 84). I will argue that many of the conclusions drawn by Deleuze in outlining this alternative are echoed in the work of Beckett. *Malone meurt* in particular, written in 1948 (Bair, 1990: 400) (towards the end of the *épuration* or purge of Nazi collaborators) and published in the author's translation as *Malone Dies* in 1956, poses problems for the notion of judgement, and in formulating those problems indicates elements of an alternative response which strike a chord with the work of Deleuze and Guattari.[2]

---

[2] For a reading of the importance of ethics in the work of Deleuze and Guattari and Foucault, see Patton, 1986.

Michael Hardt has suggested that on one fundamental philosophical point Deleuze was out of step with his age, just as Spinoza (because of the same philosophical point) was out of step with his. That point is the above-mentioned concept of parallelism: the rejection of the priority of the mind over the body. In both cases the thesis of parallelism is intimately connected with what Deleuze calls, 'the great theoretical thesis of Spinozism: a single substance having an infinity of attributes, *Deus sive Natura*, all "creatures" being only modes of these attributes or modifications of this substance' (Deleuze, 1988b: 17). That is to say 'the univocity of Being': the concept that all Being is one.

In the introduction above I describe how Beckett, like Deleuze, seems to posit a univocity of Being in his writings. Further, for both Beckett and Deleuze, the univocity of Being seems tied to 'chaos': that is, the one thing of which everything partakes, univocal Being, is, in effect, chaos. Writing in post-war France, Beckett keenly felt the chaotic nature of things and endeavoured to accommodate this chaos, tied to variable immanent existence rather than transcendent terms, into his art. He stated:

The confusion is not my invention . . . It is all around us and our only chance now is to let it in. The only chance of renovation is to open our eyes and see the mess. It is not a mess you can make sense of . . . What I am saying does not mean that there will henceforth be no form in art. It only means that there will be new form, and that this form will be of such a type that it admits the chaos and does not try to say that the chaos is really something else. (Driver, 1961: 22–3)

The chaos will not be ordered through judgement but accommodated by the kind of form that the artist brings into existence. As for Deleuze, his identification of Being with chaos is clear in *What is Philosophy?* in particular, and has been noted by a number of critics; to quote from his contemporary Jean-Luc Nancy: '[Deleuze's] thought does not have "the real" for an "object" – it has no "object": it is another effectuation of the "real", admitting that the real "in itself" is chaos, a sort of effectivity without effectuation' (Nancy, 1996: 110).

The adoption of the concept of immanence, of the full, indivisible, density of Being produces a number of effects, some of which radically affect the notion of judgement and the moral order. In the first place, as Deleuze has noted, the thesis of univocity combines pantheism and atheism: that is, the judging God of monotheism is no longer in the equation; there is no prior being to Being and so, in adopting this thesis, we have finished with the judgement of God. Indeed we have finished with judgement of any sort because there can be no judgement where there is no possibility of comprehension and there is no possibility of comprehension in an aesthetic system which claims to admit no relation.

A BOOK OF RECKONING AND A BOOK OF LIFE

Malone Dies might be seen to both highlight problems inherent in the system of judgement and to indicate the necessity of an alternative system. In the English medieval morality play *The Summoning of Everyman* the idea of judgement is illustrated through a materialistic metaphor, the metaphor of accounting, of reckoning. God is portrayed not so much as a judge as an accountant; a case is decided by a simple compilation of the credits of good deeds, against the debit of bad deeds:

> On the thou must take a longe iourney.
> Therefore thy boke of counte with the thou brynge,
> For tourne agayne thou can not by no waye.
> And loke thou be sure of they rekenynge,
> For before God thou shalte answere and shewe
> Thy many badde dedes, and good but a fewe –
> How thou hast spente thy lyfe and in what wyse –
> Before the chefe Lorde of Paradyse.
>   (*The Summoning of Everyman*, 1992: 13)

A similar use of metaphors of accounting might be found in the biblical parable of the talents. Among other things, *Malone Dies* presents itself not as a book of reckoning, but as a book of existence and bringing into existence which demolishes the idea of judgement.

There are a number of interrelated ways in which *Malone Dies* could be said to resemble a book of reckoning. Firstly, Malone is writing and, like Molloy and Moran, to an extent at least, he is writing his own story. Secondly, Malone expresses the desire to make an account of the possessions which remain to him before he dies. Thirdly, Malone is keen, from time to time, to describe his present state. All of these things might be considered to refer to Malone's life and therefore be read as offering an account, report, or reckoning of that life. In addition, of course, Malone spends much of his time telling stories, yet even these seem to be stories about himself (Beckett, 1956: 12), as he multiplies the number of characters who take his place and experience the world (both in other possible pasts, as with Sapo, and other possible presents, as with Macmann) on his behalf or in his place. This kind of fictional substitution is played on by Beckett, as Malone claims to be the inventor of Beckett's characters Murphy, Molloy, Moran, Mercier and Camier and so on (63). The stories, too, might be understood to stand in for Malone, as documents through which one might interpret and judge his life. However, I would suggest that all of these are not means of (failed) reckoning, but rather they involve existence and bringing into existence: the writing is not an adding up of past deeds, but a form of creation; so too, the evolving list of possessions brings new aspects of Malone (whose being is linked to theirs) into being; the present state and the stories are intertwined with the immanence of Malone's existence. That is, Malone's present state not only includes the possessions which remain to him, but also the stages of the stories he tells and the process of writing them, and these are things which must be brought into existence.

Firstly, then, one might consider how the process of writing overturns the notion of the book of a life, or existence, being a book of reckoning (through which judgement might take place). Malone states that he must have begun his story because he felt he had something to say about the nature of life and death, though that something continues to escape him (51–2). He suggests that he writes 'in order to know where I have got to, where he has got to' (32). The interrelation between Malone's book and Malone might be said to be even more forceful than those of Molloy and Moran and their books; at one point Malone states that the exercise-book in which he writes *is* his life (105). Indeed, once he loses his stick it is, along with the pencil with which he writes, his last remaining possession (100), and the act of writing, towards the end, is the only act he performs. His book, then, is equated with his life and so in a certain sense might be called a book of reckoning (which also seeks to encompass a life). Yet the 'life' which is expressed by Malone is a life of immanent existence; that is, Malone does not and could not encompass his own life: he has no memory of how he came to be where he is, the past is even more dimly seen by Malone than it is by Molloy, and he continues to forget as he proceeds: 'At first I did not write, I just said the thing. Then I forgot what I had said. A minimum of memory is indispensable, if one is to live really' (32). The life Malone expresses, then, is not the 'life story' recounting one's past in its entirety (so far as is possible); rather, it is the life of the moment, the life of immanent existence. So too, while a conventional book of reckoning would involve the calculation of credits and debits of good and bad deeds over the course of a life, Malone is wholly unable to do this. Indeed, what he writes turns back on itself in ineluctable contradictions which lead not to judgement but rather to aporia: 'my notes have a curious tendency, as I realize at last, to annihilate all they purport to record' (88).

When one considers the possible events which occur in this novel, the events which affect Malone, it becomes still clearer how *Malone Dies* is a book about *a* life which shows how simple processes of judgement through reference to moral codes with their (momentarily) stable orders of Good and Evil cannot encompass or even shed light on the nature of such a life. Without being exhaustive, it is worth listing some of the events which affect Malone: the woman who had once come to feed him no longer enters the room, now it is only a hand which brings him food and takes away his chamber pot (8); he 'loses' his book (33); he drops his pencil (48); the room whitens (49); his body dilates (62); he witnesses lovers at a window opposite his (65); he loses his stick (82); he experiences a 'thousand little things' among which he only mentions an 'extraordinary heat' (88–9); an intruder enters his room and strikes him (97–9); he swells, feels the room rising and falling (114); he experiences 'Gurgles of outflow' (119). Finally, one must remember that all of these events occur within two overarching events: the event of writing and the event of dying. That is, all of these events occur within what might be called the event of pure aporia, the threshold of the unknowable which is reached in dying. Despite the assurances and feigned certainties of certain religions (who claim their own orders are modelled on those of the heavens), the moment of death and what is beyond death remain undecidable; that is, the process of dying is precisely that process through which no judgement is possible, and where all human judgement loses all meaning (the meaning on which it had been built as if upon stone). So too, taken in isolation, all of the other events defy 'comprehension', if that comprehension hopes to lead us towards certainty as to the meaning of events, certainty as to how we might judge a life.

I wrote in the introduction of how I would be concentrating mostly on sensations and possible events in comparing literature to philosophy, and it is interesting to consider how all of the events listed above *affect* Malone (changing who he is, his capacity to act). The hand which brings food and takes excrement allows him to continue to live; the book and pencil allow him to write (a process which modifies his manner of existence); the stick allows him to do many things; witnessing the lovers adds to experience and perhaps contributes to the story of Malone and

Moll; the blow delivered by the stranger affects his senses (99). Further, however, many of the 'events' I have listed above are in fact sensations: the room whitening; the body dilating; the 'thousand little things'; the swelling and rising and falling room; the gurgles of outflow are all sensations, percepts and affects that emerge as discrete events which divide the overarching event of dying. Events and sensations are conflated, then, and, post-Cartesians that we (with Beckett) remain, we remember, if little else from our lessons, that we should be suspicious of the senses which are constantly deceiving us. Rather than being fixed signs which we might interpret on the way to judgement (a judgement as to the meaning or value of a life, for example), such sensations can do nothing (and need do nothing) other than speak of immanent existence.

The other ways in which *Malone Dies* resembles a book of reckoning is through Malone's constant returning to his present state, his desire to make an account of his possessions, and more subtly, in his telling of stories. At the beginning of the novel Malone puts forward two general tasks which he hopes to undertake while getting on with dying. Firstly, he decides he should tell himself stories while waiting to die. Secondly, he will speak of his 'present state' and finally he promises himself he will speak of the things that remain in his possession: 'It will be a kind of inventory. In any case that is a thing I must leave to the very last moment, so as to be sure of not having made a mistake' (3).

TELLING STORIES: CHAOS AND ORDER

In the previous chapter I identified a series of dichotomies which are all isomorphic with that between chaos and order: death and life; earnestness and play; darkness and light; decomposition and wholeness. Rather than one term simply overcoming the other (say, chaos overcoming order, death overcoming life) as a simple reversal of the order of judgement which endeavours to see order drive out chaos completely, Beckett's treatment of these terms is complex. The terms do not simply negate one another; rather, they often pass into one another. To look at it another way; rather than simply working with one pole and the next, Beckett stresses the space between the poles: it is well known, for example, how Beckett is interested in the grey area between black and white, light and dark, rather than either light or dark alone (and I will return to this point in a moment).

Stories of reckoning (such as *The Summoning of Everyman*) concern themselves, ultimately, with the judgement of God. What is presupposed in such stories is that the order of man exactly reflects the order of God: the executioner sends you from human to divine judgement. Divine judgement differs from human judgement only in that it is more comprehensive (as God, more even than the operator of the panopticon, sees and knows all). To indicate that this neat identification of human law with divine law is a matter of hubris (with God created in the image of Man), we do not need to move beyond death (where presumably we might meet God and His Judgement and see for ourselves); rather we only need to move *towards* death. This is because in moving towards death, in paying attention to the nature of our own existence, it becomes clear that human orders and the judgements on which they depend (such as the orders based on the transcendental Good of the state and the Evil of its other which I have discussed in the previous chapter) are contingent and partial. Such 'orders' never succeed in banishing chaos (and who today would claim the judgement of the Nazi order, or the Vichy order, or even the order of, say, the Catholic church over the ages, directly mirrors the order of any just God). Life itself exceeds such human order on all sides; indeed such orders are powerless to truly judge a life (any and every life), which they barely understand. Chaos – the limit of human order and judgement – shows us that death inhabits life; that darkness, the unknowable, surrounds and penetrates the narrow circle of light around which we still huddle as we have always done. Malone, as I have mentioned, wishes to exist in such a way that 'My story ended I'll be living yet' (115), and this is the only possible existence (for a complete surrendering to order, were such possible, would involve the total subjection of all one's life to that order); to live immanently; bringing into existence which involves laying some kind of form over the chaos, with life passing into death at every moment.

EARNESTNESS AND PLAY

To return to the dichotomies I alluded to above, it is clear how many of these terms are closely interrelated, death and life are involved with decomposition and wholeness and darkness and light. Each of these themes (to which Beckett returns throughout *Malone Dies*) might be conceived both simply on a physical level and on a symbolic level, and all illustrate how existence exceeds judgement and cannot be encompassed by it. The opposition between earnestness and play, I would suggest, is equally involved with these other terms; however, the nature of the interrelation in this case is not as immediately apparent and so I will treat it first.

From the beginning of *Malone Dies* it is clear that Beckett associates the notions of play and earnestness with the process of story telling itself:

All went well at first, they all came to me, pleased that someone should want to play with them. If I said, Now I need a hunch-back, immediately one came running, proud as punch of his fine hunch that was going to be asked to perform. It did not occur to him that I might have to ask him to undress. But it was not long before I found myself alone, in the dark. That is why I gave up trying to play and took to myself for ever the shapelessness and speechlessness, incurious wondering, darkness, long stumbling with outstretched arms, hiding. Such is the earnestness from which, for nearly a century now, I have never been able to depart. (2)

Here, then, some of the interrelatedness of themes I spoke of become apparent. Play involves performance, the telling of stories, but rather than this play ending happily and comforting all by leaving all with a sense of self-satisfaction and importance, the play has ended badly. The playmates have fled, leaving Malone alone with his earnestness, his darkness. Such darkness, such earnestness, is then clearly aligned with what I have been calling 'chaos': 'shapelessness and speechlessness' (as opposed to the 'Forms' of Platonic order); 'incurious wondering' (op- posed to the certainties and fixed truths of order and judgement). It is worth noting again how Beckett has often been accused of being too dark, too depressing, too distressing, perverse in short (when all he has ever attempted has been to show *how it is*). When Tom Driver asked Beckett whether aspects of his work did not deal with the same facets of existence as religion, Beckett is attributed to have replied:

Yes, for they deal with distress. Some people object to this in my writing. At a party an English intellectual – so called – asked me why I write always about distress. As if it were perverse to do so! . . . I left the party as soon as possible and got into a taxi. On the glass partition between me and the driver were three signs: one asked for help for the blind, another help for orphans, and the third for relief for the war refugees. One does not have to look for distress. It is screaming at you even in the taxis of London. (Driver, 1961: 24)

Malone does not end here, however, with the earnestness; rather he suggests that he now wants to pass on to play. He has always played badly in the past because he did not know how to play: that is, he never understood the rules (because even and especially games have rules; even and especially games speak of order). Now he wants to play again, but not so as to 'win', according to the rules, but rather so as to defeat the game itself by ignoring or obliterating the rules: 'I know the game is won, I lost them all till now, but it's the last that counts . . . I began again, to try and live, cause to live, be another, in myself, in another . . . But little by little with a different aim, no longer in order to succeed, but in order to fail' (Beckett, 1956: 17–19). The game is equated with life, then, with bringing into existence ('to try and live, cause to live'), but playing, winning, does not necessarily mean winning by the rules: when the rules are exceeded on all sides (just as chaos exceeds the order of judgement), when one fails to recognize them, it is the game itself (the order, the judgement) that is beaten, that loses its point, that is shown up as trivial and vain.

LIGHT AND DARK, LIFE AND DEATH

Imagery of darkness and light permeates *Malone Dies*. James Knowlson, following a lead offered to him by Beckett in conversation, has discussed the use of Manichean imagery of light and dark, black and white; focusing on the play *Krapp's Last Tape* in particular (cf. Knowlson, 1976, 1980). In *Malone Dies*, as we have seen, darkness is aligned with earnestness, and with decomposition and death; yet it is not a simple matter of saying darkness is equated with death and light with life. Rather, either we find ourselves moving between these two poles or witness these terms passing into one another: that is, light passes into darkness, just as decomposition passes into wholeness, life passes into death and chaos into order (and vice versa). Malone's world is grey and his days and nights proceed in anything but an orderly fashion (46–8). Malone's world is full of darkness, shadow and light, like that of Sapo and Mrs Lambert in the Lamberts' kitchen (27, 42); that is, there is darkness within life as much as without. So too, strangely, as Malone approaches death he encounters light as much as darkness, feeling an 'extraordinary heat' (88), experiencing an 'incandescent migraine' (104). He foretells the moment of death by speaking in terms of a confusion of light and darkness: 'one day, soon, soon, one earthlit night, beneath the earth, a dying being will say, like me, in the earthlight, Not even, not even that, and die, without having been able to find a regret' (94). And further, in the last moments of his narrative, as he apparently approaches death, while telling the story of Lemuel and the five inmates he speaks of 'absurd lights' (119). There is, then, light in darkness just as there is death in life and life perhaps, in death. The world of judgement is a black and white, Manichean world, yet Malone's experience of life clearly punctures the seals through which light is kept from dark and shows how each term, in fact, seeps into its other. As Beckett told Tom Driver: 'if life and death did not both present themselves to us, there would be no inscrutability. If there were only darkness, all would be clear. It is because there is not only darkness but also light that our situation becomes inexplicable' (Driver, 1961: 23).

So chaos passes into order and vice versa and this is our problem. Darkness, however, is aligned with chaos, and it is this darkness which seems to be encroaching throughout. Even more than Molloy, Malone sees darkly; a darkness tied to decomposition and the tricks it plays on perception (which Malone considers at length once the stranger comes into his room (104)). He cannot perceive properly, and so his experience becomes fragmented by periods of dark. It is worth emphasizing, for readers of the English editions, how most of the editions fail to reproduce the gaps between paragraphs which appear in the original French (cf. *Malone meurt* (Beckett, 1951)); see also *L'innommable*, which also has gaps in the early sections (Beckett, 1953)). The gaps between paragraphs, which do not appear in *Molloy*, seem to coincide with pauses, representing moments of darkness or silence, periods in Malone's life which we can know little about; for example, once he loses his pencil he tells us there has been a gap of two days of which he now remembers 'nothing' (48), although in fact he does go on to recount some memories of this time (50). It is in these gaps, one assumes, that he loses things, that his possessions change; further, most of the events I discuss above which affect and change him also take place in these gaps. His life, then, is not the ordered life of cause and effect required by judgement. He experiences *affects* but cannot grasp their cause; rather than an orderly continuity, his life is a series of barely connected fragments. Indeed, his characters experience similar shifts: after gaps, Sapo becomes, or is brought into existence as Macmann, Macmann then moves to St John of God's, bringing another Macmann into existence, and then again moves to a new self with Moll, then again a new self with Lemuel.

All this time, through the encroaching darkness, death is passing into life (yet all this time, we must remember, Malone continues to live, continues to bring into existence). There is a good deal of imagery throughout of the process of being born into death (cf. 12, 114); so too Moll and Macmann find love (something generally considered to come with regeneration and spring) in their autumn and its only issue is

Moll's death. Such a reversal, perhaps, involves turning from the notion that birth is followed by subjectification and the moving of the child into order, to the notion that birth involves a moving away from such order to the reality of chaos. That which is brought into being, then, is not the child who will be named, made whole, judged, but the old person before the second childhood of death who forgets their name, decomposes, and moves beyond human judgement. The process underlines the fact that to exist is to disobey (whether one intends to or not). Clearly Malone disobeys, the blow from the stranger attests to this, yet just as clearly he is quite unable to do otherwise as he continues to live on his way to dying.

PRESENT STATE

The stories, of course, are not the only subjects of Malone's narrative. He constantly returns to describe his 'present state' and continually threatens to make the list of his possessions: but these do not serve as entries in a book of reckoning. Rather, they call into question such a process.

Malone's 'present state' is constantly changing; at times he feels himself as large as the world (62), at times he feels himself so hard and contracted that he would be lost in the eye of a needle (51), at times he has felt himself go liquid and become like mud (51). There is no possibility of comprehension, of judgement as to the meaning of his life. Although such judgements will inevitably be made, they will just as inevitably be revoked or superseded. While groping to recover his pencil he is treated to a revelation:

And during this time . . . in my head I suppose all was streaming and emptying away as through a sluice, to my great joy, until finally nothing remained, either of Malone or of the other. And what is more I was able to follow without difficulty the various phases of this deliverance and felt no surprise at its irregular course, now rapid, now slow, so crystal clear was my understanding of the reasons why this could not be otherwise. And I rejoiced furthermore . . . at the thought that I now knew what I had to do, I whose every move had been a groping, and whose motionlessness too was a kind of groping. (50)

But the illusion of insight, of understanding, is only momentary. Malone continues to reflect on his moment of revelation:

And here again naturally I was utterly deceived, I mean in imagining I had grasped at last the true nature of my absurd tribulations . . . For even as I said,

How easy and beautiful it all is!, in the same breath I said, All will grow dark again. And it is without excessive sorrow that I see us again as we are, namely to be removed grain by grain until the hand, wearied, begins to play, scooping us up and letting us trickle back into the same place, dreamily as the saying is. (50)

In summarizing much of the above one might claim that, in *Malone Dies*, Beckett creates sensations of the concept of the immanent existence of the individual (Malone). It is useful, then, to compare Beckett's sensations to Deleuze and Guattari's concept of 'haecceity', which might be described as a concept of the sensation of the immanent existence of the individual.

HAECCEITY: A CONCEPT OF SENSATION

The *Compact Oxford English Dictionary* defines 'haecceity' with reference to the Scholastic philosopher Duns Scotus as: 'The quality implied in the use of *this*, as *this man*; "thisness"; "hereness and nowness"; that quality or mode of being in virtue of which a thing is or becomes a definite individual; individuality.' Deleuze and Guattari qualify this definition, suggesting that haecceity 'is sometimes written "ecceity" deriving the word from *ecce*, "here is." This is an error, since Duns Scotus created the word and the concept from *haec*, "this thing." But it is a fruitful error because it suggests a mode of individuation that is distinct from that of a thing or a subject' (Deleuze and Guattari, 1987: 540–1). The term is intimately connected with the concept of the univocity of Being, which Deleuze and Guattari have adapted from Spinoza:

The plane of consistency of Nature is like an immense Abstract Machine, abstract yet real and individual; its pieces are the various assemblages and individuals, each of which groups together an infinity of particles entering into an infinity of more or less interconnected relations. There is therefore a unity to the plane of nature, which applies equally to the inanimate and the animate, the artificial and the natural . . . It is a fixed plane, upon which things are distinguished from one another only by speed and slowness. A plane of immanence or univocality opposed to analogy. The One expresses in a single meaning all of the multiple . . . Being expresses in a single meaning all that differs. (Deleuze and Guattari, 1987: 254)

Haecceity provides a means of determining an individuation which, *at the same time*, maps a differentiation *and* a unity of being. 'At most', Deleuze and Guattari suggest, 'we may distinguish assemblage haecceities . . . and interassemblage haecceities . . . But the two are strictly inseparable' (262–3).

The concept of 'longitude' defines 'elements' (that is, ultimate – sub-atomic – particles) 'solely by movement and rest, slowness and speed' (Deleuze and Guattari, 1987: 254). It is a Spinozian conception of individual things defined in terms of motion.[3] Bodies (either animate or inanimate) are the composition of different elements. Elements are not atoms but 'infinitely small, ultimate parts of an actual infinity' (254). They are not defined by number because they come in infinities. They belong to a given individual (which might be part of a larger individual, part of a still larger individual, etc.) because of 'their degree of speed or the relation of movement and rest into which they enter' (254). Among other things, 'longitude' is useful in that it provides an anonymous frame of reference for defining a physical concept of individuals through which, 'each individual is an infinite multiplicity, and the whole of Nature is a multiplicity of perfectly individuated multiplicities' (254).

This movement of elements might be compared to the hand stirring in Malone's grains of being; the hand which defines and redefines that being:

to me at least and for as long as I can remember the sensation is familiar of a blind and tired hand delving feebly in my particles and letting them trickle between its fingers. And sometimes, when all is quiet, I feel it plunged in me up to the elbow, but gentle, and as though sleeping. But soon it stirs, wakes, fondles, clutches, ransacks, ravages, avenging its failure to scatter me with one sweep. (50–1)

'Latitude' is the concept of individual bodies understood in terms of the degrees of power to act which that body possesses equated with affects:

To the relations composing, decomposing, or modifying an individual there correspond intensities that affect it, augmenting or diminishing its power to act . . . Affects are becomings . . . We call the *latitude* of a body the affects of which it is capable at a given degree of power, or rather within the limits of that degree. (Deleuze and Guattari, 1987: 256)

The tick is given as an example of a body defined by affects: 'the Tick, attracted by the light, hoists itself up to the tip of a branch; it is sensitive to the smell of mammals, and lets itself fall when one passes beneath the

---

[3] Spinoza's theories of bodies from which Deleuze and Guattari extrapolate these concepts can be found in the *Ethics*, Book 2, Prop. 13, note.

branch; it digs into its skin, at the least hairy place it can find' (Deleuze and Guattari, 1987: 257).[4] Deleuze and Guattari respond to the protest that the tick's three affects are actually manifested in organs and functions, legs, snout, etc., with the point that this is indeed true from the standpoint of physiology but not from the standpoint of ethics. They relate 'ethics' here to 'ethology', playing on the meaning of the latter which refers at once to 'the science of ethics' to 'the science of character-building' and to 'That branch of Natural History which deals with the actions and habits of animals, and their reaction to their environment' (*COED*).

A body defined by the affects of which it is capable might remind us of Malone's understanding of himself: 'a mere local phenomenon is something I would not have noticed, having been nothing but a series or rather a succession of local phenomena all my life' (61). Malone is not defined by a comprehension, or judgement of his value through a simple reckoning of his deeds. Rather, his sense of self comes in relation to the affects of which he is capable. He is mostly 'impotent',[5] bedridden. He experiences life between the 'two poles' of eating and shitting (7). Examples of intensities which affect him, augmenting and diminishing his power to act, are his pencil and his book, and his stick. Quite simply, we cannot imagine Malone without his pencil and book; writing is a crucial affect of which he is capable, he could not exist for us without it. At the very least the Malone we know is the assemblage, Malone (awake and writing), pencil and book; an interdependence of which the narrator is aware and with which he plays:

I fear I must have fallen asleep again. In vain I grope, I cannot find my exercise-book. But I still have the pencil in my hand. I shall have to wait for day to break. God knows what I am going to do till then.

I have just written, I fear I must have fallen, etc. I hope this is not too great a distortion of the truth. (33)[6]

So too Malone's stick, with its hook, is an intensity which augments

---

[4] Deleuze and Guattari also discuss this idea of the tick, an example they have taken from the biologist von Uexküll, in regard to types of molecular 'perception' (which is described in a manner not inconsistent with the notion of 'apprehension' we have examined in chapter 2, above) in Plateau 3 of *A Thousand Plateaus* (51).

[5] 'My body is what is called, unadvisedly perhaps, impotent. There is virtually nothing it can do' (8). Drawing a long bow, perhaps, this statement might be compared to Spinoza's famous statements concerning the functioning of the body in the *Ethics*: 'no one has thus far determined the power of the body, that is, no one has yet been taught by experience what the body can do merely by the laws of nature, in so far as nature is considered merely as corporeal and what it cannot do' (Part 3, Prop. 2, note). The importance of this 'declaration of ignorance' is stressed by Deleuze, 1988b: 17–18.

[6] See also the passage concerning the dropping of the pencil and book (48).

his power to act. With it he can control the farthermost recesses of his room (8), pulling his possessions to him and putting them from him at will. Indeed he defines his possessions as those things he can bring to him and put from him at will, and when he loses his stick late in the novel he considers that he no longer owns those things he used to be able to reach with his stick.

Together then, 'longitude' and 'latitude' define an haecceity, just as an haecceity might define the multiple through the One:

It should not be thought that a haecceity consists simply of a decor or backdrop that situates subjects, or of appendages that hold things and people to the ground. It is the entire assemblage in its individuated aggregate that is a haecceity; it is the assemblage that is defined by a longitude and a latitude, by speeds and affects, independently of forms and subjects, which belong to another plane. It is the wolf itself, and the horse, and the child, that cease to be subjects to become events, in assemblages that are inseparable from an hour, a season, an atmosphere, an air, life. The street enters into composition with the horse, just as the dying rat enters into composition with the air. (Deleuze and Guattari, 1987: 262)

The concept allows for a much greater exactitude in the ethical definition of a body. Rather than positing a fixed and stable self moving through time and space, haecceity defines the individual as inseparable from time and space; part of the time and space of which it, in part, is assembled. Judgement requires order, order as imperative, the order of, among other things, the readily interpreted, stable self. But Malone suggests he cannot grasp what might constitute this 'order', 'For I have never seen any sign of any, inside me or outside me' (35). Order requires meaning, it requires an end, a project, and therefore the need for the idea of order generates endless comprehension, endless justifying through systems of judgement, which endlessly model themselves on a perceived relation with the Judgement of God. Haecceity and the univocity of Being have no need of human order.

Intuitively Malone recognizes that he consists of 'unformed particles' and 'a set of nonsubjectified affects' (Deleuze and Guattari, 1987: 262). He is an haecceity. It is therefore impossible for him to provide a book of reckoning, to offer himself for judgement. He enters into assemblages with his possessions, but we cannot use them to establish his 'worth' or 'value': they are, in economic terms valueless. He cannot properly list his possessions, and he recognizes that the formulation of such a list is impossible. He states that, 'only those things are mine the whereabouts of which I know well enough to be able to lay hold of them, if necessary'

(77). But his possessions are constantly changing. Each time he looks some have gone and some have appeared, 'So that, strictly speaking, it is impossible for me to know, from one moment to the next, what is mine and what is not, according to my definition' (79). Malone then, never completes his inventory of all he has by way of 'chattels personal' (20).

COMBINATION AND RELATION

While it seems clear that the identification, 'relation involves comprehension involves judgement', is, on its own terms reasonable and stable, we are now able to provide an alternative to this formulation. We have already seen how 'judgement' might be opposed to an 'ethical practice' of seeking bodies which suit and avoiding bodies which do not suit your own, and how 'comprehension' might be opposed to 'understanding'. We might take this opposing chain further now to include 'combination'.

'The art of combining is not my fault. It's a curse from above. For the rest I would suggest not guilty' (Beckett, 1984a: 140). Relation involves – always involves – the drawing of an analogy. As we have seen, haecceity, the univocity of Being, is opposed to analogy (Deleuze and Guattari, 1987: 254–5). Analogy is always a *perceived* analogy, a *fiction*, a *possibility* which is made, through relation, comprehension and judgement to masquerade as a universally applicable fact: the fatherland is (fact) Good; the Outsider is (fact) Evil. Through a process of judgement analogy reduces the necessarily unstable relation 'A is (from a certain point of view) like B' to the totalitarian imperative, the order, 'A is (must be) B.' Combination, in which all possibility is admitted, is not perceived; combination, with its exhaustivity, its inclusive disjunctions (this or that, *and* this and that, *and* that and this, *and* that or this . . .), with its 'perhaps', its 'may be', *is*. Opposed to the formulation, 'comprehension involves relation involves judgement', then, we now have, 'understanding involves combination involves ethical practice'.

THE ORDER OF TIME

In 'Pour en finir avec le jugement' Deleuze states: 'it's the act of differentiation, of taking to the infinite, which makes judgement possible: it achieves its condition from a supposed relation between existence and the infinite in the *order* of time. Whosoever takes part in this relation is given the power to judge and to be judged' (Deleuze, 1993a: 159). In modern European history time has most commonly been conceptualized as an arrow; a visualization which seems to confirm it as an aspect of the notion of time as *Chronos*, 'the time of measure that situates things and persons, develops a form, and determines a subject' used by Deleuze and Guattari in *A Thousand Plateaus* (262). I will be using the crude distinctions 'time as an arrow' and 'time as a circle' because they both seem aspects of the *Chronos* (and need to be distinguished from one another in the following discussion) before turning to the opposition of *Chronos* to *Aeon* which Deleuze and Guattari propose.

The notion of the progress of history has only recently been challenged; and, I would suggest, it was the events of World War Two in particular which threw this conception of time into crisis. 'Progress' was (is), of course, tied to science and technology: to the *accumulation* of knowledge. Progress was (is), like judgement, a matter of accounting, of credits and debits; however, the debit column was little regarded as the credit column of Western civilization seemed to grow more and more formidable. In the order of time as an arrow, progress as accumulation was conflated with telos. In general terms the telos was one of the will to dominate, to conquer or convert the rest of the world to Western values and Western civilization, which had accumulated far more knowledge (in terms of empirical data, and mechanical invention) than any other civilization and was, therefore, superior. The telos of the West was easily converted to the telos of the separate European nations, who announced their goals or ambition as destiny, a destiny intimately linked to their own inherent superiority among the European races which had proven themselves inherently superior to all other races. The analogy was with the theory of evolution; with natural selection. Races such as the Australian Aboriginals were seen as inferior, weak and moving naturally towards extinction.[7] The whole logic of the fatherland as transcendental Good within the moral code of the states of Europe, the whole logic of state judgement, was linked with a faith in the *order* of time; a faith in progress, in destiny, in telos.

In *Malone Dies*, the characters of Malone, Sapo and Macmann have finished with judgement in part because they have no faith in the order of time, the order of progress through accumulation. Opposed to the fixed self with its immortal soul, these characters appear as haecceities. They do not move in the dimension of time as an arrow, rather they exist as haecceities, as becomings, as bodies without organs; they do not

---

[7] On this point see Katharine Susannah Prichard (who was opposing it) in her novel, *Coonardoo*, and in the novel's preface (first published, 1929).

move through time and space, they are strictly indivisible from the time and space in which they exist and vice versa: 'To make yourself a body without organs, to find your body without organs is the way to escape judgement. It was already the project of Nietzsche: to define the body by becoming, by intensity, as power to affect and to be affected, that is to say *Will to Power [puissance]*' (Deleuze, 1993a: 164). The 'infinite' with which the system of Judgement claims to be in close relation is not absent from the experience of the haecceity. On the contrary the system of Judgement has little to do with the infinite which it merely cites as an authority (itself oppressive) to justify the oppression of judgement. The judging God is spoken of as existing in a 'world beyond', to which mortals have no access except through the values that world beyond has allegedly managed to pass on to those in power. The haecceity, on the other hand, as a becoming, is an aspect of the infinite, of the univocity of Being: 'To become is not to achieve a form (identification, imitation, Mimesis), but to find the zone of vicinity, of indiscernibility or indifferentiation so that one can no longer distinguish oneself from *a* woman, from *an* animal, from *a* molecule' (Deleuze, 1993a: 10).

The becoming is always 'between' or 'among', indistinguishable and so in a sense imperceptible (Deleuze, 1993a: 10–11), indefinite, communing with the infinite of which one is an aspect. 'And it is doubtless the case that every intensity is extinguished at the end, that every becoming is a becoming-death!' (Deleuze and Guattari, 1983: 330). One thinks of Malone. But this turning to death is not a turning from the infinite. While becoming is a process and death as a final fixed point is therefore never achieved, the character does change and finally is no longer recognizable or perceptible. Deleuze underlines this point in an essay on Samuel Beckett's *Film*:

Nothing ends in Beckett, nothing dies . . . When a character dies, as Murphy says, it's that he has already begun to move into the spirit. He proceeds as easily as a cork in a raging sea. He doesn't move, but he is in an element which moves . . . Becoming imperceptible is Life 'without end or condition', reaching (at last) the cosmic and spiritual sea-swell. (Deleuze, 1993a: 39)

The end of *Malone Dies*, with Malone's apparent death, leaves Macmann, Lemuel and the other escaped lunatics drifting aimlessly in their boat, which bobs on the open sea like a cork.

The *order* of time (which is time as *Chronos*) is satirized and subverted in Malone's stories of Sapo and Macmann. The story of Sapo is effectively broken into two parts: that which deals with Sapo within the world of his parents, and that which deals with Sapo among the peasant farmers, the

Lamberts. In the former, the order of time is present as the idea of progress; the time as arrow of modern (capitalist) society. In the latter, it is present with regards to an earlier, seasonal notion of time, a time which is repeating itself but getting tired in doing so.[8]

Sapo 'was the eldest child of poor and sickly parents' and so his parents are obsessed with money and with their health (10). The plans of the Saposcats are balanced between their dual obsessions; they oscillate between the topics of their health and their lack of money and thus remain inert. They look to the order of time to solve the problems they are incapable of facing. Mr Saposcat cannot do extra work because there will be no one to look after the garden. They cannot grow vegetables in the garden because the price of manure is too high. Mrs Saposcat cannot work more because of her health. To save money they might move to a smaller house. But they are already cramped:

And it was an understood thing that they would be more and more so with every passing year until the day came when, the departure of the first-born compensating the arrival of the new-born, a kind of equilibrium would be attained. Then little by little the house would empty. And at last they would be all alone, with their memories. It would be time enough then to move. He would be pensioned off, she at her last gasp. They would take a cottage in the country where, having no further need of manure, they could afford to buy it in cartloads. And their children, grateful for the sacrifices made on their behalf, would come to their assistance. It was in this atmosphere of unbridled dream that these conferences usually ended. It was as though the Saposcats drew the strength to live from the prospect of their impotence. (10–11)

The end of life for the hard-working can only be the well-earned pleasures of retirement in material comfort: thus the delusions of suburban or bourgeois dreams are ridiculed.

The order of time will not only fix things through the joys of retirement however; the Saposcats also believe in investment, and Sapo is their

---

[8] While he does not discuss the idea of time as an arrow, Martin Esslin speaks of kinds of 'infinity' found in Beckett's works and discusses two concepts which come close to the seasonal notion of time and the progressive tiredness mentioned here. Esslin highlights the obvious concept of infinity as repetition, the circle that runs into itself and thus can have no end (Esslin, 1986: 113–14), but, more interestingly, he also sees infinity represented in Beckett as 'entropy'. Entropy – the second law of thermodynamics – describes the gradual running down of the universe, yet, Esslin states, because absolute zero can never be reached, this running down must go on *dim innuendo*, forever. From this point, Esslin argues that once there is consciousness of being, that being can never consciously become aware of having ceased to be. A being, then, is trapped in an infinity of being (that is, suffering). 'The last moment of consciousness, thus, must inevitably linger in the void forever', and this, Esslin claims, is the meaning of the final scene of *Endgame* (114). See also Cohn, 1979: 193; Schwab, 1984: 195; Dobrez,1986: 29.

major investment. Ignoring the evidence that suggests he is a simpleton, they decide to leave him at school so that he might become a professional, a doctor for preference, rather than sending him out to earn his living. 'He will look after us when we are old, said Mrs Saposcat.' Thus they combine their two obsessions in a vision of Sapo's future: a well-paid professional capable of curing illness, though Mr Saposcat tempers the optimism: 'And her husband replied, I see him rather as a surgeon, as though after a certain age people were inoperable' (12).

From the point of view of his parents, the education of Sapo makes perfect sense within the order of time. His studies have a given end, which (the judging) God willing, will come to pass with time, all that is required is patience and perseverance. Unfortunately, from their point of view, their hopes with regards to Sapo are wildly misplaced. He is incapable of adapting himself to the order and thereby resists it. In this way his stupidity becomes a kind of blessing or insight. 'He was a *precocious* [my italics] boy. He was not good at his lessons, neither could he see the point of them' (9). He is impudent at school and does not study as his parents wish. Sapo's resistance to the order of time is intimately tied to his failure; it is unimportant whether he does not pursue his studies towards the goal his parents envisage because he cannot or will not. Sapo does not recognize the goal. In attempting to comprehend, the young Sapo (whether precocious or imbecile) sees no order, only chaos, and so is unable or unwilling to obey any order (cf. 13).

Rather than working towards academic success as his parents wish, he aimlessly ranges the countryside and here he encounters the Lamberts. Ruby Cohn has noted that the name 'Lambert' (which replaces 'les Louis' used in *Malone meurt*) refers to the Balzac novel, *Louis Lambert* (1973: 94). Elsewhere she has highlighted a passage from *Dream of Fair to Middling Women* in which Beckett's narrator criticizes Balzac's so-called 'realism' and suggests that nothing is less realistic than the clockwork, transcendentally stable, characters Balzac describes.[9]

Malone's story of Lambert might be said to parody this kind of 'realist' characterization. The Lamberts, and Big Lambert in particular, give themselves over to the order of time. Time for these peasants – who may be French peasants, perhaps similar to those encountered by Beckett while hiding out in Roussillon during World War Two (cf. Bair, 1990: 340–6)[10] – is not seen in terms of the arrow, the progress of the

---

[9] Samuel Beckett, *Disjecta*, edited by Ruby Cohn, 1983: 47. See also Beckett, 1993.
[10] This point, is, of course, highly debatable. John P. Harrington, though he makes no attempt to disengage the passage from Balzac, suggests that it relates to the *Irish* peasantry (1992: 142). Here,

industrialized world. The farmers inhabit a world not yet invaded by technology; they use traditional methods and draw upon traditional knowledge. The order of time in this pre-industrial society is circular; it is dominated by the repetitive movement of the seasons, by the natural ebbing and flowing of the forces of life and death. Big Lambert is greatly sought after by his neighbours to kill pigs in pig-killing season, a period which lasts from December to January, and for the rest of the year looks forward to its return. He is a practised pig-killer and relishes each new kill, which, although different from the former, holds at its core a similarity, like the similarity of one winter to the next, 'For all pigs are alike, when you get to know their little ways, struggle, squeal, bleed, squeal, struggle, bleed, squeal and faint away, in more or less the same way exactly, a way that is all their own and could never be imitated by a lamb, for example, or a kid' (25).

The joys and disappointments of the clockwork order of time the Lamberts obey seem as petty and illusory as those of the Saposcats. Malone emphasizes the squalor rather than beauty of the natural order of time; the crushing mundanity rather than the comfort of the order of time as circle or repetition: the 'natural' urges of Big Lambert and his son make them look towards their daughter/sister with incest on their minds, just as Big Lambert had looked at his sister with the same intent years before (41); Mrs Lambert is driven to distraction by her daily chores to the extent that she gives way to compulsive gestures and ejaculations of frustration just as repetitive and apparently meaningless as those very chores (27, 39).

Like the Saposcats, the Lamberts are concerned with 'values'; especially material values. Lambert praises himself for his sense of economy: he buys all his mules at the knackery and screws a last few years of service out of them (37–8). They are pleased by the small and useful gifts Sapo leaves them (29). Big Lambert is proud of his physical strength and extols the virtues of hard work (38). He is miserly towards the pigs he attempts to fatten and blames them for turning out lean (25). Such virtues, anchored in the 'natural' order of time, like the 'natural' hierar-

---

as elsewhere when it is a matter of what Harrington terms 'local phenomenon' (alluding to the comment by Malone quoted above: 61), the truth is no doubt partial. Harrington's work (notably Harrington, 1991) is an important contribution to Beckett criticism. To his credit he has stated that his concentration on an aspect of Beckett's works is not intended to disallow all other possibilities (1991: 4), as is indeed the case with my own work, for given the extent of Beckett's experience of French as well as Irish (as well as German and English) 'local phenomena', it is hoped that no one blunders into the argument that the truth is partisan. The question of 'where we are' in Beckett's texts is an important one: indeed it might be argued that what makes it important is the very uncertainty surrounding the identity of the space which is traversed.

chies promoted by Vichy, are intimately tied to a moral order. Big
Lambert is a tyrant in his small kingdom, keeping his family in check
with his physical force: 'they feared him. Yes, at an age when most
people cringe and cower, as if to apologize for still being present,
Lambert was feared and in a position to do as he pleased' (24). The idea
of the ruler of great age is well known to most peoples; in France, when
Malone meurt was published Marshal Pétain, who came to power in 1940
at the age of eighty-four, would have been fresh in people's memories.
The 'natural' moral order here seems based on the transcendental
principle of might being right. It is an elemental order but one which
leaves the Lamberts, with the exception of Big Lambert, frustrated: they
are subject to the order of time which will suffer them to live under his
tyranny until he gives way to that order and weakens or dies.

Amidst all this – the worlds of the Saposcats and the Lamberts – Sapo
stands apart. He escapes the order of time as an arrow obeyed by his
parents through movement, like the schizo-flows cutting across the
various bodies of the socius described by Deleuze and Guattari in *The
Anti-Oedipus* (280–3). Ironically the submission of the Saposcats to the
order of time as an arrow is characterized by their inertia. They have
faith in progress and so they do nothing. Sapo, then, escapes this static
world through movement: he sets out on his walks. The submission of
the Lamberts to the order of time as a circle, on the other hand, is
characterized by their incessant repetitive movement. Sapo, then, escapes this treadmill through inertia: he sits in the Lamberts' house and
watches the day pass. In each case Sapo lives in the 'present', the time he
experiences is immanent, it is part of him; time for him is that concept of
time defined by Deleuze and Guattari as *Aeon*:

> the indefinite time of the event, the floating line that knows only speeds and
> continually divides that which transpires into an already-there that is at the
> same time not-yet-here, a simultaneous too-late and too-early, a something that
> is both going to happen and has just happened. (Deleuze and Guattari, 1983:
> 262)[11]

---

[11] At first glance the concept of *Aeon* might call to mind the work of a number of Beckett critics who
have suggested that time in Beckett's works is often presented as involving a perpetual 'now'.
Robbe-Grillet has commented that in Beckett's theatre 'Everything is present in time as in space.
The ineluctable "here" is confronted by an eternal "now"' (1965: 114). Lyons, 1986 has pointed
out that drama can represent only the immediate moment, or sequence of immediate moments
(96). Rosen claims that the ideal state of being (as opposed to non-being) for both St Augustine
and Beckett is the sustained present moment (Rosen, 1976: 180). Yet the present and presence
these critics insist on is not reconcilable with the movement involved in the being of the event
described here by Deleuze and Guattari which eludes immobilized notions of the 'present'.

LIQUID MOVEMENT – THE FLOW, THE SWELL

The flowing of the river and the rise and fall of the sea swell might both be used to indicate either capture or escape. The flowing of the river might be identified with the flow of time; the tyranny of the order of time of *Chronos*; the river of Heraclitus watched by the protagonist of *Ohio Impromptu* as it carries away his love in death; Charon's river, full of slaughtered bodies however innocent. On the other hand it might be identified with the schizo-flows of escape described by Deleuze and Guattari; lines of flight that cut through and exceed the various bodies of the socius with their moral orders, which attempt to fix subjects into stable relations.

The cork bobbing on its sea swell might be compared to the order of time as repetition, exemplifying lack of movement within movement. Or it might indicate an escape on to the plane of consistency (where time is *Aeon*), through which you stop perceiving yourself as a stable subject moving through time and space on the plan(e) of organization (where time is *Chronos*) and apprehend as an haecceity. The plane of consistency 'is a fixed plane . . . Here fixed does not mean immobile: it is the absolute state of movement as well as rest, from which all relative speeds and slownesses spring, and nothing but them . . . a kind of molecular [sea swell]' (Deleuze and Guattari, 1983: 267).[12]

The plan(e) of organization or development is a plane of transcendence, of analogy, it is a teleological plane and it 'always concerns the development of forms and the formation of subjects'. It is 'a hidden structure necessary for forms, a secret signifier necessary for subjects', 'a hidden principle, which makes visible what is seen and audible what is heard, etc., which at every instant causes the given to be given, in this or that state, at this or that moment' (Deleuze and Guattari, 1987: 265). Because it is concerned with telos, with analogy, with the transcendent, this plan(e) supports the development of the moral order and judgement.

The plane of consistency or composition is an altogether different plane: 'Here, there are no longer any forms or developments of forms; nor are there subjects or the formation of subjects. There is no structure, any more than there is genesis . . . There are only haecceities, affects,

---

[12] Brian Massumi translates 'clapotement moléculaire' (Deleuze and Guattari, 1980: 326–7) as 'molecular lapping'. While this is a good translation, I have preferred 'sea swell' for stylistic reasons: I feel it better evokes the moving surface of a body of water possibly far from shore which is the sense conveyed in *Critique et Clinique* where Deleuze again uses 'clapotement' (Deleuze, 1993a: 39) in a passage I quote below.

subjectless individuations that constitute collective assemblages' (266). It is the existence of this plane which requires that one find an ethics outside the system of judgement.

The relationship between the two planes is complex. It is an inclusive disjunction. Both planes *exist*, they are in opposition one to the other (Deleuze and Guattari, 1987: 267–9), but the opposition is difficult to define concretely because 'one continually passes from one to the other, by unnoticeable degrees and without being aware of it, or one becomes aware of it only afterward. Because one continually reconstitutes one plane atop another, or extricates one from the other' (269). On the other hand there is no possibility of conciliation between the two; the opposition of the two planes can be insisted upon and the plan(e) of organization, that plane which allows the constitution of oppressive power (what both Foucault and Deleuze and Guattari would term *pouvoir* or 'power over') might be opposed through the acceptance of the existence of the plane of consistency, which allows the constitution of power to act (what Deleuze and Guattari term *puissance* or 'power to'). This process is an active one, it is a matter of decision and resistance:

> We must avoid an oversimplified conciliation, as though there were on the one hand formed subjects, of the thing or person type, and on the other hand spatiotemporal coordinates of the haecceity type. For you will yield nothing to haecceities unless you realize that that is what you are, and that you are nothing but that . . . You are longitude and latitude, a set of speeds and slownesses between unformed particles, a set of nonsubjectified affects. You have the individuality of a day, a season, a year, a *life* (regardless of its duration). (Deleuze and Guattari, 1987: 262)

Midway through *Malone Dies* Malone loses Sapo, then finds him again metamorphosed into another, soon to be called Macmann: 'How did I know it was he, I don't know. And what can have changed him so? Life perhaps, the struggle to love, to eat, to escape the redressers of wrongs' (52). He has been changed by the order of time, perhaps, as one might have been by the France of the forties with its food shortages and recriminations. He finds Macmann seated beside a river:

> he does not stir. Since morning he has been here and now it is evening . . . His back is turned to the river, but perhaps it appears to him in the dreadful cries of the gulls that evening assembles, in paroxysms of hunger, round the outflow of the sewers, opposite the Bellevue Hotel . . . But his face is towards the people that throng the streets at this hour, their long day ended and the whole long evening before them. The doors open and spew them out, each door its contingent. For an instant they cluster in a daze, huddled on the sidewalk or in the gutter, then set off singly on their appointed ways. (56)

Here Macmann is fixed between two flows, cutting across them as if he inhabits another plane: the flow of the river and its ravenous gulls and the flow of the people of the city caught up in the order of time as an arrow. Macmann, like Malone, is an haecceity, and generally (they, of course, oscillate) inhabits the plane of consistency. As such he fails to understand the hidden relations of the plan(e) of organization that holds together the throng of society or sets their various itineraries which, as if catching them in a strong current, they can only follow. The possibility that Malone is inhabiting a different plane, that he apprehends rather than perceives, perhaps explains why he fails to understand or hear the angry words shouted at him by the stranger who infiltrates his room and strikes him towards the end of his narrative; a stranger he imagines merging into the infinite variety of the faces of the masses who inhabit the plan(e) of organization Malone has begun to leave (103).

RESISTANCE TO ORDER

The gulls of the river are not only scavengers, they are threatening creatures whose malevolence is concentrated in their hungry eyes. Sapo has gull eyes which disconcert not only his father[13] but Malone:

I don't like those gull's eyes. They remind me of an old ship-wreck, I forget which. I know it is a small thing. But I am easily frightened now. I know those little phrases that seem so innocuous and, once you let them in, pollute the whole of speech. *Nothing is more real than nothing.*[14] They rise up out of the pit and know no rest until they drag you down into its dark. But I am on my guard now. (16; see also 18)

The ship-wreck of which Malone is thinking is perhaps one in which (the story is one I remember being told in my childhood) the half-dead sailors wash ashore only to be eaten alive by the gulls, their eyes (the softest tissue) pecked out first. Perhaps Malone fears being devoured by his character, eyes first. Though Gods might eat the creatures they have made, just as Malone expects to do[15], such an answering back is not expected of the creature. The suspicious gulls reappear at St John of God's, the asylum where Macmann is interned.[16] As Macmann sits by

---

[13] The father, told his eyes resemble Sapo's, inspects them in the mirror (14).

[14] This might also be said to imply an inversion of Spinoza's ontology, where God, the univocal substance who is everything, is the most real of all things.

[15] 'I shall try and make a little creature, to hold in my arms, a little creature in my image, no matter what I say. And seeing what a poor thing I have made, or how like myself, I shall eat it' (52).

[16] 'The gulls were many in stormy weather which paused here on their flight inland. They wheeled long in the cruel air, screeching with anger, then settled in the grass or on the house-tops, mistrustful of the trees' (107). Cf. Cronin, 1996, who talks of Beckett's fear of the hostile indifference of the natural world.

the river, his back to the gulls and facing the flow of society, it is his penetrating gaze which helps him to cut across that flow. The gaze is mute, unexplained, but powerful. It is difficult to say in what this power consists, but its invocation is worth remarking. It is with such a gaze that Malone watches, his eyes on stalks, the stranger who has entered his room; an unwavering and disconcerting gaze. It is at once a gaze of incomprehension and, even if unintentionally so, of resistance.

Macmann's story might be read as a struggle between a social order (existing on a plan(e) of organization) which attempts to corral or impede the counter-movement of one who exists on the plane of consistency. A story of resistance. An early image is of Macmann on a shelterless field lying static under heavy rain. He decides at last to move by rolling sideways (65–74).

He finds himself interned in St John of God's, an institution for the mentally ill which is, striking a chord with Foucault's descriptions in *Discipline and Punish*, a kind of prison (Beckett, 1956: 108). Like Molloy, Macmann is also contained by love, though Macmann is more responsive than the passive Molloy. Macmann's love for Moll – his keeper who, while she loves him a great deal, loves the rules more than he (97) – is a fetter in a way more profound than the institution, calling him back to the order of time he felt he had escaped (92–6). Perhaps for this reason, Malone kills off Moll, making escape once more a possibility for Macmann. On Moll's death Macmann is given over to Lemuel and it is then he begins to escape; leaving his room for the first time and hiding in a bush in the grounds of the asylum. It is an escape he repeats exactly so that after a few times no search is necessary. He is joined in his bush by his keeper Lemuel, himself little adapted to the order of the institution at which he works. In some ways Lemuel's relationship with Macmann resembles Murphy's with Mr Endon in *Murphy*; Lemuel is, however, unlike Murphy, plagued by angst which leads to uncontrolled gesticulations not unlike those of Mrs Lambert, and to fits of violence – mostly directed against himself (96–7, 105–10). It might be suggested that such unhappiness stems from Lemuel's entering into an unethical alliance with the order of the institution. Imposing their rules is not good for him, as he too is forever exceeding the boundaries set by the plan(e) of organization.

The charity of Lady Pedal again reminds us of the structures of oppression described by Foucault in *Discipline and Punish*. According to Foucault's analysis, and as we have already seen with regard to *Molloy*, charity plays a prominent role in the imposition of discipline (Foucault,

1991: 212). She offers to take Lemuel's group of inmates out for boat ride. It is clear, however, that the major point of the exercise is Lady Pedal's process of affirmative self-subjectification. Neither Lemuel nor the inmates have any desire to go boating nor do they have any say in the matter. If the process is for anyone's benefit, it is for Lady Pedal's. The act of philanthropy underlines her intrinsic 'goodness', a still fashionable goodness worn by members of high society like jewellery: 'No sound save the oars, the rowlocks, the blue sea against the keel. In the stern-sheets Lady Pedal, sad. What beauty? she murmured. Alone, not understood, good, too good. Taking off her glove she trailed in the transparent water her sapphire-laden hand' (117). What follows, on reaching the island of Dublin harbour, which is their destination (O'Brien, 1986: 89–93), has often been read as an example of inexplicable violence. An inexplicable violence repeated in the Trilogy by Molloy and Moran (Beckett, 1955: 113; 207–10). I would suggest, on the contrary, that the act is more one of violent resistance: rebellion. The violence is tied to a desire to escape capture. No attempt is made to justify these actions which are, more often than not, committed with relish. Mercier and Camier's murder of a policeman springs to mind (Beckett, 1988a: 92–4).

The question of the use of the violence in resistance is a difficult one, and one I lack the space to deal with here. Suffice it to say that the fictional murders are often as funny as they are shocking; indeed they are more shocking because funny and more subversive of the plan(e) of organization, or the moral order, of judgement, because of these attributes:

Lemuel released Macmann, went up behind Maurice [one of Lady Pedal's assistants] who was sitting on a stone filling his pipe and killed him with the hatchet. We're getting on, getting on. The youth and the giant took no notice. The thin one broke his umbrella against the rock, a curious gesture. The Saxon cried, bending forward and slapping his thighs, Nice work, sir, nice work! A little later Ernest came back to fetch them. Going to meet him Lemuel killed him in his turn, in the same ways as the other. It merely took a little longer. Two decent, quiet, harmless, men, brothers-in-law into the bargain, there are billions of such brutes. Macmann's huge head. He has put his hat on again. The voice of Lady Pedal, calling. She appeared, joyous. Come along, she cried, all of you, before the tea gets cold. But at the sight of the late sailors she fainted, which caused her to fall. Smash her! screamed the Saxon. She had raised her veil and was holding in her hand a tiny sandwich. She must have broken something in her fall, her hip perhaps, old ladies often break their hips, for no sooner had she recovered her senses than she began to moan and groan, as if she were the only being on the face of the earth deserving of pity. (118–19)

With this Lemuel, Macmann and the other 'inmates' set forth from the shore on their boat.

This tangle of grey bodies is they. Silent, dim, perhaps clinging to one another, their heads buried in their cloaks, they lie together in a heap, in the night. They are far out in the bay. Lemuel has shipped his oars, the oars trail in the water. The night is strewn with absurd
  absurd lights, the stars, the beacons, the buoys, the lights of earth and in the hills the faint fires of the blazing gorse. Macmann, my last, my possessions, I remember, he is there too, perhaps he sleeps. (119)

As Malone drifts towards death they huddle together, an interassemblage haecceity with the night, becoming imperceptible as Malone becomes dead, bobbing like a cork upon the sea swell of the 'fixed' plane of consistency.

That is, perhaps, the secret: to bring into existence, not to judge. If it is so disgusting to judge, it isn't because everything is of equal merit, but on the contrary because everything that is worthwhile can only be and distinguish itself in defying judgement . . . We do not have to judge other beings, but sense whether they will suit us or will not suit us, that is to say whether they bring us strength or rather take us back to the miseries of war, to the poverty of the dream, to the strictness of organization. As Spinoza said, it's a problem of love and hate, not of judgement. (Deleuze, 1993a: 169)

CHAPTER 5

Voices and stories: the translator and the leader

VOICES, STORIES AND THE WORLD

In her biography of Beckett, Deirdre Bair describes how Beckett told her the use of a tape recorder was strictly forbidden in her dealings with him (Bair, 1990: xii). In a bookshop in Sydney in 1994, after reading a passage touching on this prohibition, Bair suggested that she felt Beckett had a horror of hearing his own voice recorded, had a horror of the idea of his voice living on after his death.

In 'The Exhausted' Deleuze describes the process of exhausting the possible in Beckett through a distinction of three kinds of language. *Language I* exhausts the possible with words. Words are used as atoms, names which might be exhausted in the way that a permutation might be exhaustive, listing all possible combinations of elements. He gives the examples of the sucking stones from *Molloy*, the biscuits from *Murphy*, and the many permutations found in *Watt* where combinations of articles of clothing and the positions of furniture are listed exhaustively (Deleuze, 1995: 3–7). Before going on to describe *language III*, which is the language of images, Deleuze discusses *language II*, which is the language of voices. Whereas words refer to names, to names of things, voices refer to 'Others'. These 'Others' in turn carry with them possible worlds, worlds created by the stories that the voices convey:

the Others are the *possible worlds*, to which voices confer a reality which is always variable, following the force that the voices have, and revocable, following the silences that they make. They are sometimes strong, sometimes weak, till they fall dumb for a moment (a silence of tiredness). Now they separate and even oppose one another, and now they merge. The Others, that is to say the possible worlds with their objects, with their voices which give them the only reality to which they can lay claim, compose 'stories'. The Others have no reality other than that which their voice gives them in their possible world. (Deleuze, 1995: 7)

What needs to be underlined here is the relation between voices, stories and the composition of the world, a relation which holds not only in what we commonly call fiction, but which is also central to what we commonly call the 'real' (the pragmatic social or political world). The molar world of nation states like the molar world of subjects is built upon the stories which give those worlds reality.

Few would consider it a bold assertion to claim that *The Unnamable* is, speaking loosely, the most 'philosophical' of the three novels under consideration here. Firstly, there is clearly a greater level of abstraction involved in *The Unnamable*, and abstraction itself presupposes some kind of overlapping between art and philosophy (cf. Deleuze and Guattari, 1994: 198). Secondly, the unnamable himself reminds us from time to time how he has been 'reduced' to reason (Beckett, 1958: 70, 169): that is, his method involves proposing suppositions (about his state, the nature of his being) which are then tested, more or less, through a process of affirmation and negation ('invalidated as uttered, or sooner or later': 3). Further, his task seems to be somehow, purely through recourse to language, to establish (so as to be able to extinguish) his own being. The questions that arise, then, are questions of being in its abstract state, and such questions are generally dealt with in philosophical texts. *The Unnamable*, however, is a work of literature, and as such the abstract state is rendered particular so that it predominantly offers us sensations rather than concepts. Given its proximity to philosophical questions, however, the sensations developed here often seem sensations of concepts. In general terms the sensations involve consternation and refer to that aspect of chaos which might be termed 'groundlessness'. To speak more specifically, however, the sensation of the concept of groundlessness is directly related to the question of language. *The Unnamable* clearly concerns attempts to identify the self through recourse to language; that is, the sensations the book conveys concern the nature of the relation between language, the world at large, and the construction of the self. The unnamable feels that language comes from outside, that it does not belong to him, that it is not his, and so can in no way constitute him.[1]

COUNTERPOINT: TOTALIZING AND PRAGMATIC STORIES

Throughout this chapter I will examine two kinds of storytelling. Firstly, there is the story of the leader which is the attempt to impose a Form or

---

[1] These are questions that I will discuss at length in the next chapter.

a constant. As we will see, however, there are other kinds of stories, stories which might be aligned with what Deleuze and Guattari call 'pragmatics', and which I will discuss later in terms of the stories of the 'translator' (Deleuze and Guattari, 1987: 82). The stories of the leader largely pertain to the state's attempt to impose constants and might be termed 'totalizing'; they involve a form of storytelling which orders through exclusion, building up myths of national identity to which one is expected to adhere if one wishes to partake of the greater national identity. The second kind might be considered to undermine or provide counter-narratives to these totalizing political myths. Whereas the first kind work through determinacy – determining or fixing identity through Forms or constants – the second work through indeterminacy; by recognizing continuous variation. While the first might be considered in relation to totality which homogenizes all difference (either casting out or effacing difference) the second might be understood in relation to an infinity which insists on the heterogeneous; insists on difference, which always lurks within and decomposes identity. While the first imposes order through judgement, the second seeks an always elusive justice.

To clarify what I mean here it might be useful to place this chapter and what it hopes to achieve in relation to that which will follow. The next chapter draws on readings of Beckett, Levinas and Derrida in discussing the relation of the same (the self, the subject or individual) to the other (or others). Briefly, for Levinas the central conflict involves the opposed conceptions of totality and infinity. Totality involves the same reducing all difference to itself, while the concept of infinity, which Levinas opposes to totality, expresses the infinite (irreducible) difference between the same and the other. The other can never be reduced to the same because it is absolutely other. Further, these concepts will be more clearly brought into counterpoint with the sociohistorical context from which *L'innommable* emerged (written in Paris, in French, in 1949) by examining in this chapter the role of France's leaders during and after the war. Both Pétain and de Gaulle attempted to 'embody' France and thereby unify it through the process Levinas describes as totalizing. Each of these leaders sought to efface difference in reducing the others that comprised France to the totality which was their idea of France.

Pétain sought to unify France by excluding those elements judged not to be French enough, those considered too other: the politically other, the racially other, the ideologically other. Laws were drafted to this effect (laws which were felt by Derrida, for example, excluded from school in Algeria because he was Jewish (cf. Derrida, 1991a: 300)). De Gaulle, on the other hand, sought to unify France through inclusion: all sins might be forgiven, all who believed themselves French could be unified within his Republic, old wounds could be healed. To this order by totalization I will, both here and in the next chapter, oppose the notions of alterity clearly apparent in the works of Beckett and Derrida and Levinas.

An example of pragmatic, non-totalizing storytelling might be found in Beckett. In *L'Entretien infini*, Blanchot describes the peculiarity of Beckett's emphasis on voices. He suggests, in discussing *How It Is*, that what is most challenging to a reader is Beckett's refusal to frame the narrative, as is traditional, in relation to what the protagonist/narrator has seen, stressing instead – thus striking a chord with Deleuze and Guattari's descriptions of the order-word (cf. Deleuze and Guattari, 1987: 76–82; Uhlmann,1997: 39–41) – what he has heard: 'I say it as I hear it.'[2] Blanchot suggests that this emphasis has the effect of seeming to confound the process of reading with the process of writing[3] (Blanchot, 1969: 481–2). The story is told to us, we hear tell. The narrator of *How It Is*, like that of *The Unnamable, Texts for Nothing, As the Story Was Told* and *Company*, for example, mimics the reader. He translates what he hears, relates the story as it was told him rather than claiming to bear witness, to have seen what we hear. This procedure removes the link with a material world we might have supposed had or could have existed. The stories are built on stories, on void. The very foundations of identity (whether social or personal) are undermined. There is no ground. We are forced to gaze uneasily at certain implications of a link between the description of reality given to us through language and voices, and fiction. A link we generally overlook, suspending our disbelief.

PETAIN AND DE GAULLE: TOTALIZING STORIES

We might take a step back, then, and consider the first kind of story: the totalizing narratives of political order and national identity which might be equated with specific voices telling stories. Two figures dominated

---

[2] See Beckett, 1964. This phrase is repeated numerous times throughout the text.
[3] Leslie Hill has discussed this passage from Blanchot to slightly different purpose in his fine book, *Beckett's Fiction in Different Words* (see 134–5). Thomas Trezise argues for the contiguity between the works of Beckett and Blanchot (Trezise, 1990: 117). Apart from this, of course, Blanchot has written one of the best-known pieces of criticism of Beckett's *L'innommable* (an essay originally published in 1953); see Blanchot, 1986.

French history during World War Two: Marshal Pétain and General de Gaulle. Pétain, born in 1856, had been a high-profile national identity since the battle of Verdun in World War One. He won a reputation as one of the great, perhaps greatest, French heroes of that war, a reputation given added gloss in the eyes of the *anciens combattants* (and those who simply heard tell) because of his reputation for being both careful of the lives of his troops and willing to share danger with them; a reputation which was indeed rare among the leaders in that war, where men were sent by the million over the top and into enemy machine-gun fire by generals usually positioned well behind the front lines. Between the wars Pétain became perhaps the most admired public figure in France and exerted considerable influence on French military policy. He was lauded as the man to save France by large sections of the French press as World War Two came to seem more and more inevitable. He easily won an opinion poll in 1935, asking the readers of a popular French daily newspaper who, given the apparent failure of the French Third Republic to ensure the protection of France, should be made dictator of a government of national safety (Griffiths, 1970: 173). Pétain, however, was not prepared to challenge the Republic; rather he awaited the call of his country, which he felt sure would come, and indeed it did come after the catastrophic defeat of June 1940. He was made Prime Minister of the Third Republic, which evacuated from Paris to Bordeaux and then eventually to Vichy, negotiating an armistice with the Nazis on the way, and then, under pressure from Pierre Laval (a complex figure more often than not constrained to taking the large measure of blame for Vichy's collaboration, complicating the Pétain/de Gaulle equation), voting itself out of existence in conferring dictatorial powers on Pétain, then in his eighty-fifth year (see Griffiths, 1970).

De Gaulle, born in 1890, was a young captain in World War One. He served under Pétain at Verdun, where he was wounded for a third time and captured by the Germans after a sortie with his men which was reported in heroic terms by Pétain in dispatches – though Pétain's description of events bore little resemblance to what actually seems to have taken place (Lacouture, 1990: 37–41). Between the wars he developed his unfashionable military theories, which sharply contradicted the notions of defensive strategy adopted by the French military command (among whom Pétain was prominent). For a time the young de Gaulle was taken under Pétain's wing. They fell out over a book de Gaulle had ghost-written at Pétain's request: a matter of stories and the naming of stories. De Gaulle became a revolutionary military theoretician, being among the first to notice the potential for using tanks as an offensive weapon in divisions of their own. His books were studied by the Germans, who benefited from his ideas in building the Panzer divisions which were, along with the Luftwaffe, to devastate French forces when the war came, but they were largely ignored (until it was too late) by French strategists. As the crisis of the coming war loomed, Colonel de Gaulle (provisionally promoted to General after commanding his tanks with distinction early in the war) was brought into Paul Reynaud's government. He was passionately against an armistice with Germany, passionately for France continuing to fight the war, from North Africa if necessary. Thwarted by events, he removed to England and contacted Churchill, who aided him in setting up a (at this stage at least) mock counter-authority to the French government and allowed him to broadcast messages to France calling for continued resistance. Charged with desertion by the French command, he was, *in absentia*, stripped of his newly given rank, forcibly retired, and eventually sentenced to death (a sentence Pétain later maintained he would not have seen carried out), decisions which, by this stage, de Gaulle considered to be without interest. Pétain announced the armistice with Germany on 16 June and de Gaulle broadcast his plea to continue the struggle on 18 June. In simplified versions of the French itinerary in World War Two, each man has become identified in turn with these dates. Pétain the man of 16 June the man of the armistice, collaboration. De Gaulle (though his post-war career was such that he was also known for many other things) the man of 18 June the man of resistance, the saviour of French honour (see Griffiths, 1970; Lacouture, 1990, 1991).

Pétain and de Gaulle have frequently been compared. They were both military men. Both assumed a kind of power which reminded some either of the old monarchy or of Bonaparte. Both, taking to their regal status, have been described as 'incarnating' France. As leader of Vichy, Pétain felt he *was* France, a feeling which Richard Griffiths has claimed led to a certain intoxication, a certain delirium which convinced him that he was capable of things which were in reality beyond his all too human powers. To illustrate his point Griffiths quotes the following passage from Céline (Griffiths, 1970: 341):

Say what you like . . . I can speak freely because he detested me . . . Pétain was our last King of France. 'Philip the Last! . . .' the stature, the majesty, the works . . . and he believed in it . . . first as victor at Verdun . . . then, at the age of seventy and then some promoted to Sovereign! Who could have resisted? . . . A pushover! 'Oh, Monsieur le Maréchal, how you incarnate France!' That incarnation jazz is magic . . . if somebody said to me: 'Céline, damn it all, how you incarnate the *Passage*! the *Passage* is you! all you!' – I'd go out of my mind! take any old hick, tell him to his face that he incarnates something . . . you'll see, he'll go crazy . . . you've pierced his heart! . . . he won't know which way is up . . . Once Pétain incarnated France, he didn't care if it was fish or flesh, gibbet, Paradise or High Court, Douamont, Hell, or Thorez . . . he was the incarnation! . . . that's the only real genuine happiness: incarnation . . . you could cut his head off . . . he'd go right on incarnating . . . his head would run along all by itself, perfectly happy, seventh heaven! Charlot shooting Brasillach![4] he was in seventh heaven too! another incarnator! both in seventh heaven, both incarnations! . . . And Laval? (Céline, 1987: 149–50)

De Gaulle's notion of incarnating France was stressed frequently throughout his career as leader. Jean Lacouture suggests that during the war Pétain and de Gaulle provided rival incarnations. He suggests in fact that both *were* France, Pétain incarnating the actual France, the France of Occupation, of Vichy, France as it then existed, while de Gaulle incarnated France as it once was and would be again, in all its glory, France as it should be, the essential France (Lacouture, 1990: 282).

What is involved with the notion of incarnating something such as France? How might a leader be said to incarnate a country? The state is a conception imagined by and brought into existence by the minds of people, it has rarely been mistaken for a natural relation. Laval designed the initial structure of executive power at Vichy, for example – badly, as it gave Pétain more power than Laval (Lacouture, 1991: 198) – just as the constitution of the Fifth Republic, which gave de Gaulle the power and stability of government he required, was something he himself designed. 'And this brings us to the heart of the second Gaullism. The constitution was "sacrosanct" in that it brought all individuals together into a collective person, by which the French merge together to form that ideal whole that is called France' (Lacouture, 1991: 198).

The body of the state, then, is an imaginary body given an actual existence, and it is given this existence primarily by the voice of the leader who claims to be able to speak for the state and for all who pertain to it. One of de Gaulle's most famous pronouncements, written on the first page of his *Memoires de guerre*, affirms: 'Toute ma vie, je me suis fait une certaine idée de la France' (*All my life I have had / made a certain idea of*

[4] De Gaulle declined to pardon the writer Robert Brasillach, who was sentenced to death during the purge for collaborating with the Nazis (cf. Lacouture, 1991: 80–1). In 1945 de Gaulle told Minister of State René Brouillet he could never delegate the power of clemency over death penalties: 'It is the royal prerogative par excellence, the highest responsibility of a head of State, the only one that he cannot delegate. For that, and for nothing else, do I have to account only to God' (Lacouture, 1991: 79).

France) (Lacouture, 1990: 284). This idea is something he has not only had but something he has made. He has built the idea and with *Memoires de guerre* and *Memoires d'espoir* he gave the idea to others, just as, in coming to power in 1958, in designing the constitution in accordance with his idea, in identifying that idea, through himself, with that state, he gave that idea to the country as a whole. The way we see France, the way the French still see it, carries the residue of that Gaullist idea.[5]

That idea was not only made, it was not only incarnated, it was, above all, pronounced. All of this, perhaps, brings us back to possible worlds whose reality rests upon voices and the stories these voices invent. Both de Gaulle and Pétain invented France, at least as much through their pronouncements as through their 'actions'. Indeed, can a head of state bring about an action, officially tied to his function as head of state, that does not involve a pronouncement, his voice? When asked by General Madon, the officer responsible for the French strategic nuclear force, how he would recognize the validity of an order to use nuclear weapons,[6] de Gaulle responded, 'Come now, Madon, you know my voice don't you?' (Lacouture, 1991: 433).

Here then, we see the importance of stories, of fiction, of voices, and the relationship between these stories and the foundations of a state. In formulating his pronouncements the voice of the leader is also constituting a reality, a reality given form by the constitution he composes. In doing this he develops a single story, a grand narrative (incorporated into earlier stories of the nation) which becomes that of national identity. An important end of this process is the effort to subjectify. If one can design a state by developing a narrative of national identity, one can also design or develop through education the kinds of order-words and so the kinds of subjects which exist within that state. It becomes clear, then, how counter-narratives, pragmatic stories of being, stories *tout court* insofar as they offer a different picture of the real, are always political.

The idea of the leader incarnating a country might be related to the notion of 'totality' developed by Levinas. It involves the reduction of the otherness of the individual citizens of France to the sameness of the single coherent body: France. In *Totality and Infinity*, Levinas talks of totality in terms of the same appropriating or *including* the other within itself.[7]

---

[5] The 'Gaullist' R.P.R., especially their leader, the French President Jacques Chirac, frequently invoke the spirit of de Gaulle.
[6] And the fact of having an independant nuclear deterent was one of the cornerstones of the France which de Gaulle brought into being.
[7] This is discussed in more detail in the next chapter.

The definition of the body of the state involves notions of inclusion and exclusion. Vichy propaganda stressed how foreign elements and divisive internal elements had combined to throw France into the disarray, the division which led to the defeat of June 1940. The goal of Pétain's National Revolution – a programme which barely managed to get off the ground due to Nazi interference (Griffiths, 1970: 254–65) – was at once to purify and unify the country. The strong hand that was to sweep out the garbage and bring together the people was that of Pétain. An early Vichy poster displays Pétain pointing to the reader with a look of strong resolve: 'Français! vous n'êtes ni vendus ni trahis ni abandonnés. Venez à moi avec confiance' (French! you have neither been sold nor betrayed nor abandoned. Come to me with confidence) (Rousso, 1992: 29). Here, we witness purification and unification, the expelled (or excluded) and the included, Beckett's Molloy and Moran for example. The world of the National Revolution was the world of the possible as described by Deleuze in 'The Exhausted'. The possible being that which always involves exclusion: 'Language states what is possible, but in preparing it for a realization ... But the realization of what is possible always proceeds through exclusion, because it presupposes preferences and goals which vary, forever replacing predecessors' (Deleuze, 1995: 3).

From 1944 to 1946, with the Liberation which involved the end of Vichy, de Gaulle was in power; in 1958 he returned to power; at both times his preferences and goals replaced those of his predecessors. The leader was he who made possible through exclusion and inclusion, purification and unification. In 1944 de Gaulle made a pronouncement suggesting that the French had liberated themselves, officially installing what has been called the Gaullist 'myth of resistance', a myth which reached back to 18 June 1940 and invented a France whose majority had never ceased to fight alongside de Gaulle. This myth, along with the *épuration* he brought to bear, sought both to purify French history of what might have been seen as a shameful episode, and to unify a France deeply divided by civil war (Lacouture, 1990: 574–5; Morris, 1986; 71–83). In 1958, recalled to power to confront the crisis in Algeria which had brought the Fourth Republic to its knees, de Gaulle went to Algiers and made another of his more famous pronouncements to the French Algerians:

De Gaulle approached the microphone, breathed in, like a diver before his brief effort, and declared, in two stages, separated by a slight pause: 'Je vous ai (three words that were inaudible) compris!' There was stupefied silence for two or three seconds, followed by a yell of collective joy . . . These words, 'seemingly spontaneous but in reality carefully calculated, which I hoped would fire their enthusiasm without committing me further than I was willing to go' were his tour de force. (Lacouture, 1991: 186–7)

'Je vous ai compris!' means firstly, 'I have understood you', but also 'I have included you.' De Gaulle went on in that speech to outline his goals for Algeria, goals which would ultimately (and ironically) lead to the decolonization of Algeria and therefore the exclusion of French Algeria from France. The slogan, which may have drowned out the rest of the speech for many, perhaps struck such a chord with the French Algerians because they felt themselves included, as they wished to be, in the greater French state which they feared was about to expel them.

OPPOSING ORDER: THE EXILE

Here the figure of the outcast, the exile, the excluded or the expelled becomes important. These are other to the totalizing same of the state, they are obviously different, insisting on the continuous variation of the words and their meanings, whereas order is maintained by the insistence on similarity and constants. So too the refugee or foreigner becomes an other within the body of national identity, a foreign body within that body. It is indeed interesting how so many of the thinkers aligned with or whose ideas seem in sympathy with the critical programme of post-war French thought might be considered outsiders. Levinas, the Russian Jew, Derrida, the Algerian Jew, Beckett the Irishman, Genet the homosexual, Sarraute the Russian *émigré*, Foucault the homosexual, Irigaray, an immigrant and woman, and so on. Yet it is important to note that this sense of being in the minority need not be limited to those who somehow came from outside or became outsiders: Deleuze and Guattari have written at length about becoming minoritarian, urging us to become the bastard rather than the pure breed with purity here considered not only with regard to the purity of the individual which is the state (the state understood as a constant), but with regard to the purity which resides in the individual who is the fixed subject (the self understood as a constant). In this they follow Rimbaud, who coined the slogan 'je est un autre' (I is an other) (cf. Deleuze and Guattari, 1987: 100–10, 379). Otherness, difference, continuous variation, is ineluctably part of the self-divided, indeterminate, self; and such a 'self' in perhaps its quintessential (that is, absolutely indefinite) form is Beckett's unnamable.

While enough is known of Beckett's foreignness within France, it is worth briefly touching on the specific itineraries of Derrida and Levinas, as the work of these thinkers will be considered in relation to Beckett in the next chapter. As for Levinas and the idea of his own exile, this has been well summarized by Fabrice Pliskin in a recent obituary of Levinas:

Born in Lithuania in 1905, this errant Jew placed the errant at the heart of his thought. Heir to Russian, French and German cultures, he knew exile in the Ukraine, the exodus in France and captivity in Hanover not far from the extermination camp of Bergen-Belsen. Neither *normalien* nor graduate of the *agrégation* examination, he was never at home, even at the university which he did not become part of until he was 55. With this Lithuanian émigré, philosophy itself became emigrant, nomadic, stepping outside itself. (Pliskin, 1996: 54)

The theme of exile, of not being at home even in oneself and the powerful critical potentialities this continuously varying position allows in the face of oppressive order might be further developed with regard to the wanderings of both Beckett and Derrida, and Beckett's fascination with tramps. The power of the vagabond, the outsider, to decompose the constants of totalitarian order which I discussed with reference to Foucault in chapters 1 and 2 might be further underlined here with reference to Pliskin, who illustrates the importance of the relation between this critical position and the idea of the homeland (the constant made manifest). To quote Pliskin:

in 1946 . . . Levinas offered his hospitality to the extraordinary M. Chouchani. Chouchani was a brilliant Talmudist, juggler of verses, a genius more rabbinical than the rabbis. He was also a well-travelled tramp whose origins were known to no one . . . One thing alone was certain, that he was errant. Chouchani lived for three years at Levinas's college, then disappeared all of a sudden, like he came, with his small bag, without leaving any trace. / Under the depths of Levinas's thought, then, there is Chouchani, the man without horizon, without country, without home – 'that home whose conquest and jealous defence constitutes European history', as Levinas writes in *Otherwise than Being or Beyond Essence*. (54)

This not being at home in oneself (a being in continuous variation) might be further underlined with reference to the life of Jacques Derrida. We might easily trace Derrida's errant nature in considering what might be commonly called facts (which are often used as constants). Born in Algeria on 15 July 1930 to Jewish parents, Derrida was already an outsider in France. In an interview given to François Ewald of *Magazine Littéraire* he tells how he was given the name Jackie (after an American actor) but changed it when he began to publish (Derrida, 1991b: 20).[8] He went to France at the age of nineteen to study for the *khâgne* at Louis-le-Grand for two years, where, living in exile and suffering from having taken part in what he considered monstrous national competitions in order to enter the Ecole normale supérieure, the young Derrida found life hard and unhappy. What is most interesting, perhaps, is how the notion of a fact such as being born (a date which identifies the self as a constant) and the importance of exile to his own critical project, are underlined by Derrida in this interview. With regard to exile he states: 'I had the impression that I could never "write" while living "at home" (chez moi) and already for political reasons. From the beginning of the fifties politics and above all colonial society had become unbearable to me' (20). With regard to the 'fact' (the constant) of being born he states: 'The consternation which surrounds this subject will never cease. Because the event designated in this way might only announce itself to me in the future tense "I am (not yet) born", but in the future in the form of a past in which I will never have been present and which will remain for this reason always promised – and moreover always multiple. Who said that one is only born once' (18). These comments not only indicate a profound sense of the importance of continuous variation within the self, a variation seen also in the vagabond, but might remind us again of Samuel Beckett, who was not unhappy to leave his date of birth open to question, and who, according to Bair, and others, felt that he had never been properly born (Bair, 1990: 1, 221–2; Cronin, 1996: 220–2; Juliet, 1986a: 14). The exile exists within individuals, then, both as an other within the individual that is the state and as an other within the individual who is the self.

VOICES: THE LEADER AND THE TRANSLATOR

Here then, one might oppose to the ideal of the leader (whose voice stands in for and drowns out all other voices) an ideal of the translator, one who comes between voices, one who voices pass through. The first is aligned with judgement: a 'comprehension' through an inclusion which presupposes exclusion (I comprehend you insofar as your inten-

---

[8] For more on Derrida's life see Bennington and Derrida, 1991.

tions are similar to mine). The second is aligned with justice: the desire to understand by taking difference (precisely those things which are not identical to me) seriously, by attempting to preserve rather than efface difference.

After the Liberation Beckett returned to Ireland to see his family, then discovered on attempting to return to France to live that foreign nationals were not being allowed in at that time. As a way of getting back into France Beckett volunteered to serve as a translator and storekeeper for the Irish Red Cross Hospital in Saint-Lô on the Normandy coast (Bair, 1990: 362–6). According to Dougald McMillan, on 10 June 1946 he read a script he had written entitled *The Capital of the Ruins* on Irish radio. This would have been one of the few occasions that Beckett's voice was heard in public. This assertion, however, has been challenged by Stan Gontarski, who shows there is no proof for McMillian's claims and no record of such a broadcast having taken place (Gontarski, in Beckett, 1995: 285–6). Still, even the written voice is a voice attempting to interpret between others. As McMillan explains:

The practical occasion of the radio script was public Dublin disparagement of the equipment and conditions of the Hospital implying criticism of the French for not making better provision . . . *The Capital of the Ruins* is a rare piece of polemic attempting to correct Irish parochialism. But it is also an even more rare direct personal statement about the significance of his experience in war-ravaged France. (McMillan, 1990: 15–16)

In addressing his Irish audience Beckett makes interesting use of the pronouns of inclusion and exclusion, 'we' and 'they':

When I reflect now on the recurrent problems of what, with all proper modesty, might be called the heroic period, on one in particular so arduous and elusive that it literally ceased to be formulable, I suspect that our pains were those inherent in the simple and necessary and yet so unattainable proposition that their way of being we, was not our way and that our way of being they, was not their way. It is only fair to say that many of us had never been abroad before. (Beckett, 1990a: 24–5)

These statements are interesting for a number of reasons. In the first place Beckett clearly aligns himself with the Irish people to whom he is speaking, the Irish people of whom, no matter what, he will necessarily remain. There is a subtle contradiction in those pronouns of inclusion, however. 'Many of us', he suggests, 'had never been abroad before.' Here Beckett identifies with those among his group who were unlike himself: Beckett had not only travelled a fair deal in Europe, but had lived in France for the last eight years and was absolutely at ease in the French language.[9] He stands outside this 'us', even as he pronounces it. This sense of inclusion, an inclusion whereby one allows oneself to appear included while not quite believing in the process, an inclusion which stresses the imaginative or fictional element involved in the notion of inclusion, is further underlined in the suggestion 'that their way of being we, was not our way and that our way of being they, was not their way'. This seems to work on two levels, whereby, firstly, the French make an effort of imagination to feel themselves at one with the Irish who in turn make a corresponding imaginative effort. On another level, there is the sense of inclusion which is taken for granted, no doubt because the listeners would have taken it for granted, whereby the Irish are a discrete cultural unit as are the French, and it is over this cultural difference that further attempts at inclusion stumble. Inclusion turns upon comprehension, as is indicated by de Gaulle's famous words, and comprehension primarily involves a linguistic process. The anglophone Irish could not comprehend the francophone French and vice versa, and therefore they often failed, despite best intentions, perhaps, to include one another, to relate to one another as one people: all this is easily conceived.[10] They require a translator, if they are not simply to exclude one another.

Where would this leave Beckett, who was not only the storekeeper but above all a 'translator' for the Irish mission? While the leader imposes meaning, enforces order in judging between two sides by excluding one of them, the translator attempts to justly include by oscillating between the two sides. Such a position also involves the being outside of the translator: if the leader is in some senses set apart from, above, or beyond the crowd he unites, the translator is between, neither the one nor the other, apart. But while the leader attempts to erase all difference

---

[9] The question of Beckett as translator of his own works is an extremely interesting one, and one adjacent to the notion of the interpreter described here. Much good work has already been done on the question of self-translation, the best of them being Brian Fitch's *Beckett and Babel*, Steven Connor's chapter 'Repetition and Self-Translation' (in Connor, 1988) and Leslie Hill's chapter 'The Trilogy Translated' in his book *Beckett's Fiction*.

[10] In speaking of his memories of the original production of *En attendant Godot*. Roger Blin has stated: 'There is no theatre without ambiguity . . . Robert Kanters has even said that *Godot* was the first Christian play. It was elsewhere under a misunderstanding of this order that Beckett received the Nobel Prize . . . Faced with the enormous success of Godot, Beckett was really floored and quite perturbed. He wondered whether it wasn't proof that he had not been understood. But, on the contrary, I think that the public had understood perfectly ' (Blin, 1986: 85–6).

by making over the nation in his own image or imaginings, the translator does not seek to dissolve differences by valuing one over the other but rather to consider them to be of equal value, in part, paradoxically, by bringing them to the surface, by in a sense being that surface, the linguistic surface that allows the same to converse with the other. While I have stated above that Beckett addresses the Irish as one of their own because this is an identification which he cannot help but make, it is also apparent that, as McMillan states, he is only addressing the Irish at all because he felt the need to intercede on behalf of the French. The role of the translator, then, is a true between, an attempt at inclusion which involves the being neither of the one who makes the attempt. He attempts to persuade the Irish by dramatizing conditions from the other side (that of the French), generating empathy by imagining the gratitude and future gratitude of the French people. On the other hand he is able to speak for the French by virtue of the fact that he is attached to the other side (that of the Irish), pretending to talk about the other from within, the French from within the English spoken by the Irish in a voice complete with the Dublin accent Beckett never lost.

In *Totality and Infinity* Levinas discusses the same and the other. The same is identified with the self, consciousness, the ego, and the relation between the same and the other is said to be infinite. The leader, the pure breed who attempts to fix truth, might be aligned with totality (with determinacy or the constant) while the translator, the exile, the bastard, the refugee, the lunatic or otherwise minoritarian, is aligned with the infinity (of indeterminacy or continuous variation). The first becomes totalizing through recourse to judgement and its exclusions, the second opens towards infinity by bringing into existence and seeking justice. This justice is to be found between two sides,[11] and the translator too is a kind of between: a decentred subject.

Yet what if the translator were not just between two totalized bodies representing national identities, but also between all the particular bodies within each state and also between those relations which go to make up his own conception of self? The exile, then, would also be within: and this is precisely the decentred subject. The between inhabits all the individuated bodies: the self, the state, the between states. The between is bastard, minoritarian, following Rimbaud, 'je est un autre.' This surely is a Beckettian formulation, reminiscent of that described in the prose piece, *neither*

---

[11] This point will be examined in more detail in the next chapter.

to and fro in shadow from inner to outer shadow
from impenetrable self to impenetrable unself by way of neither
as between two lit refuges whose doors once neared gently close,
once turned away from gently part again
beckoned back and forth and turned away
heedless of the way, intent on the one gleam or the other
unheard footfalls only sound
till at last halt for good, absent for good from self and other
then no sound
then gently light unfading on that unheeded neither
unspeakable home (Beckett, 1995: 258)

This between is a beyond more than an outside. The translator is beyond: he is beyond the two voices which merge in him in order to communicate, he is the space in which their communication becomes possible, but they communicate through him rather than in him; he is neither one nor the other, in actualizing the process he remains between the actual process which must take place within the same and within the other who form the dichotomy inside/outside. The between is the fact of the linguistic surface, the being of that surface come to a knowledge of itself. As a translator, for example, you are the linguistic surface between a same and an other who could not communicate without you. But you are also a cipher, a process, a medium which words pass through in order to be understood. The translator is the medium of voices but has no voice, no story of his/her own, unless it be the story of mediation, the story of the sensation of being a conduit through which words, voices, course, raging through and causing its being to vibrate, the story of being *a channel* but not *a source*. And such, perhaps, might be the experience of the unnamable who asks, 'Is it possible certain things change on their passage through me, in a way they can't prevent?' (Beckett, 1958: 81).

And if every experience of being in language were the experience of being a translator? This is where the unnamable's indefinite abstract state is important – it shows us the groundlessness involved in extracting our identities from languages which are always tied to social bodies 'outside' our selves (cf. Deleuze and Guattari, 1987: 77–82).

THE VOICE

Imagery of being outside recurs in Beckett. Being outside, in an infinite outside, traversing empty space, be it covered in flowers or mud or grass.

In *Enough, How It Is, Lessness, Afar a Bird*, for example. Yet images of being inside also haunt his work, be it in small rooms which may resemble the insides of a skull, alone or with a single companion, or a cylinder with numerous others. In *All Strange Away, Imagination Dead Imagine, Ping, The Lost Ones, Closed Space*, for example. There are also images of the inside opening to the outside, the same to the other, be it the pure inside of one in his room opening to the pure outside of one in a field empty and endless to the horizon, or the supposed inside of one on his back in the dark opening to the supposed outside of memories of the fields and streets of childhood (and here it might not even be clear which is really inside and which is really outside). In *Stirrings Still* and *Company*, for example. Important to the notions of the inside/outside is that of being neither, the between which is beyond these dichotomies. In the narratives, be they of the inside or the outside, the neither, the between, which is also that which translates them for the reader, is the voice, the medium of the story:

> I say it as I hear it . . .
> A voice comes to one in the dark. Imagine.
> Closed place. All needed to be known for say is known. There is nothing but what is said. Beyond what is said there is nothing.[12]

It is important to recognize that the voice telling stories, the *language II* of Beckett described by Deleuze in 'The Exhausted', might be read as more than just an analogy to the workings of stories produced outside literature. It is important to recognize the fictionalization of the real which takes place in history, for example; in particular, for our purposes, in that history through which Beckett lived during World War Two in France. In constituting rival incarnations of France, de Gaulle and Pétain also developed rival narratives, rival stories which they pronounced, each as the authentic voice of patriotism, tradition and order.

A story is always told by a voice, although that voice is never a voice in isolation: it refracts the possible world of the other to which it pertains, but by means of language that is always the language of others. The voice, like the being to which it is attached, is partial, a link on an infinite chain, largely ignorant of the other links. The story is a means of recuperating what is other to it. This is how Spinoza talks of the imagination. We relate to and make sense of the world beyond ourselves through recourse to imagination, language works through imagination

[12] Samuel Beckett, *How It Is, Company*, in *Nohow On* (1989: 5); *Closed Space*, in *Collected Shorter Prose* (1984a: 199).

(cf. *Ethics*, especially Part 2, Props. 40–9). In speaking you are, through force of imagination, recuperating the world to yourself; in imagination you encompass within yourself a world. You are a possible world to another. It is your voice which confers reality on your world, it is the stories constituted by this voice which describe this reality for others.

Like the counter-narratives which oppose one universal with another, one totalization with another, the particular truth also involves totalization. The individual's truth becomes *the truth* thereby excluding everything which is other to it. It is here that the non-totalizing story of the translator might be said to be more just. It refrains from fixing the truth or establishing any ground through which such truth might be fixed. As such, it is a more just portrayal of complex and contradictory events.

What, then, are the political implications of stating 'I say it as I hear it' (rather than 'I describe what I saw'); of the notion that our sense of the real is built upon the stories we hear and retransmit more than on our own (partial and difficult to interpret) perceptions? To illustrate what is at stake it is worth turning to a short Beckett piece, *As the Story was Told.* This describes a process of torture.[13]

As the story was told me I never went near the place during sessions. I asked what place and a tent was described at length . . . I asked what sessions and these in turn were described, their object, duration, frequency and harrowing nature. I hope I was not more sensitive than the next man, but finally I had to raise my hand. I lay there quite still for a time, then asked where I was while all this was going forward. In a hut, was the answer, a small hut in a grove some two hundred yards away, a distance even the loudest cry could not carry, but must die on the way . . . As the story was told me the man succumbed in the end to his ill-treatment . . . finally I asked if I knew . . . what exactly was required of the man, what it was he would not or could not say. No, was the answer . . . I did not know what the poor man was required to say, in order to be pardoned, but would have recognized it at once, yes, at a glance, if I had seen it. (Beckett, 1990a: 103–7)

What is the effect of this voice that comes between, telling the story? Not only telling the story but telling the protagonist of the story both what it was he knew and remembered and who he was? Beckett, if he ever witnessed, took part in or heard tell of a process of torture was most likely to have done so during the war, when working with the Maquis in Roussillon, perhaps (cf. Bair, 1990: 351–4). Here there is detachment,

---

[13] Other Beckett texts which describe processes of interrogation are: *Rough for Radio II*, *Play* and *What Where* (all in Beckett, 1990b).

but rather than this providing the basis for objective truth, this detachment seems tied to groundlessness, a disconcerting groundlessness, the
groundlessness of fiction. With Beckett the voice which intercedes,
intercedes not only within the fiction itself, but within the story; it tells
the story, moreover, it intercedes within the voice which is telling the
story, telling it the story. It is everywhere between individuals: the
national individual, the individual called the self. It translates but lacks
the guarantee of the real of which the named individual, as eye-witness,
is the guarantor. In Beckett's text what the narrator's voice states has
already been translated by another voice always at one remove, but the
words of the translator carry with them no guarantee of truth, or
comprehension, and this is a cause for consternation.

Yet what if such a play of voices were the condition of all human
interaction? What if even the testimony of the Gospels were open to
question? Such is shown to be the case in *Waiting for Godot* where
Vladimir and Estragon discuss the discrepancies among the four Evan-
gelists with regard to the story of one of the thieves, crucified with
Christ, being saved (Beckett, 1990b: 14–15). What if even the truth of
your own voice were brought into question, or further still, the existence
of your *own* voice? Your own voice as source that is, the source of your
own story. How could the voice be said to be your own when it merely
recounts stories which may concern you, but always at one remove?
One begins to feel the ground fall away. Such a groundless homeland,
resembling, perhaps, a sojourn in war-torn France, is traversed by
Beckett in *The Unnamable*. For, as Beckett states in *The Capital of the Ruins*:

I may perhaps venture to mention . . . the possibility that some of those who
were in Saint-Lô will come home realising that they got at least as good as they
gave, that they got indeed what they could hardly give, a vision and sense of a
time-honoured conception of humanity in ruins, and perhaps even an inkling of
the terms in which our condition is to be thought again. These will have been in
France. (Beckett, 1990a: 27–8)

CHAPTER 6

Language, between violence and justice: Beckett, Levinas and Derrida

THE SAME AND THE OTHER

The theme of the relation between the same and the other is one which Vincent Descombes identifies as being central to contemporary French philosophy.[1] I intend, here, to build upon the notion of the problem-field discussed in the introduction by supposing that the nature of the relation between the same and the other and the questions of justice and ethical behaviour it brings with it constituted a problem which seemed pressing after World War Two in France, and in making this supposition I will assume that insights into the nature of these problems might be gained by comparing contiguous but separate responses to it.

One of the philosophers working in post-war France who has thought most closely about this relation between the same and the other and the question of justice is Emmanuel Levinas. This theme is, arguably, also central to *The Unnamable*. As we have seen, Jacques Derrida has suggested that there are close affinities between his own work and that of Samuel Beckett.[2] Derrida has also closely engaged with the work of Levinas[3] in considering the problem of the relation between the same and the other and in developing his own response to the problem of justice. I will attempt, here, to read through these problems in comparing the manner in which they are treated in Beckett's *The Unnamable*, Levinas's *Totality and Infinity* and Derrida's 'Violence and Metaphysics', 'Force of Law' and *Spectres de Marx*. In each a central concern is the

---

[1] His book *Modern French Philosophy* is entitled *Le même et l'autre*, 'the same and other', in its French version.
[2] Asked why he had never written on Beckett, Derrida replied, 'This is an author to whom I feel very close, or to whom I would like to feel myself very close' (Derrida, 1992: 60).
[3] The usefulness of reading Beckett through Levinas has been noted before. Steven Connor delivered a paper at the international symposium, Beckett in the 1990s, entitled 'Beckett in the Face of Levinas' (Connor, 1992), and Trezise (1990) and Locatelli (1990: 230) mention Levinas in passing.

problem of justice and accordingly this chapter will orbit around this problem. My reading, is necessarily partial and focused: I will not attempt to discuss other works by Levinas or Derrida's second essay on Levinas because I feel that, for my purposes, the concepts developed in *Totality and Infinity* and discussed by Derrida in 'Violence and Metaphysics' shed more light on the sensations which appear in *The Unnamable*. The 'Levinas' I will be treating here is the Levinas of *Totality and Infinity*.

In *Spectres de Marx*, developing the concept of 'justice' Derrida cites Levinas from *Totality and Infinity*: 'the relation with others [autrui] – that is to say, justice'.[4] It is apparent how the problems of the relation between the same and the other and the problem of justice might be closely linked. Further, as will be discussed below, both these concerns are tied in with the question of language in Beckett, Levinas and Derrida.

In *Totality and Infinity*, the 'same', which is most clearly represented by the ego, is set against the 'other', most clearly represented as others.[5] The other, however, is *absolutely* other. To briefly clarify this point, for Levinas the central conflict (between justice and injustice) involves the opposed conceptions of totality and infinity. Totality (injustice) involves the same reducing all difference to itself, while the concept of infinity (justice), which Levinas opposes to totality, expresses the infinite (irreducible) difference between the same and the other. The other can never be reduced to the same because it is absolutely other. What is infinite then, is the *relation between* the same and the other. The infinity is an irreducibility, the same can never contain or reappropriate the other, the distance between the two can never be effaced, their difference is that which can never be reconciled, is difference itself. This is a relation through which the terms cannot form a totality: totality rests crucially distinct from infinity (Levinas, [n.d.]: 39).

At the end of section one of *Totality and Infinity* Levinas notes that his own thesis, which insists that a metaphysics[6] precedes ontology, is at the antipodes of Spinozism (42-8). In the *Ethics* Spinoza outlines an ontology which commences with what he claims is the most apparent, the most

---

[4] Derrida, 1993: 49, citing Levinas, *Totalité et Infini*, p. 62 ('la relation avec autrui – c'est-à-dire la justice').

[5] Derrida shows how this adequation constitutes a break, not only with 'the Greek and most modern philosophies of subjectivity', but also with Levinas's earlier works, 'which were most careful to distinguish the Ego from the same and Others from the other' (Derrida, 1978: 109–10).

[6] Derrida summarizes Levinas's use of the term 'metaphysics' as follows: 'Levinas calls the positive movement which takes itself beyond the disdain or disregard of the other, that is, beyond the appreciation or possession, understanding and knowledge of the other, *metaphysics or ethics*. Metaphysical transcendence is *desire*' (Derrida, 1978: 92).

real of all things: that is to say everything, the absolutely infinite and unique substance, God. God is the first principle, the first cause. Levinas begins from the other pole: rather than starting from God and working down to Man as a finite mode among all the other finite modes which are modifications of God's infinite substance, Levinas expounds a philosophy based on the lived experience of humans. To quote Derrida: '[Levinas's work] seeks to be understood from within a *recourse to experience itself.* Experience itself and that which is most irreducible within experience: the passage and departure towards the other; the other itself as what is most irreducibly other within it: Others' (1978: 83). Perhaps God is just too big: Beckett, like Levinas, draws the line at human experience, attempting to think the relation of same and other.

> The master . . . we don't intend . . . unless absolutely driven to it, to make the mistake of inquiring into him, he'd turn out to be a mere high official, we'd end up by needing God, we have lost all sense of decency admittedly, but there are still certain depths we prefer not to sink to. Let us keep to the family circle, it's more intimate, we all know one another now, no surprises to be feared, the will has been opened, nothing for anybody. (Beckett, 1958: 122)

In *The Unnamable* it might be claimed that at times Beckett finds himself wandering this country which Levinas has positioned at 'the antipodes of Spinozism'. The analogy is loose. Beckett does not systematically reject Spinoza or any other philosopher; rather I will argue that in a certain sense *The Unnamable* might be read as a kind of parody of philosophical discourse in general[7] while remaining an oscillating critique which might be read against certain philosophical positions and be said to converge with others. That is to say that at times, for example, he might resemble Levinas and at other times differ from him, and at times he might resemble Derrida and at other times differ from him (just as Derrida and Levinas overlap at times and move apart at times).

LITERATURE AND PHILOSOPHY, AGAIN

It might be useful to again briefly sketch the status which will be attributed to Beckett's novel in relation to works of philosophy here. The problem is recognizably a philosophical one; that is, one conceived through concepts: what is the nature of the Being which this being is experiencing, what constitutes the 'I' who experiences and the space

[7] Butler, 1984 (2) and Adorno, 1988 also speak of Beckett's works parodying philosophy.

that is inhabited? It is also a literary one; that is, one felt through sensations: how does the unnamable escape being, the pain commensurate with being, how does he exit the labyrinth of language he finds himself in? Importantly, the theme of the interrelation between conception and sensation is one with which Beckett plays in *The Unnamable*. Worm, for example, does not feel or sense, yet he exists because he is 'conceived' by others (82). The question of the nature of being, then, is raised between philosophy and literature: does one have to be 'conceived' (with the obvious pun on sexual reproduction on the one hand, and philosophical or rational speculation on the other) in order to be? Is not feeling itself enough to account for life? Indeed, Worm cannot properly speaking be said to exist until he comes to feel (and at this point he stops being Worm, who does not feel, who is only conceived). The opposite problem to that of Worm plagues Mahood. Mahood feels but, finally, he is no longer conceived, the others fail to believe in him and so he ceases to exist. Philosophy and art, then, encounter one another necessarily on the ground laid down on which one considers the nature of being.

Further, in common with a philosophical text the work has a 'methodology': 'What am I to do, what shall I do, what should I do, in my situation, how proceed? By aporia pure and simple? Or by affirmations and negations invalidated as uttered, or sooner or later?' (Beckett, 1958: 3).

If it were a philosophical text we might note that Beckett seeks to proceed neither by affirmation (as in a purely positive ontology such as that of Spinoza) or negation (as in the progression by negation Derrida identifies in the work of Levinas[8]) nor by the synthesis of thesis and antithesis as in Hegelian dialectic, but through the more or less pure positing of a question mark. The procedure of this questioning apparently marks a limit where the unnamable veers away from philosophical discourse: he proceeds, in fact, through unsubstantiated supposition. This pure supposition, however, is always haunted by aporia: the narrator constantly reminds us of the provisional nature of his guesses. The suppositions never serve as a stable ground on which to build but carry with them and draw attention to the question mark of the question. While this use of supposition makes it impossible to extract this or that affirmation or negation in support of any thesis, the aporetic haunting establishes, through irony, a rigorous and constant *modus*

---

[8] 'It could doubtless be shown that it is the nature of Levinas's writing . . . [to progress] by negations, and by negation against negation. Its proper route is not that of an "either this . . . or that" but of a "neither this . . . nor that"'(Derrida, 1978: 90).

operandi which allows one to draw an analogy between this and a philosophical methodology.

While Beckett and Levinas might be said to be, at times and to a certain extent, thinking the same relation, a crucial difference is in how the two writers understand language. For Levinas language is the link between the same and the other which is, in turn, justice:

> We shall try to show that the *relation* between the same and the other – upon which we seem to impose such extraordinary conditions – is language . . . The relation between the same and the other, metaphysics, is primordially enacted as conversation, where the same, gathered up in its ipseity as an 'I', . . . leaves itself. (Levinas: [n.d.] 39)

Metaphysics then, like justice, is originally dependent on the play of language. Levinas's assertion that metaphysics (the relation of the same to the other) precedes ontology is based on an understanding of an originary language. That is, for beings such as ourselves, which comes first, consciousness of Being (with a capital *B*, the Being of ontology, of Spinoza's substance), or consciousness? Now, consciousness, for Levinas, involves the relation of the same to the other which opens consciousness, and what is consciousness of Being other than consciousness

> already the comprehension of Being is said to the existent, who again arises behind the theme in which he is presented. This 'saying to the other' – this relationship to the other as interlocutor, this relation with an *existent* – precedes all ontology; it is the ultimate relation in Being. Ontology presupposes metaphysics. (47–8)[9]

Derrida notes that, through the concept of the face of the other, and the face-to-face of the same and the other, Levinas equates language with thought. The face-to-face might stand for an originary language, a flickering into consciousness that is already language and is still not language, a strange 'language' that escapes the category of language, a non-signifying 'language':

> the face-to-face eludes every category. For within it the face is given simultaneously as expression and as speech. Not only as glance, but as the original unity of glance and speech, eyes and mouth, that speaks, but also pronounces its hunger. Thus it is also that which *hears* the invisible, for 'thought is language' and 'thought is in an element analogous to sound and not to light'. This unity of

---

[9] Derrida quotes this, (1978: 98).

the face precedes, in its signification, the dispersion of senses and organs of sensibility. Its signification is therefore irreducible. Moreover, the face does not signify. It does not incarnate, envelop, or signal anything other than self, soul, subjectivity, etc. Thought is speech, and is therefore immediately face. In this, the thematic of the face belongs to the most modern philosophy of language and of the body itself. The other is not signalled by his face, he is this face: 'Absolutely present, in his face, the Other – without any metaphor – faces me.' (Derrida, 1978: 100)

A similar equation of thought to language is apparent in Beckett in the narrative of Worm. Worm as Worm, in his integrity, is pure existence, pure Being; he sleeps, without knowing, without sensing. He only comes into being as Worm once he begins to sense: he hears, a noise. A noise he later realizes or imagines has been going on for a long while, a long while before he was able to recognize it. A noise he later recognizes as language, a noise he later recognizes as, perhaps, his own voice. He is given an eye with which to weep and be pained by the light a throng of others shines into his face. But in coming into consciousness he has stopped being Worm (81–120): 'Feeling nothing, knowing nothing, he exists nevertheless, but not for himself, for others, others conceive him and say, Worm is, since we conceive him, as if there could be no being but being conceived, if only by the beer. Others. One alone, then others' (Beckett, 1958: 82).

How close is this to Levinas? Rather than an other, who is face, which is 'simultaneously expression and speech', radiating this relation to the same as a kind of discourse, we have others prodding a same (who is still more other to 'they') into existence by plying him with language. At one point the unnamable imagines Worm baited like an animal, others linking hands to dance about him, flinging words across their circle at the most other of all things: seemingly, a same existing in itself, the true core of an individual being. This relation seems an inversion to that presented in Levinas. Worm is brought into consciousness through language, and this language emanates from the other and to this extent we might make analogies with Worm's story and Levinas. But the movement of injustice is far different here in Beckett to Levinas; rather than injustice arising from the efforts of the same to reappropriate the other into its totality, it appears in inverted form with the other moving to appropriate the I (or the same) by plying it with its language and hauling it into the light of its day. This is the light of language-based relations between the same and the other, those inexhaustibly painful relations the unnamable, in searching out silence, non-being, is seeking to escape. While language is primarily aligned with justice by Levinas, here it is primarily aligned with injustice by Beckett.

DERRIDA, LEVINAS AND BECKETT

One of Derrida's essays on Levinas, 'Violence and Metaphysics', might be used to think through some of these problems. Derrida's reading of Levinas through Husserl provides insights into the workings of *The Unnamable*, even though Beckett's text is never mentioned, because the difficult themes of language, silence, the same and the other, the same as other, which circle the unnamable in his unknowable space are all addressed. It is the coherence of Levinas's system and the rigour of Levinas's thought itself which allows Derrida to read against the grain of Levinas's texts to indicate the principles of questions that arise from those texts, as Levinas's thought is already engaged with these questions (Derrida, 1978: 109, 151.) Derrida suggests that the questions indicated are 'questions of language and the question of language'. The other is infinitely other and the *relation between* the same and the other which comprises justice is language. Derrida questions the infinity Levinas thereby requires of language to achieve this relation.[10] If language were infinite, would it not be able to *state* the infinite relation? The unnamable hopes to be able to escape the torment of talking interminably by stating (through sheer chance) something which is required to be stated to end that torment. The supposition that recurs most often is that he is supposed to express his own being in his own voice. He ends the narrative claiming he must go on. We are not able to assert with assurance either that his torment has stopped or that it will never stop, but we are certain that he has not succeeded in stating his self: he remains unnamable and the question remains in suspension, we are unable to think language as either finite or infinite. What Derrida says concerning history seems to go equally well for language: 'A system is neither finite nor infinite. A structural totality escapes this alternative in its functioning' (Derrida, 1978: 123).

If language is not infinite, perhaps 'the meaning of alterity is finite, is not positively infinite' (Derrida, 1978: 114). Levinas proposes a positive

---

[10] 'To say that the infinite exteriority of the other *is not* spatial, is *non*-exteriority and *non*-interiority, to be unable to designate it otherwise than negatively – is this not to acknowledge that the infinite (also designated negatively in its current positivity: in-finite) cannot be stated? Does this not amount to acknowledging that the structure "inside-outside" which is language itself, marks the original finitude of speech and of whatever befalls it?' (Derrida, 1978: 113.)

Infinity (God) which is also infinitely other. Derrida contends that there can be no possible otherness within a positive infinity:

If one thinks, as Levinas does, that positive Infinity tolerates, or even requires, infinite alterity, then one must renounce all language, and first of all the words *infinite* and *other*. Infinity cannot be understood as Other except in the form of in-finite. As soon as one attempts to think Infinity as a positive plenitude (one pole of Levinas's nonnegative transcendence), the other becomes unthinkable, impossible, unutterable . . . The other cannot be what it is, infinitely other, except in finitude and mortality (mine *and* its). It is such as soon as it comes into language, of course, and only then, and only if the word *other* has a meaning – but has not Levinas taught us that there is no thought before language? (Derrida, 1978: 114–15)

It might be claimed that if Levinas describes a reciprocal relation (between the same and the other) as moving in a single direction (from the same to the other), a similar, but inverted, claim might be made concerning *The Unnamable*. Derrida later sums up an aspect of the problem as follows: 'That I am also essentially the other's other, and that I know I am, is the evidence of a strange symmetry whose trace appears nowhere in Levinas's descriptions' (128). The 'they' which the unnamable describes are beings of a different order; initially, at least, there seems no symmetry between the unnamable and these others. 'They' suffer as much as he but are sometimes seen to be at a higher level, they are part of an hierarchy set up to torment the unnamable. This question, too, turns about language. Whereas in Levinas language moves between the same and the other, setting out from the same and involving either totality (injustice) where the same tries to annex the other to itself, or infinity (justice), where the same opens itself to the absolute otherness of the other, the unnamable often supposes that language comes to him purely from the other, that it passes through him and does not belong to him.[11]

It must not be forgotten, sometimes I forget, that all is a question of voices. I say what I am told to say, in the hope that some day they will weary of talking of me . . . Do they believe I believe it is I who am speaking? That's theirs too. To make me believe I have an ego all my own, and can speak of it, as they of theirs. (Beckett, 1958: 81; see also 111)

---

[11] On this point it is worth noting Knowlson and Pilling's account of Beckett's high regard for the essay 'On the Marionette Theatre' (1810) by the German dramatist and theorist Heinrich von Kleist (Knowlson and Pilling, 1979: 277–85). Apart from Knowlson and Pilling, the only reading of Beckett in relation to Kleist of which I am aware is Peter Gidal's brief but thought-provoking piece (Gidal, 1986: 187–92).

In writing of Beckett and his use of language, Gilles Deleuze has
suggested that 'it is always an Other who speaks, since words have not
expected me and there is no language other than the foreign' (Deleuze,
1995: 7).[12] As with Levinas, there seems no symmetry here. The unnamable is separated from this 'they' in an originary and infinite way. 'They'
are not like the unnamable who cannot be born in order to die. It is
supposed that they are waiting for him to come into being: 'perhaps
that's all they're waiting for . . . to give me quittance, waiting for me to
say I'm someone, to say I'm somewhere, to put me out, into the silence'
(Beckett, 1958: 173–4).

   Yet this reading of 'they', though often encouraged, is also revoked.
In an important way the chimerical 'they' are identified with the
unnamable. They are pure supposition, there is no evidence for their
reality other than the (admittedly convincing) circumstantial evidence of
the existence of a language which the unnamable knows he has not
invented and which fails to represent him adequately to himself. The
they, which the unnamable posits, are powerless and suffer. His suppositions concerning them amount to stories, and like all his characters,
once they are investigated, they are recognized as impotent and passive.
If they are in an hierarchy above the unnamable then at times it seems
an impossible power-free hierarchy of the impotent and passive, a
pyramid stretching all the way to God, and if, in their impotence, they
come to resemble the unnamable, with the establishing of the resemblance they are recognized as inadequate copies, inadequate to a proper
identification of the unnamable, and disappear (sometimes to reappear).
Such, at one point at least, is the fate of they:

> where are the others, who is talking, not I, where am I, where is the place where
> I've always been, where are the others, it's they are talking, talking to me,
> talking of me, I hear them, I'm mute, what do they want, what have I done to
> them, what have I done to God, what have they done to God, what has God
> done to us, nothing, and we've done nothing to him, you can't do anything to
> him, he can't do anything to us, we're innocent, he's innocent, it's nobody's
> fault . . . I can't go on, poor devil, neither can they, let them say what they want,
> give me something to do, something doable to do, poor devils, they can't they
> don't know, they're like me, more and more, no more need of them, no more
> need of anyone, no one can do anything. (Beckett, 1958: 138–9)

This impotence is related to the unnamable's ignorance. All he knows is
the emanation of a voice, perhaps his own, which is trying to say, or

---

[12] This comment seems similar to that of Lacan quoted by David Watson in his book on Beckett,
   'that it is from the Other that I received the very message I transmit' (Watson, 1991: 88).

make him say, that he *is*, trying to make him say 'I' and mean himself, and failing. All he senses is a silent being free of language that cannot be expressed by a language stripped of referent. While the existence of language suggests that there is an other (because while the being that is sensed is itself a being prior to language, the existence of language has preceded his existence), the language palpably fails to express either this other or this being. Perhaps an important element of the problem is the lack of referent other than that imagined by the language. There is no face here, nothing that might not simply speak but express, not simply signify but *be*:

> there must be something else, to go with this grey, which goes with everything
> . . . A face, how encouraging that would be, if it could be a face, every now and
> then, always the same, methodically varying its expressions, doggedly demon-
> strating all a true face can do, without ever ceasing to be recognizable as such
> . . . That would be nice. A presence at last . . . And even should the notion of
> time dawn on his [Worm's] darkness, at this punctual image of the coun-
> tenance everlasting, who could blame him? Involving very naturally that of
> space, they have taken to going hand in hand, in certain quarters, it's safer. And
> the game would be won, lost and won, he'd be somehow suddenly among us,
> among the rendezvous, and people saying, Look at old Worm . . . Fortunately
> it's all a dream. For here there is no face, nor anything resembling one, nothing
> to reflect the joy of living and succedanea, nothing for it but to try something
> else. (105–6)

If we are to state the problem, perhaps crudely, in non-reciprocal terms, then perhaps Beckett and Levinas offset one another, each showing different and apparently (and apparently paradoxically) mutually exclusive aspects of the same relation: where language constitutes, at once, justice (the infinite relation between the same and the other in Levinas) and injustice (the infinite non-relation, or failure to relate, between a shadowy same and an equally shadowy other in Beckett).

THE SAME AS THE OTHER

The game of the same and the other is, in the world of the unnamable's pure (save the crucial impurity of language) consciousness, like all the games here, apparently unplayable, there are too many pieces seemingly missing. And there is little possibility of renouncing and going home. Yet with regard to the same and the other and Derrida's critique of Levinas's critique of Husserl, we have not yet completed one of the most telling moves. The possibility of the same itself involving (paradoxically, *within* finite existence) the infinitely (irreducible) other: 'I hear, somewhere, if all has been said, all this long time, all must have been said, but it's not my turn to know what, to know what I am, where I am, and what I should do to stop being it, to stop being there, that's coherent, so as to be another, no, the same' (Beckett, 1958: 176).

Levinas criticizes Husserl for reducing the other to a phenomenon of the ego: 'by making the other, notably in the *Cartesian Meditations*, the ego's phenomenon, constituted by analogical appresentation on the basis of belonging to the ego's own sphere, Husserl allegedly missed the infinite alterity of the other, reducing it to the same' (Derrida, 1978: 123). Derrida objects that it would be easy to show the pains Husserl takes to respect the alterity of the other. An important point is that Husserl, too, is concerned with describing lived experience and as such he 'is concerned with describing how the other *as other*, in its irreducible alterity, is presented to me. It is presented to me . . . as originary nonpresence' (Derrida, 1978: 123). It is important not to lose sight of that with which *The Unnamable* seems to be concerned, as in this regard it seems at once to turn from and converge with Phenomenology: 'One could neither speak, nor have any sense of the totally other, if there was not a phenomenon of the totally other, or evidence of the totally other as such' (Derrida, 1978: 123).In what sense is there such a phenomenon in *The Unnamable*? The only 'things' or 'objects', the only phenomena, are words, ideas of things. If the commonplace of Beckett studies – that Beckett's book parodies, to a certain extent, Cartesian first philosophy – is accepted, then we should not be so surprised that we are in a realm where all sensation has been suppressed or is being ignored, all sensation other than consciousness, and crucially this is a consciousness which retains language, language which finds itself in the paradoxical situation of being at once other than and constitutive of this consciousness, such a paradox is illustrated by the unnamable who uses words to find himself when those words could only be made from the echoes of the voices of others (which is all he knows): 'Who would ever think, to hear me, that I've never seen anything, never heard anything but their voices' (Beckett, 1958: 50). 'Even if one neither seeks nor is able to thematize the other *of which* one does not speak, but *to whom* one speaks, this impossibility and this imperative themselves can be thematized (as Levinas does) only on the basis of a certain appearance of the other as other for an ego. Husserl speaks of this *system*' (Derrida, 1978: 123). In *The Unnamable* there is no phenomenon of the other, but for *a system*, which (as Derrida suggests here) is all phenomena itself is able to constitute. The implication (which Derrida does not state so unequivocally) is that the face only communicates in relation to a system, that *it* is not what is expressed to the same, rather it is what is *signified*. The world as it is presented to me, the world of other as other, the world of phenomena, is always mediated, is always signified, a kind of language.

The otherness of language is stressed in *The Unnamable*, and here Beckett seems very close to Derrida: language is the relation to/of originary non-presence and this non-presence moves symmetrically (to/of) between the same and the other. Language carries with it the trace of the other even where (in the Cartesian supposition of a consciousness in language but divorced from sensation) there is no phenomenon of the other. Furthermore, though other, language is used as an instrument to define the self or the same (to which language bears no 'natural' relation). As language can describe only through signifying rather than being, it cannot bring the same into true present being, only to a non-presence always at one remove from a 'true presence' that can only ever be 'sensed' (with this intuition itself constituting a sensation which is a phenomenon that can only signify):

> I'll soon know if the other is still after me. But even if he isn't nothing will come of it, he won't catch me, I won't be delivered from him, I mean Worm, I swear it, the other never caught me . . . I am he who will never be caught, never delivered, who crawls between the thwarts, towards the new day . . . The third line falls plumb from the skies, it's for her majesty my soul, I'd have hooked her on it long ago if I knew where to find her. That brings us up to four, gathered together. I knew it, there might be a hundred of us and still we'd lack the hundred and first, we'll always be short of me. (Beckett, 1958: 71–2)

According to Derrida, in Husserl others are other egos, other subjects who can experience me just as I experience them. The appearance of the other as 'that which I can never be', which Derrida calls an 'originary non-phenomenality', is that which Husserl examines through the concept of the ego's *intentional phenomenon* (Derrida, 1978: 123). Through this intentional phenomenon, 'the other appears as other, and lends itself to language, *to every possible language*' (125). In *The Unnamable* no other subjects appear. But might there not be said to be an originary non-phenomenality here in the realization that I can never be identical to language (which carries the trace of the other which has lent itself to that language)?

For Derrida Levinas seeks to show that the other is not only an alter
ego but also, and most importantly 'what I myself am not' (Derrida,
1978: 125). Husserl, on the other hand, talks of the other only as alter
ego, another ego which is like my ego in that it is other to other egos:
'The other as alter ego signifies the other as other, irreducible to my ego,
precisely because it is an ego, because it has the form of the ego. The
egoity of the other permits him to say "ego" as I do; and this is why he is
Other, and not a stone, or a being without speech *in my real economy*'
(Derrida, 1978: 125). In *The Unnamable* it seems that the concept 'ego' is
inherent in the language, in the words which pass through the unnamable, but he seems to feel that this ego does not correspond to the silent
self present at the core of his being. The unnamable senses that the ego
proper to these words, this language, is the ego or the egos of others, and
thus supposes the existence of 'they'.

The same problem leads also to a somewhat different supposition, a
somewhat different description of what *may be*. Towards the end of *The
Unnamable* the idea is put forward of a double at the core of self, a double
ego, a pair of alter egos within the absent ego of the unnamable, a
doubling which in effect prevents the being-present of the absent ego. At
one pole there is 'he whose voice it is', the one who speaks through the
unnamable:

he speaks of me, as if I were he, as if I were not he, both, and as if I were others
. . . it's he who speaks, he says it's I, then he says it's not . . . he wants me to be he,
or another . . . I nearly believed him, do you hear him, as if he were I, I who am
far, who can't move can't be found, but neither can he, he can only talk, if that
much, perhaps it's not he, perhaps it's a multitude, one after another, what
confusion. (Beckett, 1958: 163–4)

It is important to note that even the one who speaks is plagued by
aporia, an aporia which is at the heart of language, an aporia which, in
language's efforts to unravel itself, thinking that it can, leads to confusion.

At the other pole is the being who is far, the absentee, he who 'is made
of silence' just as his double is 'made of words': 'he is made of silence . . .
he's in the silence, he's the one to be sought, the one to be, the one to be
spoken of, the one to speak, but he can't speak, then I could stop, I'd be
he, I'd be the silence' (177). What is sought is the impossible reconciliation of the irreducible alterity of the same. The task is to get the one
who is, by definition, 'silence' to speak, to enunciate the silence he is,
thereby merging with his double who is the one who speaks; to convert

the originary non-presence inherent in the other within the self into a complete self-presence. That such a reconciliation is impossible implies a break with Levinas, for whom the same is the same and the absolutely other by definition has no part in this same. That the same itself contains alterity, otherness, in any sense where that term has sense, is a position Derrida's reading tends towards:

> the expression 'infinitely other' or 'absolutely other' cannot be stated and thought simultaneously; that the other cannot be absolutely exterior to the same without ceasing to be other; and that, consequently, the same is not a totality closed in upon itself, an identity playing with itself, having only the appearance of alterity, in what Levinas calls economy, work, and history. How could there be a 'play of the Same' if alterity itself was not already *in* the Same, with a meaning of inclusion doubtless betrayed by the word *in*? (Derrida, 1978: 127)

A BEING-AT-WAR: LANGUAGE AND VIOLENCE

Between the two poles of the supposed double ego we find a being-at-war. Derrida discusses an analogous war in relation to Levinas and his discussion of the concepts of 'violence' and 'nonviolence'. Derrida notes that Levinas acknowledges a debt to Eric Weil, for his identification of the opposition between discourse and violence. Simply put, a certain sort of discourse is non-violence, and violence is the moving away from this discourse. Derrida, however, underlines the radical difference between Weil's and Levinas's conceptions of that which constitutes the proper non-violence of discourse. For Weil, non-violent discourse is identified with the project of ontology, 'Harmony between men will be established by itself if men are not concerned with themselves, but with what is.'[13] The non-violent discourse of ontology, which Derrida suggests is Hegelian at least in style, has infinite coherence as its polarity. For Levinas, on the other hand, this coherence, which hopes to instigate a totality, is violence itself. Ontology is violence itself. For Levinas, it is not coherence but the separation of absolutes (the same and absolutely other, with no attempt to reduce the other to the same) which constitutes non-violent discourse or peace. Therefore Levinas's peace equals Weil's violence and vice versa. For Weil, violence is reduced by the reduction of alterity but for Levinas the reverse is true. For Levinas, coherence is finite and alterity infinite

---

[13] Derrida, 1978: 315, footnote, Derrida quoting Weil.

whereas, for Weil, the opposite is true. 'But for both, only the infinite is
non-violent, and it can be announced only in discourse' (Derrida, 1978:
315).[14] Now, in *The Unnamable*, on the other hand, silence, which in
relation both to Levinas's and Weil's systems comprises 'the worst sort
of violence', is exactly that which the unnamable most avidly seeks.
According to Derrida, Levinas's discourse is in violent opposition to
such silence:

Discourse [although it is itself originally violent] . . . is the least possible
violence, the only way to repress the worst violence, the violence of primitive
and prelogical silence, of an unimaginable night which would not even be the
opposite of day, an absolute violence which would not even be the opposite of
nonviolence; nothingness or pure non-sense. Thus discourse chooses itself
violently in opposition to nothingness or pure non-sense, and, in philosophy,
against nihilism. (Derrida, 1978: 130)

How, then, are we supposed to read the unnamable's desire for
silence? As nothingness, pure non-sense or nihilism? Perhaps, but also
perhaps as a critique of systems of thought which insist that 'justice' is
already latent within the system we have (language), so long as that
system is used in a certain way, driven to a given end (coherence for
Weil, alterity for Levinas)? Such scepticism is certainly apparent in *The
Unnamable*. According to Derrida:

Speech is doubtless the first defeat of violence, but paradoxically, violence did
not exist before the possibility of speech. The philosopher (man) must speak and
write within this war of light, a war in which he always already knows himself to
be engaged; a war which he knows is inescapable, except by denying discourse,
that is, by risking the worst violence. (Derrida, 1978: 117)

To pose the question again, would the unnamable say that this worst
violence was in fact peace? It is silence the unnamable desires, but it is
not just any silence, 'For it is all very fine to keep silence, but one has also
to consider the kind of silence one keeps' (Beckett, 1958: 28). The silence
he desires may be the seemingly irretrievable silence that is the silence
before speech, the silence before the possibility of violence: 'For he who
has once had to listen will listen always, whether he knows he will never
hear anything again, or whether he does not. In other words . . . silence

---

[14] Derrida's note on the philosophical significance of these diametrically opposed readings of the
same relation should perhaps be noted: 'One should examine the common presuppositions of
this convergence and divergence. One should ask whether the predetermination, common to
these two systems, of violation and of pure logos, and above all, the predetermination of their
incompatibility, refers to an absolute truth, or perhaps to an epoch of the history of thought, the
history of Being' (1978: 315).

once broken will never again be whole' (Beckett, 1958: 110). Once speech has appeared could there ever be a return to such silence, an impossible return to the before which would erase the after through which that before has returned to being? 'Is there then no hope? Good gracious, no heavens, what an idea! Just a faint one perhaps, but which will never serve' (Beckett, 1958: 110). The being of silence, too, is a centreless being. It is no more self-identical than the being of language. There are varying kinds of silence, one could speak of a violent silence, a silence which resides in speech, a silence of speaking and saying nothing as words course through a being, words that do not belong to him and so fail to break his silence when breaking this silence is exactly what is required, perhaps, to end the torment: 'In their shoes I'd be content with my knowing what I know, I'd demand no more of me than to know that what I hear is not the innocent and necessary sound of dumb things constrained to endure, but the terror-stricken babble of the condemned to silence' (Beckett, 1958: 94).

Looked at this way we return to paradox, which seems at the heart of the matter. In *The Unnamable*, paradoxically, language, without which violence would not have been brought into existence, provides the only possibility of achieving the impossible telos (which is not a telos, an end which comes before the beginning an end which would erase both beginning, and the end). In *The Unnamable*, too, language might be related to justice through this movement between this beginning and this end, which, while destined to fail, provides the closest approximation to a gesture which would recover that which is both before the beginning and after the end (another between).

THE BETWEEN I : THE STEP NOT BEYOND

The effort to move towards this between[15] of before the beginning and after the end (which doubles the between of silence and language) might be compared with Blanchot's notion of *le pas au-delà* ('the step not beyond'). The word 'pas' means 'step' and 'not' at once, *le pas*

---

[15] Chambers establishes a dualism between (eternal) essence and (finite) existence; stating that Beckett's characters exist between (1965: 152–7). Hill's work on Beckett is particularly impressive where it deals with sexual difference, which he conceptualizes through reference to 'the neuter', a between (1990: 34). Still more relevant here is Steven Connor's description of the voice of the unnamable as a between: 'it is very difficult to speak of the voice as existing anywhere but in the movement of play between the different versions of itself – or in the action of repetition itself rather than in what is being repeated. This sense of being-between is itself dramatized by the voice' (Connor, 1988: 76–7).

au-delà, then, is a step beyond which at the same time is not beyond, an impossible movement 'beyond' an infinity, a step taken and erased at once. How can there be a movement beyond all Being? In discussing Giordano Bruno's cosmology, Alexandre Koyré describes Bruno's interpretation of Aristotle's notion of space: 'We can pretend, as Aristotle does, that this world encloses all being, and that outside this world there is nothing; *nec plenum nec vacuum* [neither plenum nor vacuum].[16] But nobody can think, or even imagine it' (Koyré, 1957: 47). Bruno's criticism of Aristotle involves the repetition of 'the classical objection: what would happen if somebody stretched his hand through the surface of heaven?' While Koyré contends that the question itself should not be posed as it involves a misunderstanding of Aristotle's concept of the 'place-continuum', he suggests that nevertheless Bruno gives 'a nearly correct answer'. He goes on to quote Bruno: "BURCHIO – Certainly I think that one must reply to this fellow that if a person would stretch out his hand beyond the convex sphere of heaven, the hand would occupy no position in space, nor any place, and in consequence would not exist" (47). What would happen if you threw a spear at the edge of the Infinity? Would it simply fall at your feet? How can there be a beyond of a system which defines the limits of what you might know? For Spinoza, to talk of a threshold to the absolutely infinite would be nonsensical, the absolutely infinite is that which, by definition, has no threshold. There is, however, finite existence within this infinite existence, finite modes which exist as modifications of the absolutely infinite substance, and it is of this finite existence that creatures such as ourselves partake. We are modes. We may exist outside time as essences and are modifications of the infinite substance of God which is itself eternal, but we have duration. The question becomes one concerning the relation of the finite to the infinite. The question of threshold concerns the threshold between the finite and the infinite, duration and eternity. Duration is that which concerns time, beginnings and endings, whereas eternity is conceived outside time, time has no meaning in the eternal which 'cannot be explained by duration or time, even though the duration is conceived as wanting beginning and end' (*Ethics*, Part I, Def. 8, Explanation). For finite beings the threshold between the finite and infinite is non-life: either pre-existence or death. The before the beginning or after the end which equates to the be-

---

[16] Earlier in this book, Koyré, describing the development of seventeenth-century conceptualizations of the nature of the universe, alludes to the ancient 'struggle between the "plenists" and the "vacuists"' (Koyre, 1957: 3).

yond. The step not beyond time, the threshold, is a gesture of pure undecidability, an irreducible undecidability which might be related to an understanding of 'infinity' as Levinas seems to use the term in referring to the irreducible difference between the same and the absolutely other. The step not beyond is a beyond all beginnings and endings which have no meaning outside time. Such a step is impossible, but in a specific sense. It is not impossible to take, in fact it is a condition of being, or rather a condition *for* being, because being (as finite, modal existence, that which has an essence which does not involve existence) follows from Being (the absolutely infinite substance whose essence involves existence: (*Ethics*, Part 1, Props. 22–7)), the finite follows from the infinite: therefore we must all take a step beyond the beginning and the end. The step is impossible in that it is impossible for us (who are not beyond) to *know*. The step is impossible in that it is impossible for us to *be* in this beyond, as being with a small *b* is finite being and to step beyond is to leave the finite.

The Unnamable has traditionally been read as a narrative from beyond death. This novel, insofar as the three novels under study here comprise a Trilogy, follows, of course, *Malone Dies*. But while this reading is valid to an extent, it is important to note that the beyond death here is not beyond, it involves language, consciousness, it is tied to being and lived experience (stories, imagination too, are lived experience, it might even be argued they comprise the large part of lived experience). The narrative of the unnamable is a narrative of the threshold, the undecidable threshold, but it is clearly situated (and could only be situated) before that threshold (that is, before any 'befores' or 'afters' cease to have meaning). For this reason a reading of *The Unnamable* simply as an after-death narrative is inadequate as being before the threshold might be related with equal validity to life as to life after death (the notion of life after death being a useful dramatic convenience). The narrative still involves and concerns language and time, but it also involves a trying to kick free of these things, and in this it seems close to Blanchot's notion of a step that has and has not been taken:

Time, time: the step not beyond that is not accomplished in time would lead outside of time, without this outside being intemporal, but there where time would fall, fragile fall, according to this 'outside of time in time' towards which writing would attract us, were we allowed, having disappeared from ourselves, to write within the secret of the ancient fear. (Blanchot, 1992: 1)

THE BETWEEN 2: POLES

There are still other thresholds and others not beyond. Proceeding by pure supposition, one of the strategies the unnamable uses in encountering paradox (which might be said to resemble the structure of the limit or threshold) is by defining poles, extreme possibilities between which (with this between standing in for the beyond, this between itself a kind of 'not beyond') the truth might somehow fall, only because everything should fall into the category of this between. The structure of 'between' as a kind of 'not beyond' is important in Beckett's work. In *Molloy*, Molloy and Moran might be said to form two poles, Molloy is one attempting to exist outside of society, outside therefore the laws of society, while Moran is one attempting to exist within society through being an agent of the law of that society. Molloy's narrative might be said to describe a movement back within (he is looking for his mother and is narrating at the behest of others) which constitutes a kind of escape, and Moran's narrative might be said to describe an attempt at capture (the capture of Molloy) which constitutes a kind of expulsion (Moran's). Expulsion and escape: the between of each of the characters might be read as different views of the same process. *Malone Dies* describes a process of dying. Between life and death, taken as poles of finite existence comes living or, without splitting hairs, dying. Dying is a kind of being-towards-death if you like, a between. *The Unnamable* might be read as a different look at a problem similar to that encountered in *Malone Dies*, with the finite existence, or life, read as a between the infinite (pre-finite existence and post-finite existence, if we consider the infinite as in-finite).

This between should not be confused with the synthesis of Hegelian dialectic[17] (if synthesis is understood as involving a kind of reconciliation implying the production of a more or less durable truth). The between cannot be fixed: it is aligned with aporia, the question mark of the question, with non-presence. Rather, the process might be compared to a reading of Derrida's deconstruction. The strategy seems to involve the reading of a text and finding a reading which is 'other' to and contradictory of the self-identical authorized meaning, or intended meaning of the original.[18] *Différance* is, in part, the play between these two readings,

---

[17] For a sustained comparison of Beckett's works to Hegelian dialectic see Schulz, 1973, and Butler, 1984.
[18] In 'Tympan', Derrida discusses the deconstructive process of questioning the idea of the limit and suggests that this 'implies that the text ... functions as a writing machine in which a certain

these two polarities of meaning. The deconstructive reading, then, would still contain the trace of the authorized reading and vice versa.

An example of this use of poles might be found in the stories of Mahood and Worm, the 'anti-Mahood' (82). Mahood is Basil before he is Mahood, Basil, who tells the unnamable things about himself wishing the latter to believe that this self is the unnamable's self. Basil belongs with 'they' and then becomes Mahood whose story is recited by the unnamable sometimes using the first person. Mahood's first incarnation exemplifies a notion of circular (impossible) telos. Mahood presses on (towards a goal?), but his course is curved not straight, and so describes a spiral. It is imagined that the spiral covers the whole earth and that Mahood is winding back towards his original point of departure, his place of birth. In one version of events he circles his family, who die of food poisoning while awaiting his return; he continues however, winding in ever-tighter circles as he enters the house, treading the rotting corpses of his relatives underfoot as he winds in to the end of the spiral before springing back out and returning to his journey in the opposite direction. This story might be said to describe the spiral as a between of the notions of time expressed as a straight line or arrow, and time as a circle. The spiral might be read as a synthesis of the circle and the straight line. If such is the case, it should be noted that this dialectical spiral is not allowed to stand. Mahood's story is later modified so that it is claimed he has never left the island where he was born, and that he moved in aimless loops rather than a spiral, a modification which seems to sabotage any attempt to extract meaning, dialectical or not, from the earlier story.

Mahood next reappears in a jar on the street outside a restaurant near a shambles in the rue Brancion, a street around the corner from where Beckett was living while writing this novel.[19] In his former incarnation Mahood lacked an arm and a leg but now all his members but one (the 'virile') are gone; he is a trunk and a head in his jar. The unnamable describes (at times in the first person) Mahood's existence in the jar, and his relationship with Marguerite/Madeleine, the woman who looks after him. After a time, however, he begins to wonder why no one other than she acknowledges his existence. He should be a curiosity but he is

number of typed and systematically enmeshed propositions (one has to be able to recognize and isolate them) represent the "conscious intention" of the author as a reader of his "own" text, in the sense we speak today of a mechanical reader' (1986: xi).

[19] Cf. *Paris par Arrondissement*, for rue Brancion, in the 15ème arrondissement. The street runs on to rue des Favorites, where Beckett lived (cf. Bair, 1990, Knowlson, 1996, Cronin, 1996).

ignored by passers-by. Accordingly he begins to doubt his own existence, and Marguerite/Madeleine too begins to doubt until finally she
loses her faith in Mahood completely. While Levinas suggests that the
same is incapable of apostasy with regard to its self ([n.d.]: 37), Mahood
too loses faith and stops existing, at least for the unnamable.

The stories of Mahood and Worm might be said to describe loosely
two philosophical poles: Idealism and Materialism. The story of Mahood in his jar might be read as a parable following the ideas of Beckett's
compatriot, Bishop Berkeley. Beckett was later to use Berkeley's most
famous premise *Esse est percipi* (to be is to be perceived) as a point of
departure for his screenplay *Film* (Beckett, 1990b: 323).[20] To be is to be
perceived: once Mahood feels himself no longer perceived he disap-
pears: a state of matter is reduced to a state of mind. But this disappearance suggests that Mahood has no self-perception, that the state of mind
of this same is not his own state of mind but that of others; Mahood stops
existing because 'they' no longer believe in him, not because he no
longer believes in himself. To this extent he is like Worm: 'Worm is,
since we conceive him, as if there could be no being but being conceived' (82). Neither the Idealism nor the Materialism is pure, then, but the
opposition seems clear enough.

At an opposite pole to Mahood, Worm is a materialist being. His is a
state of mind reduced to a state of matter, he is pre-conscious being, a
thing, a creature that sleeps, pure matter without mind, pure matter
which has mind brutally branded upon it. Worm begins life as 'pupil
Mahood', a blank slate 'they' attempt to inscribe with language. Between these two poles, Mahood and the anti-Mahood, comes the
unnamable, just as he comes between silence and language, the same
and the other, the inside and the outside:

perhaps that's what I feel, an outside and an inside and me in the middle,
perhaps that's what I am, the thing that divides the world in two, on the one
side the outside, on the other the inside, that can be as thin as foil, I'm neither
one side nor the other, I'm in the middle, I'm the partition, I've two surfaces
and no thickness, perhaps that's what I feel, myself vibrating, I'm the tympanum, on the one hand the mind, on the other the world, I don't belong to
either. (134)[21]

---

[20] Gilles Deleuze has dedicated an essay to this piece in *Critique et Clinique*, and Watson has done an
interesting reading of this work in relation to Lacan in regard to voices and the Other (Watson,
1991: 87–92).
[21] Mary Bryden cites this passage in arguing for an alternative reading to the one given here, a
proximity between the unnamable and Deleuze and Guattari's Body without Organs (Bryden,
1993: 60).

Such a between, such a 'middle' might also be read as a dialectical synthesis. But the between of the unnamable cannot be fixed, it is its elusive nature, its relation to originary non-presence which allows it to stand in for the beyond. The idea of being a middle, a fixed (or dialectical) between is quickly dismissed. The above quote continues:

it's not to me they're talking, it's not of me they're talking, no, that's not it, I feel nothing of all that, try something else, herd of shites, say something else, for me to hear, I don't know how, for me to say, I don't know how. (134)

LANGUAGE AS THE LAW

If discourse is originally violent (in order to quell the worst violence of silence), does it then fundamentally involve control? Is it possible to distinguish between language used by a given discourse to tend towards the achievement of a given end and language as a system that will always exceed such control, will always carry within it the possibility of a justice distinct from law? In his essay 'Critique of Violence' (an essay discussed by Derrida in 'Force of Law'), Walter Benjamin distinguishes two types of violence which are necessarily related to the law. First there is founding violence, the originary moment of violence through which a regime authorizes its right to lay down laws. Such a moment of founding violence might be a general strike or revolution, for example, or an invasion. A second function for violence with regard to the law is the violence which conserves the law; for example, the privation of liberty, or the death penalty: punishment, in short. A between which complicates this polarity is the police, who comprise aspects of founding violence and conserving violence, and thereby can themselves be outside or above the law while still being 'the law' (Benjamin, 1971: 132) – as police are sometimes called in American movies. If discourse is originally violent, then, is it nothing less than 'the law'?

For Levinas, language, the 'relation' between the same and the other which is justice, is just because it involves the infinite difference of the same and the other, an opening towards the other which also involves a recognition of the other's absolute otherness. What makes language just, then, is its very inability to achieve complete identification: the other can never be contained by language, can never be delivered to the same by language, there is an originary irreducible distance between language and its object and this justly represents the originary irreducible difference between the same and the other. The relation between the same and the other is justice, and language, which constitutes this relation, is just because it is a just representation unless it is distorted through violence (a discourse of coherence, for example) which would have it forget itself by falsely allowing the same to reappropriate the other within a totality.

What also seems to be involved in Levinas's concept of language as justice, is the relation of justice to presence, the present. In *Spectres de Marx*, Derrida discusses justice in relation to *Hamlet*, examining Hamlet's comment that 'the time is out of joint' and he must set it right with regard to a notion of justice (equated with a time that is not out of joint, is not all wrong, but just as it should be). Examining the notion of time being out of joint Derrida turns to Heidegger.[22] To simplify: in the flux of time, the future rushes through the present into the past, we understand time as broken into segments, but, Heidegger asks, 'Where is there a single join (*nur eine Fuge*)? How can the present (*das Anwesende*) be without join, *adikon*, that is to say, disjointed (*aus des Fuge*)?' (quoted in Derrida, 1993: 51).

And Derrida responds:

Is that to say 'out of joint'? Because one can translate Heidegger, reader of Anaximander, in the language of Hamlet . . . Does the *Spruch* of Anaximander signify that the presence of the present, the *eon* of the *eonta* belong to the *adikia*, disjointure, which is usually translated, as it is by Nietzsche in this case, by injustice (*Ungerechtigkeit*)? (Derrida, 1993: 51)[23]

---

[22] For a sustained comparison of Beckett's works to Heidegger's ontology see Butler, 1984.
[23] That the concept of time broken into segments appears in Beckett's work has been clearly demonstrated by Steven J. Rosen in *Samuel Beckett and the Pessimistic Tradition*. Rosen remarks that the pattern which emerges in Beckett's works is an insistence on time, but also a slowing down of time, as if from a wish to take life instant by instant (1976: 174). A necessary consequence of this temporal 'atomism' is void; because there must be something – that is, nothing – between these discrete moments. This vision entails a discontinuity of personal being (181). That is, a being is not whole or continuous, because a being is a different entity at each moment. If there is no continuous being, there is no continuous self. Rosen goes on to note that Beckett's 'atomism' follows the tradition of Descartes, who resolves this dilemma by deducing a continuous creation. This is a short step from the 'Occasionalism' of Malebranche and Geulincx whose doctrine maintains that God must 'create us anew' at every instant of existence (Rosen, 1976: 182). We are merely an occasion through which God might exercise His omnipotence: He holds the discord of the discontinuous being together. He creates us (and so our sense of self) at every moment. Rosen suggests that, as Beckett cannot turn to God to resolve the problem of personal continuity, he turns instead to 'habit'. In *Proust*, Beckett states: 'Habit is a compromise effected between the individual and his environment . . . the guarantee of a dull inviolability, the lightning-conductor of his existence. Habit is the ballast that chains the dog to its vomit . . . Breathing is Habit. Life is habit. Or rather life is a succession of habits, since the individual is a succession of individuals' (Beckett, 1987: 18–19). Reading Rosen through Derrida, the point might be made in passing that it could be possible to identify Beckett's concept of 'habit' with the notion of injustice Derrida is developing here. A number of other critics make general mention of Beckett's work in relation to Geulincx's *Ethics*. Perhaps the most sustained and detailed reading to date is that by Rupert Wood.

In *The Unnamable* there seems to be a true between of discourse, a between which allows a double movement between the same and the other, the other involving the same and the same involving the other. An example of this is the between of an irretrievable originary silence (before the beginning) and an impossible full saying of the thing it is necessary to say to allow the emergence of the end; an after the end identical with a before the beginning. This complicated between might be compared, formally at least, to Derrida's *différance*. Derrida himself calls the relation of the same and the other *différance* (1978: 129).

In 'Tympan', the introductory essay to *Margins of Philosophy*, Derrida discusses the notion of philosophy thinking its other (Derrida, 1986: x), suggesting: 'In thinking it as such, in recognizing it, one misses it. One reappropriates it for oneself, one disposes of it, one misses, or rather one misses (the) missing (of) it, which, as concerns the other, always amounts to the same. Between the proper of the other and the other of the proper' (Derrida, 1986: xi–xii). This amounts to Levinas's notion of the totality. This 'Philosophy' (whose limits Derrida is hoping to test and breach) is a totality, a discourse of order, of the law. There seem (at least) two senses in which the idea of limit is understood in Derrida's essay. The limit as that which, by definition, cannot be crossed, that which it is impossible to go beyond (Philosophy as closed system), and the limit as border, the dividing line between an outside and an inside, the border, that is, between two powers which limit each other (Philosophy and non-Philosophy). Derrida asks: 'can one, strictly speaking, determine a nonphilosophical place, a place of exteriority or alterity from which one might still treat of philosophy?' (xii). He speaks of rupturing the tympanum within the ear of the philosopher, the tympanum which is the fixed between of the inside and the outside, and wonders if one can achieve this rupture and still be heard by the philosopher. This tympanum is the fixed between of the dialectic, the totalizing gesture, the gesture of reappropriation and stability of meaning suggested by the synthesis of thesis and antithesis. As I have suggested above, Derrida's strategic approach is altogether different.

Philosophy which fixes order and the law through the founding and conserving violence of its totalizing discourse is unjust. It is unjust because it attempts to say that that is in joint which is in fact 'out of joint', it seeks, in other words, to pass itself off as justice, justice being that (following Derrida's reading of *Hamlet*) which sets time which is out of joint, right. Things are not right, 'the time is out of joint', but Philosophy as dialectic, would have us believe otherwise. The deconstructive response is, firstly, to set *this* injustice right, paradoxically, by putting philosophical discourse out of joint, which cannot be done through direct opposition (which would allow reappropriation by the totality) but only through textual strategy: 'to *luxate* the philosophical ear, to set the *loxos* in the *logos* to work, is to avoid frontal and symmetrical protest, opposition in all the forms of anti-, or in any case to inscribe antism and overturning, domestic denegation, in an entirely other form of ambush, of *lokhos*, of textual maneuvers' (Derrida, 1986: xv).

It is, perhaps, these textual manoeuvres, testing the limits of philosophy, that have led Derrida to seek at times to blur the genre distinction between literary (non-philosophical) and philosophical discourse, a blurring which *The Unnamable* also seems to achieve through its parody of philosophical discourse. In 'Tympan', Derrida develops the metaphor of the philosopher's ear which is equated with understanding, and uses, as we have seen, the tympanum of the ear as a metaphor for a dialectic fixed between. We have quoted above the unnamable's supposition that he may be a tympanum, in the middle, but have also quoted the negation of this affirmation. The tympanum is perhaps a wrong metaphor for the unnamable because he is not a middle, of the beginning-middle-end school, but, rather, a between which is not fixed, at play between one and the other, that which ruptures the middle, putting the stable certainties we are used to associating with being out of joint. A between which resembles Derrida's *différance*:

In the one case 'to differ' signifies nonidentity; in the other case it signifies the order of the same. Yet there must be a common, although entirely differant [*différante*], root within the sphere that relates the two movements of differing to one another. We provisionally give the name *différance* to this *sameness* which is not *identical*: by the silent writing of its *a*, it has the desired advantage of referring to differing, *both* as spacing/temporalizing and as the movement that structures every dissociation. (Derrida, 1973: 129)

LANGUAGE AND A JUST SAYING

It seems that this relation between is part of what Derrida means when he speaks of 'justice'. Yet given that this between is, as Levinas suggests, discourse, how does this notion of 'justice' avoid being contradicted by the violence which, it has been suggested, is necessary to discourse, how is it not contradicted by the being-at-war which also seems inherent in the relation between. One answer might be that language is violent because it has been understood through a totality as Levinas understands it (what Derrida sometimes refers to as Philosophy with a capital *P* and what earlier I have called 'Platonism' or the philosophy of identity), which, as we have seen, privileges *a certain kind* of discourse; the discourse of one meaning. Justice, on the other hand, which Derrida claims in 'Force of Law', *is* Deconstruction,[24] reinstates equivocity, is composed of equivocity. The identification of justice and Deconstruction is complex. In the following quote, the word 'Philosophy' (with a capital *P*, philosophy as a totalizing discourse) might be substituted for the word 'law', as indeed, this Philosophy is a kind of law:

(1) The deconstructibility of law (*droit*), of legality, legitimacy or legitimation (for example) makes deconstruction possible. (2) The undeconstructibility of justice also makes deconstruction possible, indeed is inseparable from it. (3) The result: deconstruction takes place in the interval that separates the undeconstructibility of justice from the deconstructibility of *droit* (authority, legitimacy, and so on). (Derrida, 1990: 945)

The process of deconstruction then (with a lower-case *d*) takes place between law and justice. Deconstruction (with a capital *D*) would be justice were it possible fully to achieve justice. The contradiction inherent in identifying language both with violence and justice might now more easily be untangled: 'At the beginning of justice there was logos, speech or language, which is not necessarily in contradiction to another *incipit*, namely, "in the beginning there will have been force"' (Derrida, 1990: 935). Justice, like capital *D* Deconstruction, has not been achieved, cannot, perhaps, be achieved: it is the experience of the impossible (Derrida, 1990: 947). On the other hand, lower-case *d* deconstruction, which stands in for justice just as the between has been said to stand in for the beyond, involves a more just usage of language (an equivocity). Derrida suggests that there is no contradiction between the originary need to relate to justice through language, and the force or violence inherent in language. He alludes to Pascal in order to suggest that justice has need of force, that there is a practical, pragmatic element at play here, that justice will not be achieved unless it has the force to be enforced, that a powerless justice is injustice (Derrida, 1990: 937). While

---

[24] 'The structure I am describing here is a structure in which law (*droit*) is essentially deconstructible, whether because it is founded, constructed on interpretable and transformable textual strata . . . or because its ultimate foundation is by definition unfounded . . . it is this deconstructible structure of law (*droit*), or if you prefer of justice as *droit*, that also insures the possibility of deconstruction. Justice in itself, if such a thing exists, outside or beyond law, is not deconstructible. No more than deconstruction itself, if such a thing exists. Deconstruction is justice' (Derrida, 1990: 945). 'Deconstruction', here, might be aligned with the philosophies of difference.

equivocal, then, deconstruction cannot be passive, it is an active procedure and involves a free decision, or, if you like, the decision of
freedom. 'We would not say of a being without freedom, or at least of
one without freedom in a given act, that its decision is just or unjust'
(Derrida, 1990: 961). It is here, perhaps, that we might begin to gauge
the extent to which Derrida's concept of justice might be said to be
analogous to ideas apparent in *The Unnamable*.

JUSTICE, FREEDOM AND RESPONSIBILITY

To what extent might it be said that the unnamable is not free? At first
sight he might seem to be totally without freedom. If this were indeed
the case, it would be foolish to attempt to argue that his narrative
involves justice in any way. Derrida suggests that the worst form of
injustice is the (fixed) presence of the present, the life which is fully
present to itself which therefore has no conception of death and no
desire to hear it spoken of: no conception of what is past or what is to
come (Derrida, 1993: 278). According to Derrida, learning how to live
(which is the paradoxical project of any ethics, that is, just dealings with
others) can only take place between life and death. And this between
life and death involves the ghost: justice, that which is equivocal, must
be justice for all, and this all includes the ghostly figures of the not-yet-
born, and the already-dead; there can be no justice without responsibility which goes beyond the present living (Derrida, 1993: 14, 16). The
ghosts of the not-yet-born are felt in the responsibility for the consequences of our actions, consequences that will determine the hospitality of the world into which they will enter. The ghosts of the already
dead are felt in the responsibility for the interpretation of the heritage
they have left us with. We are free to choose, in interpreting, how to
read the heritage these ghosts have left behind them (Derrida, 1993:
21–40), a reading which will affect the world in which we live. A third
kind of ghost is the ghost of ourselves, the not fully present self who
must exist among the traces of the past and the hopes of the future.
The ghost, says Derrida, is a thing, an unnamable thing which watches
us (Derrida, 1993: 26):

If we have insisted so strongly . . . on the logic of the ghost, it is because it
tends towards a thinking of the event which necessarily exceeds a binary or
dialectical logic, that which would distinguish or oppose *effectivity* (present, as it
happens, empirical, living – or not) and *ideality* (regulatory or absolute non-
presence). (Derrida, 1993: 108)

As we have seen, a measure of freedom is necessary to justice. A striving for freedom is a striving for justice. Puppet that he seems, even if despite himself or involuntarily, the unnamable resists 'they'; they are unable to reabsorb him. Such a reabsorption might be compared to the French word *refoulement* (meaning 'repression', especially in a psychological sense), which is derived from *foule* (meaning 'press' or 'crowd'). Repression as reinsertion into the crowd: the molar crowd as totality, the fixed presence.

Tenuously, the situation of the unnamable might be said to exemplify a striving for justice. This is, however, by no means the only way that Derrida's 'justice' might be seen to be relevant to *The Unnamable*. As I have hoped to show above, the work in its entirety might be seen as a critique of the idea of full self-presence, the presence of the present which Derrida sees as the worst injustice. The similarity of Beckett's 'between' and Derrida's *différance*, I would hope, is also clear enough. The importance of this relation within deconstruction is well known, and the relation of deconstruction to justice has been sketched above. There seems, however, an important moment at which *The Unnamable* at once converges most closely with and verges away from Derrida's description of justice.

I noted at the beginning of this chapter how the 'methodology' of *The Unnamable* seems based on aporia. In beginning his essay 'Force of Law', a paper written in response to a request to address a conference calling itself *Deconstruction and the Possibility of Justice*, Derrida notes that the problems covered by this title are infinite. They are infinite in themselves, he suggests, 'because they require the very experience of the aporia'. By this, he says, he means two complicated things:

(1) As its name indicates, an experience is a traversal, something that traverses and travels towards a destination for which it finds the appropriate passage. The experience finds its way, its passage, it is possible. And in this sense it is impossible to have a full experience of aporia, that is, of something that does not allow passage. An aporia is a non-road. From this point of view, justice would be the experience that we are not able to experience . . . But, (2) I think that there is no justice without this experience, however impossible it may be, of aporia. Justice is an experience of the impossible. (Derrida, 1990: 947)

In addressing the question of language – which, as we have seen, is the relation between law and justice, the same and the other, the outside and the inside – critically, testing its limits through suspicion, aporia, *The Unnamable* might be said to be among the most detailed of all possible descriptions of the impossible. The impossible of *le pas au-delà,* the beyond of all these betweens. But to what extent is it a description of the *experience* of the impossible?[25] Despite or perhaps because of its methodology, the ghostly unnamable becomes irreducible, finds perhaps an irreducible seed of being which is pure ignorance and incomprehension. If such a discovery were possible, it might be claimed that the unnamable has found that stable cornerstone with which he might rebuild the universe in the likeness of himself: all interfused with pure incomprehension. But such a discovery is not possible, and it is the very insistence on this impossibility which might be said to be that through which Beckett's work is most just, most effectively a process of justice. The self is shown to be unfixable, other to itself, without core or cornerstone. Rather than accepting the same as simply self-identical, Beckett does justice to the complexity of the same, to the infinitely other within the same, and in this sense the justice he expresses is universal. The self-presence of Philosophy as totality, the presence of the present it insists upon, which Derrida considers the greatest injustice, is shattered. The resistance of the unnamable, at first sight feeble, is revealed as one of extraordinary power. It is resistance to the entire discourse of self-presence.

Yet the unnamable as pure consciousness, which itself is revealed as pure aporia, remains on the level of abstraction. *The Unnamable* is a strong critique but it does not attempt, as Derrida does, to relate this abstraction to a thinking of the *différance* between law and justice in an effort to identify a justice beyond law, a justice therefore, marked by and including law. Because of this, it might seem that this concept of justice is one that might most easily be brought to Beckett from Derrida.

Yet that Beckett was aware of the specific question of justice (an ideal justice not related to human law) might be supported with reference to his 1962 piece for theatre, *Play.* A man and two women are shown up to their necks in three jars. Both women have been lovers of the man, a situation which has caused suffering to all. The play is a kind of process of justice: but it is an aporia, a non-road, and it is not traversed. Each of the three speaks when a light of interrogation shines in his or her face; at times they all speak at once. The structure of the play suggests

---

[25] Such an 'experience' does seem to resemble that famously described by Beckett in *Three Dialogues with Georges Duthuit:* 'The situation is that of him who is helpless, cannot act, in the event cannot paint, since he is obliged to paint. The act is of him who, helpless, unable to act, acts, in the event paints, since he is obliged to paint' (Beckett, 1987: 119).

that they may go on forever, each repeating from their particular point of view the story of their relations, each attempting to expurgate his or her own guilt. At one point the man M says, 'I know now, all that was just . . . play. And all this? When will all this – [. . .] All this, when will all this have been . . . just play?' (Beckett, 1990b: 313).[26] In 'Structure, Sign, Play', Derrida describes an oscillation between (which formally resembles *différance*, justice) as 'play' (1978: 289–93). The answer to M's question may be 'never', that 'play' will be 'just play' (pure enjoyment, play alone and the play of justice) when it is infinite play: the telling of the whole story, all stories at once. Again here we have an aporia, and this, for Beckett, may be equated with justice. But Derrida is talking of a legal justice: the production of a decision as just as possible and as aware as possible of its own injustice: that is, the *experience* of aporia. Derrida suggests that the undecidable is not merely the oscillation between two contradictory or determinate rules, but the obligation to decide, to make the impossible decision while taking account of laws and rules, suggesting 'A decision that didn't go through the ordeal of the undecidable would not be a free decision' (Derrida, 1990: 963). 'Law is the element of calculation, and it is just that there be law, but justice is incalculable, it requires us to calculate with the incalculable; and aporetic experiences are the experiences, as improbable as they are necessary, of justice' (947).

To what extent might Beckett be said to make this calculation? To what extent might he be said to deal with rules and make the undecidable decision? Derrida makes such a decision in choosing, against the time, to read Marx in a certain way so as to develop a critique of the New World Order. Perhaps Beckett makes it, in the thoroughly ideologically polarized world of 1951 in choosing not to choose, in choosing the grey rather than the black or the white. But this does nothing (though this is a crucial nothing), perhaps, but show us the aporia and bring us to the threshold of calculation without calculating, of decision, without deciding. Where Derrida speaks of the experience of aporia, Beckett speaks simply of aporia. Where Derrida speaks of the ghost in its relations to the living, Beckett gives voice to the ghost. Where Derrida confronts a world in which to act, Beckett contemplates acts without worlds. At his greater level of abstraction, Beckett can lead us through a maze of language and allude to a threshold, but it cannot be crossed because there is nothing with which to cross, nothing to cross.

---

[26] The ellipses are Beckett's and do not indicate omissions, except those within square brackets, which indicate an omission I have made from the text.

We may have been taken to the edge of the universe but there is no spear to throw, no hand to stretch through the surface of heaven which encloses the unnamable like a wall, no way of telling if we are facing a void or its opposite. Nor any way of confirming the Aristotelian suggestion, 'that outside this world there is nothing; *nec plenum nec vacuum*':

may not this screen which my eyes probe in vain, and see as denser air, in reality be the enclosure wall, as compact as lead? To elucidate this point I would need a stick or pole, and the means of plying it . . . Then I would dart it, like a javelin, straight before me and know, by the sound made, whether that which hems me round, and blots out my world, is the old void, or a plenum. (Beckett, 1958: 16–17)

Conclusion

THE SHAPE OF IDEAS

It is worth briefly summarizing again the aim of each chapter before further indicating some of the book's global concerns. Chapter 1 describes how *Molloy*, when considered in counterpoint with other works of history and philosophy which approach the same questions, might help us to think through problems of freedom and surveillance; problems which were thrown into sharp relief in France by the virtual civil war experienced by the French in and around World War Two. Chapter 2 shows how order and chaos exist in inclusive disjunction, and how Beckett's works add to a tradition of thinking around the problematic of this interaction. Chapter 3 indicates how a crisis of the moral order came to the fore in the France of the 1940s; a crisis that is reflected in the novels Beckett wrote towards the end of this decade. Chapter 4 argues how, both in drawing upon certain traditions of Western thought and in response to the crisis discussed in the preceding chapter, the notion of judgement itself is brought into question by *Malone Dies* and the kinds of ethics developed by Deleuze and Guattari. Chapter 5 describes how stories affect and actualize the real, and how the totalizing stories of the leader might be contrasted with the openness of the narratives of the translator. And finally, chapter 6 deals with questions of justice with its aporias as opposed to the certainties of judgement; showing how these problems are thought in relation to language and the nature of language in Beckett's *The Unnamable* and certain of the works of Derrida and Levinas.

MOMENTS OF REASONING

But there is reasoning somewhere, moments of reasoning, that is to say the same things recur, they drive one another out, they draw one another back. (Beckett, 1984: 100)

A number of things, have been underlined by what has gone before in this book. Chief amongst them is the manner in which literature and philosophy overlap, and how literature might be seen, just as much as philosophy, to offer a penetrating and illuminating way of thinking about the world.

Firstly, literature and philosophy intersect and overlap because they emerge at specified times and in specified places: they are touched not only by other texts, but by contexts; not only by the discursive formations Foucault describes (cf. Foucault, 1989) but by the non-discursive milieux which enter into correspondence with these texts (cf. Deleuze, 1988a). Accordingly, they encounter the same sets of problems, and these problems determine the kinds of questions that need to be asked at a given time and place. The writer of fiction encounters the problems through the creation of sensations which are in response to those problems and go beyond them, while the writer of philosophy encounters the problems through the creation of concepts which also emerge in response to those problems. Yet the writer and the philosopher can and do connect with one another, as the writer creates sensations of concepts and the philosopher concepts of sensations.

Secondly, while the works of the writer of fiction and the philosopher clearly emerge from separate traditions, these traditions are not fully closed, so that the writer might be (and clearly was in Beckett's case) influenced by some of the traditions of philosophy, just as the philosopher might be influenced by literary forms and traditions (as were Derrida and Deleuze and Guattari, for example). Further, for this reason the manner of thinking of a writer of fiction might intersect with that of a philosopher and vice versa, insofar as they have encountered aspects of the same traditions, which they, at the same time, both contribute to and deform.

Thirdly, considering works of literature and philosophy together is useful insofar as the two resonate with one another in such a way that each sheds light on the other. Resonance of any sort is never simply accidental, because it announces the sorts of patterns with which we are able to attempt to make sense of things, both in works of fiction and the world at large. This phenomenon of resonance through counterpoint is sufficient in itself to justify the comparison of works of literature and philosophy; particularly if the work of literature is understood to be, as I argue in the introduction, a being of sensation, with a life of its own which necessarily varies as it encounters new ideas, new readers, new times.

Finally, all of this underlines how literature can be a powerful way of thinking, one which differs from philosophy, but which is also able to add to our understanding of the major questions which emerge from that discipline, which, like the discipline of art, concern Being and knowing; what it is to exist and what we can and cannot understand. Beckett's works not only shed light upon these questions in general, but also offer a way into thinking about certain tendencies of contemporary thought (called 'poststructuralism', for convenience); tendencies which clearly have not fallen from the sky, but which emerge from traditions that continue to mutate in answer to the problems of the moment. And, by the same token, these philosophical ways of thinking shed light on Beckett's works.

This book underlines how Samuel Beckett, as much as any contemporary philosopher, has contributed to on-going efforts to think through the problems of contemporary existence; offering us, in the manner of the artist (and certain philosophers who take their lead from such artists), an overview of the field rather than fixed solutions or plans of action. Furthermore, the ramifications of Beckett's ideas – which are expressed as sensations – still need to be further thought through. For in turning to these works one is able to both find insight into our present condition and more than an inkling of the terms in which it might be thought again.

References

Acheson, James. 1993. '*Murphy*'s Metaphysics'. *The Beckett Studies Reader*. Ed. S. E. Gontarski. Gainesville: University of Florida Press. 78–93.

Adorno, Theodor W. 1988. 'Trying to Understand *Endgame*'. *Modern Critical Interpretations: Samuel Beckett's 'Endgame'*. Ed. Harold Bloom. New York: Chelsea House. 9–40.

Alvarez, A. 1974. *Beckett*. London: Woburn Press.

The Architecture of Doom [Architektur des Untergangs]. 1989. Prod., Dir. and Script, Peter Cohen. Narrator, Bruno Gantz. POJ Filmproduktion/ AB Filminstitutet/Sveriges Television Kanal 1/Sandrew Film and Teater AB.

Artaud, Antonin. 1976. *To Have Done with The Judgement of God*. In *Selected Writings*. Trans. Helen Weaver, ed. Susan Sontag. New York: Farrar, Straus and Giroux.

Asmus, Walter D. 1975. 'Beckett Directs Godot'. *Theatre Quarterly*, 5.19. 19–26.

Astro, Alan. 1990. *Understanding Samuel Beckett*. Columbia: University of South Carolina Press.

Bair, Deirdre, ed. 1990 *Samuel Beckett: A Biography*. London: Vintage.

Barale, Michèle Aina, and Rubin Rabinovitz. 1988. *A KWIC Concordance to Samuel Beckett's Trilogy:* Molloy, Malone Dies, *and* The Unnamable. Volumes I and II. New York: Garland.

Beckett, Samuel, 1949. Ts. Letter to Georges Duthuit '9/3/49–10/3/49'. MS 2907: Samuel Beckett Collection, University of Reading. Typescript consulted May 1992. Translations from this source are mine.

1951. *Malone meurt*. Paris: Editions de Minuit.

1953. *L'innommable*. Paris: Editions de Minuit.

1955. *Molloy*. New York: Grove Press.

1956. *Malone Dies*. New York: Grove Press.

1958. *The Unnamable*. New York: Grove Press.

1964. *How It Is*. New York: Grove Press.

ed. 1973. *Murphy*. London: Picador.

1983. *Disjecta: Miscellaneous Writings and Dramatic Fragment*. Ed. Ruby Cohn. London: Calder.

1984a. *Collected Shorter Prose: 1945–1980*. London: Calder.

1984b. Letter to Dr E. Franzen, 17/2/54, cited in 'Babel 3, 1984', [magazine]. MS 2993: Samuel Beckett Collection, University of Reading. Typescript consulted May 1992.

ed. 1987. *Proust and Three Dialogues with Georges Duthuit.* London: Calder.

ed. 1988a. *Mercier and Camier.* London: Picador.

ed. 1988b. *Molloy.* Paris: Editions de Minuit.

1989. *Nohow On.* London: Calder.

1990a. *As The Story Was Told.* London: Calder.

ed. 1990b. *The Complete Dramatic Works.* London: Faber and Faber.

1993. *Dream of Fair to Middling Women.* New York: Arcade–Riverrun.

1995. *The Complete Short Prose.* Edited with notes and an introduction by Stan Gontarski. New York: Grove Press.

1996. *Eleuthéria.* Translated by Barbara Wright. London: Faber and Faber.

Benjamin, Walter. 1971. 'Pour une critique de la violence'. *Oeuvres I: Mythe et violence.* Essais traduits de l'allemand par Maurice Gandilla. Paris: Lettres Nouvelles.

Bennington, Geoffrey, and Jacques Derrida. 1991. *Jacques Derrida.* Paris: Seuil.

Ben-Zvi, Linda. 1986. *Samuel Beckett.* Boston: Twayne.

Bergson, Henri, ed. 1991. *Matter and Memory.* Trans. N. M. Paul and W. S. Palmer. New York: Zone Books.

Bernold, André. 1992a. *L'amitié de Beckett: 1979–1989.* Paris: Hermann. Translations from this source are mine.

1992b. 'Deleuze et Beckett'. Unpublished paper, delivered at the International Symposium, Beckett in the 1990s. The Hague, 8–12 April.

Blanchot, Maurice. 1969. *L'entretien infini.* Paris: Gallimard.

1986. 'Where Now? Who Now?' Trans. Richard Howard. *On Beckett: Essays and Criticism.* Ed. S. E. Gontarski. New York: Grove Press. 141–8.

1992. *The Step Not Beyond.* Translated with an introduction by Lycette Nelson. Albany: State University of New York Press.

Blin, Roger. 1986. *Roger Blin: souvenirs et propos recueillis par Lynda Bellity Peskine.* Paris: Gallimard. Translations from this source are mine.

Bourgeois, Guillaume. 1993. 'Comment Staline dirigeait le PCF'. *Nouvel Observateur,* 1500, 5–11 August. 4–9..

Bourgeois, Guillaume, and Roger Martelli. 1993. 'Nazi–PCF: maintenant on sait tout!' *Nouvel Observateur,* 1497, 15–21 July. 26–8.

Bryden, Mary. 1993. *Women in Samuel Beckett's Prose and Drama: Her Own Other.* Lantham, MD: Barnes and Noble.

Butler, Lance St John. 1984. *Samuel Beckett and the Meaning of Being.* London: Macmillan Press.

Butler, Samuel, ed. 1985. *Erewhon.* Harmondsworth: Penguin.

Céline, Louis-Ferdinand. 1987. *Castle to Castle.* Trans. Ralph Manheim. New York: Carroll and Graf.

Chabert, Pierre. 1980. 'Samuel Beckett as Director'. M. A. Bonney and J. Knowlson. *Theatre Workbook,* volume 1, *Samuel Bekcett: Krapp's Last Tape. A Theatre Workbook.* Ed. James Knowlson. London: Brutus Books. 85–107.

Chambers, Ross. 1965. 'Beckett's Brinkmanship'. *Samuel Beckett: A Collection of Critical Essays*. Ed. Martin Esslin. Englewood Cliffs, NJ: Prentice-Hall. 152–68.

Cioran, E. M. 1992. *Anathemas and Admirations*. Trans. Richard Howard. London: Quartet.

Cluchey, Rick. 1984. Beckett lecture to English Modern Drama Students at the University of Sydney, 4 July. During the 'Beckett Directs Beckett' Sydney Season. Course Lecturer Axel Kruse. Tape held at Fisher Library, University of Sydney.

Cohn, Ruby. 1973. *Back to Beckett*. Princeton: Princeton University Press.

1979. 'Words Working Overtime: Endgame and No Man's Land'. *Yearbook of English Studies*, volume IX. Leeds: Modern Humanities Research Association.

Connor, Steven. 1988. *Samuel Beckett: Repetition, Theory and Text*. Oxford: Basil Blackwell.

1992. 'Beckett in the Face of Levinas'. Unpublished paper delivered at the International Symposium, Beckett in the 1990s. The Hague, 8–12 April.

Cronin, Anthony. 1996. *Samuel Beckett: The Last Modernist*. London: HarperCollins.

Delarue, Jacques. 1992. 'La police'. *Vichy et les Français*. Ed. Jean-Pierre Azéma and François Bédarida. Paris: Fayard. 302–11.

Dearlove, Judith E. 1982. *Accommodating the Chaos: Samuel Beckett's Nonrelational Art*. Durham, NC: Duke University Press.

Deleuze, Gilles. 1983. *Nietzsche and Philosophy*. Trans. Hugh Tomlinson. New York: Columbia University Press.

1986. *Cinema 1: The Movement-Image*. Trans. Hugh Tomlinson and Barbara Habberjam. Minneapolis: University of Minnesota Press.

1988a. *Foucault*. Trans. and ed. Sean Hand. London: Athlone.

1988b. *Spinoza: Practical Philosophy*. Trans. Robert Hurley. San Francisco: City Lights Books.

1990. *The Logic of Sense*. Trans. Mark Lester with Charles Stivale. Ed. Constantin V. Boundas. New York: Columbia University Press.

1993a. *Critique et Clinique*. Paris: Editions de Minuit.

1993b. *The Fold: Leibniz and the Baroque*. Foreword and translation by Tom Conley. Minneapolis: University of Minnesota Press.

1995. 'The Exhausted'. Trans. Anthony Uhlmann. *Substance: A Review of Theory and Literary Criticism*, 24. 3. Number 78. 3–28.

Deleuze, Gilles and Félix Guattari. 1980. *Mille Plateaux*. Paris: Editions de Minuit.

1983. *The Anti-Oedipus: Capitalism and Schizophrenia*. Trans. Robert Hurley, Mark Seem and Helen R. Lane, with a preface by Michel Foucault. Minneapolis: University of Minnesota Press.

1987. *A Thousand Plateaus: Capitalism and Schizophrenia*. Trans. Brian Massumi. Minneapolis: University of Minnesota Press.

1994. *What is Philosophy?* Trans. Hugh Tomlinson and Graham Burchell.

New York: Columbia Uuniversity Press.

Dettmar, Kevin J. H. 1990 'The Figure in Beckett's Carpet: *Molloy* and the Assault on Metaphor'. *Rethinking Beckett*. Ed. Lance St John and Robin J. Davis. London: Macmillan. 68–88.

Derrida, Jacques. 1973. 'Differance'. *Speech and Phenomena and Other Essays on Husserl's Theory of Signs*. Trans. David B. Allison. Evanston: Northwestern University Press. 129–60.

———. 1978. *Writing and Difference*. Translation with introduction and additional notes by Alan Bass. London: Routledge and Kegan Paul.

———. 1981. *Dissemination*. Trans. Barbara Johnson. Chicago: University of Chicago Press.

———. 1986. *Margins of Philosophy*. Trans. Alan Bass. Brighton: Harvester Wheatsheaf.

———. 1990. 'Force of Law'. *Cardozo Law Review*. 11. 5–6 (July/August), 919–1045.

———. 1991b. 'Une "folie" doit veiller sur la pensée"'. Interview with François Ewald. *Magazine Littéraire*, No. 286 (March). 18–30.

———. 1992. '"This Strange Institution Called Literature." An Interview with Jacques Derrida'. With Derek Attridge, Trans. Geoffrey Bennington and Rachel Bowlby. *Acts of Literature*. Ed. Derek Attridge. New York: Routledge. 33-75.

———. 1993. *Spectres de Marx*. Paris: Galilée. Translations from this source are mine.

Descartes, René. 1988. *Selected Philosophical Writings*. Trans. John Cottingham, Robert Stoothoff, and Dugald Murdoch. Cambridge: Cambridge University Press.

Descombes, Vincent. 1980. *Modern French Philosophy*. Trans. L. Scott-Fox and J. M. Harding. Cambridge: Cambridge Uuniversity Press.

Dobrez, L. A. C. 1986. *The Existential and its Exits: Literary and Philosophical Perspectives on the Works of Beckett, Ionesco, Genet, and Pinter*. London: Athlone.

Doherty, Francis. 1971. *Samuel Beckett*. London: Hutchinson University Library.

Dostoyevsky, Fyodor. 1992. *Notes from the Underground*. Trans. Constance Garnett. New York: Dover.

Driver, Tom. F. 1961. 'Beckett by the Madeleine'. *Columbia University Forum*, 4, (Summer). 21–5.

Drowning by Bullets. 1992. Dir. and Prod. Philip Brooks and Alan Hayling. A Point du Jour Production for Channel Four in association with FR3 and the Centre National de la Cinématographie.

Elkaïm-Sartre, Arlette. 1992. Foreword. *Notebooks for an Ethics*. By Jean-Paul Sartre. Trans. David Pellauer. Chicago: University of Chicago Press.

Eribon, Didier. 1991. *Michel Foucault*. Trans. Betsy Wing, Cambridge, MA: Harvard University Press.

Esslin, Martin. 1986. 'Samuel Beckett–Infinity, Externity'. *Beckett at Eighty/Beckett in Context*. Ed. Enoch Brater. Oxford and New York: Oxford University Press. 110–23.

Etchegoin, Marie-France. 1994. 'Les mains sales de Maurice Papon'. *Nouvel Observateur*, 1523, 13–19 January. 50.

Federman, Raymond. 1970. 'Beckettian Paradox: Who is Telling the Truth?' *Samuel Beckett Now*. Ed. with an introduction by Melvin J. Friedman. Chicago: University of Chicago Press. 103–17.

Fitch, Brian. 1977. *Dimensions structures et textualité dans la trilogie romanesque de Beckett*. Paris: Lettres Modernes–Minard.

    1988. *Beckett and Babel: An Investigation into the Status of the Bilingual Work*. Toronto: University of Toronto Press.

Fletcher, John. 1964. *The Novels of Samuel Beckett*. London: Chatto and Windus.

    1967. *Samuel Beckett's Art*. London: Chatto and Windus.

    1970. 'Interpreting *Molloy*'. *Samuel Beckett Now*. Ed. with an Intro. by Melvin J. Friedman. Chicago: University of Chicago Press. 157-70.

Foucault, Michel. 1971. *L'ordre du discours: Leçon inaugurale au Collège de France prononcée le 2 décembre 1970*. Paris: Gallimard. Translations from this source are mine.

    1977. *Language, Counter-Memory, Practice. Selected Essays and Interviews*. Ed. Donald F. Bouchard. Trans. by Donald F. Bouchard and Sherry Simon. Ithaca, NY: Cornell University Press.

    1980. *Power / Knowledge: Selected Interviews and Other Writings 1972-1977*. Ed. Colin Gordon. New York: Pantheon.

    1985. 'Archéologie d'une passion'. Interview with Charles Ruas. *Magazine littéraire*, 221 (July/August). 100–5. Translations from this source are mine.

    ed. 1989. *The Archaeology of Knowledge*. Trans. A. M. Sheridan Smith. London: Routledge.

    1990. 'Maurice Blanchot: The Thought from Outside'. Trans. Brian Massumi. *Foucault / Blanchot*. New York: Zone Books.

    ed. 1991. *Discipline and Punish: The Birth of the Prison*. Trans. Alan Sheridan. Harmondsworth: Penguin.

Genet, Jean, ed. 1991. *Journal du voleur*. Paris: Collection Folio–Gallimard. Translations from this source are mine.

Gidal, Peter. 1986. *Understanding Beckett: A Study of Monologue and Gesture in the Works of Samuel Beckett*. London: Macmillan.

Gordon, Lois. 1996. *The World of Samuel Beckett*. New Haven: Yale University Press.

Griffiths, Richard. 1970. *Marshal Pétain*. London: Constable.

Habermas, Jürgen. 1992. *The Philosophical Discourse of Modernity*. Trans. Frederick Lawrence. Cambridge, MA: MIT Press.

Hardt, Michael. 1993. *Gilles Deleuze: An Apprenticeship in Philosophy*. London: UCL Press.

Harrington, John P. 1991. *The Irish Beckett*. Syracuse: Syracuse Uuniversity Press.

    1992. 'A Note on *Malone Dies* and Local Phenomena'. *Journal of Beckett Studies*, I. 1–2. 141–3.

Hayman, David. 1970. '*Molloy* or the Quest for Meaninglessness: A Global Interpretation'. *Samuel Beckett Now*. Ed. with an introduction by Melvin J. Friedman. Chicago: University of Chicago Press. 129–56.

Hill, Leslie. 1990. *Beckett's Fiction in Different Words*. Cambridge: Cambridge

University Press.

Husson, Jean-Pierre. 1992. 'L'itinéraire d'un haut fonctionnaire: René Bousquet'. *Vichy et les Français*. Ed. Jean-Pierre Azéma and François Bédarida. Paris: Fayard. 287-301.

Iser, Wolfgang. 1974. *The Implied Reader: Patterns of Communication in Prose Fiction from Bunyan to Beckett*. Baltimore: Johns Hopkins University Press.

Jacobsen, Josephine and William R. Mueller. 1964. *The Testament of Samuel Beckett*. New York: Hill and Wang.

Janvier, Ludovic. 1966. *Pour Samuel Beckett*. Paris: Editions de Minuit.

Jauvert, Vincent. 1993. 'Comment le Kremlin finançait le PCF (1950–1990)'. *Nouvel Observateur*, 1509, 7–13 October. 50–4.

Juliet, Charles. 1986a. *Rencontre avec Beckett*. Paris: Fata Morgana.

  1986b. 'Un Vivant'. *Magazine littéraire*, 231 (June). 16. Translations from this source are mine.

Kenner, Hugh. 1973. *A Reader's Guide to Samuel Beckett*. London: Thames and Hudson.

Knowlson, James. 1976. '*Krapp's Last Tape*. The Evolution of a Play, 1958–75'. *Journal of Beckett Studies*, 1 (Winter). 50–65.

  ed. 1980. *Theatre Workbook*, volume 1, *Samuel Beckett: Krapp's Last Tape. A Theatre Workbook*. London: Brutus Books.

  1985. 'State of play: performance Changes and Beckett Scholarship'. *Journal of Beckett Studies*, 10. 108–120.

  1996. *Damned to Fame: The Life of Samuel Beckett*. London: Bloomsbury.

Knowlson, James and John Pilling. 1979. *Frescoes of the Skull: The Later Prose and Drama of Samuel Beckett*. London: Calder.

Koyré, Alexandre. 1957. *From the Closed World to the Infinite Universe*. Baltimore: Johns Hopkins University Press.

Lacouture, Jean. 1990. *De Gaulle*, volume 1, *The Rebel, 1890–1944*. Trans. Patrick O'Brian. London: Collins Harvill.

  1991. *De Gaulle*, volume II, *The Ruler, 1945–1970*. Trans. Alan Sheridan. London: Harvill.

Lefèbre, Antoine. 1993. 'Secret d'Etat'. Interview with Antoine Lefèbre, and 'Je suis partout', a review of Antoine Lefèbre's book, *Les conversations secrètes des Français sous l'Occupation*. *Libération*. Thursday 30 September. 23–5.

Leibniz, Gottfried Wilhelm. 1973. *Philosophical Writings*. Ed. G. H. R. Parkinson. Trans. Mary Morris and G. H. R. Parkinson. London: J. M. Dent.

Levinas, Emmanuel. [n.d.] *Totality and Infinity*. Trans. Alphonso Lingis. Pittsburgh: Duquesne University Press.

Lloyd, Genevieve. 1996. *Spinoza and the Ethics*. London: Routledge.

Locatelli, Carla. 1990. *Unwording the World: Samuel Beckett's Prose Works after the Nobel Prize*. Philadelphia: University of Pennsylvania Press.

Lottman, Herbert R. 1986. *The People's Anger: Justice and Revenge in Post-Liberation France*. London: Hutchinson University Press.

Lyons, Charles R. 1986. 'Happy Days and Dramatic Convention'. *Beckett at Eighty. Beckett in Context*. Ed. Enoch Brater. Oxford and New York: Oxford

University Press. 84–101.

Mazey, Sonia, and Vincent Wright. 1992. 'Les préfets'. *Vichy et les Français*. Ed. Jean-Pierre Azéma and François Bédarida. Paris: Fayard. 267–86.

McMillan, Dougald. 1990. Introduction. *The Capital of the Ruins*. By Samuel Beckett. *As The Story Was Told*. London: Calder. 15–16.

Miquel, Pierre. 1976. *Histoire de la France: De Vercingétorix à Charles de Gaulle*. Paris: Marabout Université.

Morris, Alan. 1986. 'Attacks on the Gaullist "Myth" in French Literature Since 1969'. *The Second World War in Literature*. Ed. Ian Higgins. Edinburgh: Scottish Academic Press. 71–83.

Murphy, P. J. 1994. 'Beckett and the Philosophers'. *The Cambridge Companion to Beckett*. Ed. John Pilling. Cambridge: Cambridge University Press. 222–40.

Nancy, Jean-Luc. 1996. 'Deleuzian Fold of Thought'. Trans. Thomas Gibson and Anthony Uhlmann. *Deleuze: A Critical Reader*. Ed. Paul Patton. Oxford: Basil Blackwell. 107–13.

O'Brien, Eoin. 1986. *The Beckett Country: Samuel Beckett's Ireland*. Dublin: Black Cat.

Paris par Arrondissement. [n.d.] Paris: Coutarel.

Patton, Paul. 1986. 'Ethics and Post-Modernity'. *Futur*Fall: Excursions into Post-Modernity*. Ed. E. A. Grosz, Terry Threadgold, David Kelly, Alan Cholodenko and Edward Colless. Sydney: Power Institute.

    1994. 'Anti-Platonism and Art'. *Gilles Deleuze and the Theater of Philosophy*. Ed. Constantin V. Boundas and Dorothea Olkowski. London: Routledge. 141–56.

    1995. 'Mabo and Australia: Towards a Postmodern Republic'. *Australian Journal of Anthropology*, 6. 1 –2, 83–94.

Pilling, John, 1976. *Samuel Beckett*. London: Routledge and Kegan Paul.

    1992. 'From a *(W)horoscope* to *Murphy*'. *The Ideal Core of The Onion*. Ed. John Pilling and Mary Bryden. Reading: Beckett International Foundation. 1–20.

    1993. 'Beckett's *Proust*'. *The Beckett Studies Reader*. Ed. S. E. Gontarski. Gainseville: University of Florida Press. 9–28.

Plato. 1979. *The Portable Plato*. Trans. Benjamin Jowett. Ed. Scott Buchanan. London: Viking.

Pliskin, Fabrice. 1996. 'Le voyage de Levinas'. *Nouvel Observateur*, 1626, 4–10 January. 54–5.

Poznanski, Renée. 1992. 'Vichy et les Juifs. Des marges de l'histoire au coeur de son écriture'. *Vichy et les Français*. Ed. Jean-Pierre Azéma and François Bédarida. Paris: Fayard. 57–67.

Prichard, Katharine Susannah [1929] 1992. *Coonardoo*. Sydney: Angus and Robertson.

Prinz, Jessica. 1987. 'The Fine Art of Inexpression: Beckett and Duchamp'. *Beckett Translating / Translating Beckett*. Ed. Alan Warren Friedman, Charles Rossman, Dina Sherzer. University Park: Pennsylvania State University Press. 95–106.

Rabinovitz, Rubin. 1990. 'Repetition and Underlying Meanings in Samuel Beckett's Trilogy'. *Rethinking Beckett.* Ed. Lance St John and Robin J. Davis. London: Macmillan. 31–67.

Raffy, Serge. 1993. 'Bousquet: Les pièces du procés'. *Nouvel Observateur,* 10–16 June. 28–33.

Robbe-Grillet, Alain. 1965. 'Samuel Beckett, or "Presence" in the Theatre'. *Samuel Beckett: A Collection of Critical Essays.* Ed. Martin Esslin. Englewood Cliffs: Prentice-Hall. 108–16.

Rosen, Steven J. 1976. *Samuel Beckett and the Pessimistic Tradition.* New Brunswick: Rutgers Uuniversity Press.

Rousso, Henry. 1991. *The Vichy Syndrome: History and Memory in France Since 1944.* Cambridge, MA: Harvard University Press.

———. 1992. *Les années noires: vivre sous l'Occupation.* Paris: Gallimard–Découvertes.

Serres, Michel. 1995. *Conversations on Science, Culture, and Time.* Interviews with Bruno Latour. Trans. Roxanne Lapidus. Ann Arbor: University of Michigan Press.

Schopenhauer, Arthur. 1995. *The World as Will and Idea.* Trans. Jill Berman. Ed. David Berman. London: J. M. Dent.

Schulz, Hans-Joachim. 1973. *This Hell of Stories: A Hegelian Approach to the Novels of Samuel Beckett.* The Hague: Mouton.

Schwab, Gabriele. 1984. 'The Dialectic of Opening and Closing in Samuel Beckett's *Endgame*'. *Yale French Studies,* 67. 191–202.

Scott, Nathan A. 1965. *Samuel Beckett.* London: Bowes and Bowes.

Shenker, Israel. 1956. 'Moody Man of Letters'. Interview with Samuel Beckett. *New York Times,* section 2, 6 May. 1–3.

Smith, Daniel W. 1996. 'Deleuze's Theory of Sensation: Overcoming the Kantian Duality'. *Deleuze: A Critical Reader.* Ed. Paul Patton. Oxford: Basil Blackwell. 29–56.

'*The Sorrow and the Pity*': *The Text and Illustrations from the Marcel Ophuls Film.* 1975. Trans. Miereille Johnson. London: Paladin.

Spinoza, Benedictus de, 1992. *Ethics.* Trans. Andrew Boyle and revised with an introduction by G. H. R. Parkinson. London: Everyman.

The Summoning of Everyman. [*c.* 1510–35] 1992. Ed. Geoffrey Cooper and Christopher Wortham. Nedlands: University of Western Australia Press.

Thoumieux-Rioux, Emmanuelle. 1993. 'Les Zazous, Enfants terribles de Vichy'. *L'Histoire,* 165 (April) 32–9.

Trezise, Thomas. 1990. *Into the Breach: Samuel Beckett and the Ends of Literature.* Princeton: Princeton University Press.

Uhlmann, Anthony. 1997. 'Choice, Capacity, the Possible, and the Nightly News'. *Continuum,* 11, 2. 33–53.

Watson, David. 1991. *Paradox and Desire in Samuel Beckett's Fiction.* London: Macmillan.

White, Edmund. 1993. *Genet.* London: Chatto and Windus.

Wood, Rupert. 1993. '*Murphy*, Beckett: Geulincx, God'. *Journal of Beckett Studies,* 2, 2. Florida State University. 27–51.

Wylie, Laurence. 1974. *Village in the Vaucluse.* 3rd edn. Cambridge, MA: Harvard
    University Press.
Zurbrugg, Nicholas. 1988. *Beckett and Proust.* Totowa: Barnes and Noble.

Index

Printed in Great Britain
by Amazon